D1738731

Hypercapitalism

Steve Jones
General Editor

Vol. 15

PETER LANG
New York • Washington, D.C./Baltimore • Bern
Frankfurt am Main • Berlin • Brussels • Vienna • Oxford

Phil Graham

Hypercapitalism

New Media, Language, and Social Perceptions of Value

PETER LANG
New York • Washington, D.C./Baltimore • Bern
Frankfurt am Main • Berlin • Brussels • Vienna • Oxford

Library of Congress Cataloging-in-Publication Data

Graham, Phil.
Hypercapitalism: new media, language,
and social perceptions of value / Phil Graham.
p. cm. — (Digital formations, vol. 15)
Includes bibliographical references and index.
1. Capitalism. 2. Value. 3. Marxian economics.
I. Title. II. Series: Digital formations; v. 15.
HB501.G62756 330.12'2—dc22 2003022528
ISBN 0-8204-6217-9
ISSN 1526-3169

Bibliographic information published by **Die Deutsche Bibliothek**.
Die Deutsche Bibliothek lists this publication in the "Deutsche
Nationalbibliografie"; detailed bibliographic data is available
on the Internet at http://dnb.ddb.de/.

Cover design by Lisa Barfield

The paper in this book meets the guidelines for permanence and durability
of the Committee on Production Guidelines for Book Longevity
of the Council of Library Resources.

For my Father, William Joseph Graham

Motif

At the fairground, one encounters enormous and spectacular machines. These machines provide profit for those who invest in them. Henceforth from the time of investment they become a unique form of capital: consciousness capital. The most curious aspect of these machines is that, unlike the forms of capital that manipulate materials to produce exchangeable commodities, they are designed to produce an effect on the individuals who pay to be manipulated in them. Thus, the machines produce a change in their owners' customers. The transformative experience that each customer receives for their money is a non-exchangeable, non-returnable, and non-reversible change in their conscious states. That experience becomes the sole internal property of each individual who pays to ride, each of whom is changed by their experience in the machine. Such machines have as the objects of their production the customer's consciousness.

Contents

Preface ……………………………………………………………ix

1. Introduction …………………………………………………... 1

2. Value in history …………………………………………….15

3. Social life ……………………………………………….53

4. Hypercapitalism ……………………………………………67

5. Time, space, and new media ……………………………….. 87

6. Making value with policy …………………………………...109

7. Utopian frontiers of the digital age ………………………….135

8. Eat my head …………………………………………….155

9. Not the end …………………………………………….....165

Notes …………………………………………………….....177

Bibliography …………………………………………….....183

Index ……………………………………………………....199

Preface

The purpose of this book is twofold: it is a critique of political economic thought in the context of an emergent global knowledge economy and describes a method, based in systemic functional language analysis, for identifying important changes in social perceptions of value. The relationships that give these coherence are as follows. The widely heralded emergence of a knowledge economy indicates that more intimate aspects of human activity have become exposed to commodification on a massive scale, specifically, activities associated with thought, language, and social relatedness. Correspondingly, more abstract forms of value have developed as the products of thinking and meaning have become dominant sources of commodities. These trends rely upon new media, and are defining features of hypercapitalism, a political economic system in which products of the most intimate aspects of human activity can be technologized, alienated, and sold as commodities.

I developed my notion of hypercapitalism during postgraduate research in Australia. I first began using the word in late 1998 as terminological shorthand to denote the high-speed, global system of financial transactions I was studying, and the mass mediated hype that gave legitimacy to that system. Shortly afterwards, I found David Golumbia's (1996) "Hypercapital," a piece focusing on the implications of commodifying packets, information, bits, and bytes. The same week I saw that Ronald Sukenick (1996) had also coined the term to describe a state in which "money is like gravity" and "everything is pulled toward it." After brief discussions with both these authors, it was becoming clear to me that the term was "in the air," so to speak, and a week later I saw that Ruth Colker (1998) had published a book on American law in the context of hypercapitalism, by which she meant an extreme form of *laissez faire* capitalism. Since then, many people have published works with the word "hypercapitalism" in the title, most notably Jeremy Rifkin (2001). Unfortunately, I must pass over the various and vastly different meanings of the term as these other authors use it and move on to the formulation I have been working with these last six years.

Developing the problems and approaches

The knowledge economy is widely assumed in policy and business circles to be the result of new media that facilitate the production and exchange of knowledge between people and groups of people on a global scale. It is also assumed in these circles that the forms of social relatedness peculiar to nation-based industrial capitalism will dissolve into those more appropriate to a global knowledge economy. The nature of knowledge and its status as a commodity form are problematic at many levels. Rather than retreat into epistemology, I proceed by accepting the widespread claims that knowledge can become a dominant commodity form; that a global economy can be built on such forms; and that our new media must, in some fundamental way, underpin the emergence of this new form of political economy.

If we accept these claims, the problems of understanding a knowledge economy become analogous to the problems facing classical political economy in its day: namely to identify the historical differences in production, distribution, and consumption; circulation, exchange, and value, that characterize new forms of social relatedness peculiar to a global knowledge economy as historically unique. As a "substance," knowledge is ultimately ineffable. As a process, it is incredibly complex. Nevertheless, any knowledge economy based on the logic of capitalist commodity production must involve specific forms of labor, the products of which can be owned separately from the people that produce them. In other words, knowers and their knowledge must be separable and separated, and title in the products of conscious activity must be able to pass from person to person. New property laws and new technologies are presupposed in the full development of any knowledge economy—new laws to distinguish between the conscious activity of people and ownership in the products of that activity; new technologies for the production, distribution, circulation, and exchange of knowledge commodities.

It is here that the perceived *value* of knowledge becomes a problem. Since all people are knowers, all are potential producers of knowledge commodities, that is, creators of value in a knowledge economy. How are knowledge, knowers, and ways of knowing to be valued? Who is to say what is valuable knowledge and what is not? How would they do it? The problem then becomes one of *knowledge about the value of knowledge*. Privileged ways of knowing are implicated and the research problem becomes fully blown: not only is the legal separation between knowers and their knowledge presupposed in a knowledge economy, but a separate existence for the value of knowledge must also be assumed. Here, knowers, ways of knowing, knowledge, and the value thereof become artificially separated "things."

In historical isolation, the problem is intractable. It is a thoroughly historical problem that demands an historical explanation, not only of how socially embedded persons would turn the source of social cohesion into alienated commodity forms, but also of how certain people from certain social domains can claim—or are granted—the privilege to define what will count as valuable knowledge and which people will count as producers of valued knowledge. In the final analysis, privilege is an artifact of more or less formal relationships that are established within specific social contexts. That is to say, privilege is socially produced. As such, the production and reproduction of privilege and legitimacy are focal points for the analysis of any knowledge economy. Relations of privilege and legitimacy are deeply bound up in, and defined by, specific modes of expression—specialist dialects. That is because knowing and knowledge are socially inaccessible by means other than some form of language (meant here in the broadest sense of the word).

To establish the historical significance of a global, digitally mediated knowledge economy, the approach must grasp the relationship between language, privilege, and the perceived relative value of different classes of knowers and knowledges; to grasp the effects of new media and their relationship to changes in conceptions about the character of knowledge; and—since knowledge, new media, language, and value are perennial and dynamic influences in human societies—to identify what marks the current transition in social relations as historically significant or unique, if anything. I have therefore approached the work as an historical investigation into relationships between language, new media, and social perceptions of value.

The work presented here developed along four interdependent lines which are given coherence by the problems outlined above. These are: i) problematizing the concept of a knowledge economy in the context of capitalist political economy; ii) historicizing the phenomena that are claimed as the basis for an emergent knowledge economy; iii) identifying ways of critically analyzing dominant language practices that are, to a large extent, shaping the development of a new form of political economy, especially in respect of value-relations; and iv) examining the capacity of Marx's approach to political economy for identifying the major trajectories of the current era. The current system is typically viewed as merely an extension of capitalism. But there are strong arguments to be made that the current period is transitionary and ephemeral because of its place in a trajectory that is pre-capitalist in content and origin. The initial questions posed here arose out of a fascination with the speculative excesses and hyperbolic claims that accompanied the emergence of new digital media as an influential means of communication.

My earliest efforts in this direction were in large part a response to what are characteristic trends in contemporary political economy: the phenomena of corporate "mega-mergers"; of "globalization" in general; and of the emergence of supranational "apolitical" legislative bodies, such as the International Monetary Fund (IMF) and World Trade Organization (WTO). One direct outcome of the massive corporate mergers in recent years has been the rise of socially owned corporate entities that are perceived to be, in some cases, more powerful and valuable than whole nations. A glaring paradox of these massive entities is that they require the endorsement of national legislatures for their existence. That is, they require national governments to endorse their existence as a corporate "person" that is larger and more powerful than the nations from which they have emerged. A sense of qualitative and logical disjunctions drove my earliest analysis and theory development in the direction of trying to understand the logical assumptions of policy makers on the one hand, and the theoretical limits to human organizations on the other. Both directions implicated language as a decisive aspect in the constitution and transformation of human social systems.

Up to this point, I had treated political economy as tangential to the analysis of contemporary developments, focusing rather on the communicative and social systemic aspects of the many phenomena associated with "globalization." However, the extent to which media industries appeared to be implicated in the propagation of globalist propaganda led me towards literature concerned with the political economy of communication—in the first instance, Horkheimer and Adorno's (1947/1998) critique of the "culture industry." By way of positioning myself in the research, this piece was pivotal. As a "cultural laborer" in the media industries for some twenty years, I recognized in this and Adorno's (1991) *The Culture Industry*, a perspective that resonated with my own experiences in mass media industries. It was necessary for my own understanding of Horkheimer and Adorno to read Marx's *Capital* (1976, 1978, 1981) which provides their major perspectival underpinnings. At this point, I began to develop a notion of hypercapitalism.

I recognized in Marx a critical sensitivity to the *language* of political economy (Fairclough and Graham, 2001). Marx's analysis of language seemed to me to offer a sound method for understanding the meaning of a very large scale change, so I undertook a reading of Marx that departs from more typical interpretations. Specifically, mine was a methodological reading of Marx that drove me away from being concerned with the *logic* of policy language and toward a perspective more grounded in the problems of classical political economy: the production of values and the distribution of power—political economy—with a specific focus on communication and new media.

At this point, the problem became one of the relationships between media history, capitalist political economy, and new forms of labor that were being drawn into mainstream commodity production. In this view, it became clear that more intimate aspects of humanity had become commodified as the systemic logic of capital and its associated technologies became more refined and spread throughout humanity. Human consciousness has become the primary focus of global commodity production processes. In the context of a Marxist reading, it became necessary to explicate an essential premise to accommodate this quite obvious trend: thought and language are as material as any other aspect of human activity. A major dualism in much of the literature influenced by Marx cannot be accepted in such a view: namely the perceived split between language and thought on the one hand and material existence on the other. This is an unhelpful and, I believe, false distinction, especially in the context of what has become a form of political economy in which the most prevalent commodity forms *are* symbolic products of human imagination. Furthermore, there is no indication to me in any of his work that Marx made such a separation. In fact the opposite seems to be the case.

Assuming the idealist distinction between human consciousness and the rest of human experience is false creates problems for political economic analysis in any classical sense. But some of the more neglected aspects of Marx's critique, especially those to do with the relationship between circulation time and value, are very useful for understanding current developments in political economy. The role of media in political economy is further emphasized in this view, and language is more deeply implicated as a decisive factor in the determination of value, and in the exercise of power. Assuming that is the case, the close and intimate relations between perceptions of value, the expert dialects of power, and the contexts of their production appear to be the most logical focus for a study of contemporary political economy.

An assumption of the "newness" of new media in a global knowledge economy, and a subsequent investigation of what exactly is new about new media, draws attention to the spatial reach and speed of exchanges. Harold Innis provides an historical materialist account of the *meaning* of time and space as it pertains to new media in political economy. Understanding how new media affect perceptions of time and space is fundamental to understanding the historical character of knowledge in the formation of social perceptions of value. The close connections between the character of specific media, their associated technologies of expression, and their suitability for moving more or less valued meanings across large spaces at great speed provide insight into the qualitative changes that are affecting people everywhere.

The current system of networked digital media is biased towards disruptions in the social meaning of space because of its extreme prejudice against time and memory: conceptual time between people and places is abolished in hypercapitalist exchanges. And the circulation time of symbolic commodities is a core aspect of our new media in terms of political economy. According to the logic of capital, massive capital—capital welded to space—can be substituted by an increase in the circulation rate of money. The logic of a system oriented towards exchange-value therefore favors a mediated form of productive relationships that spans the entire planet, and which facilitates massive, continuous, high-speed transactions of symbolic commodities, especially forms of money.

Conceptions of time and space become problematic in the context of new media. The "knowledge economy" appears as the ultimate expression of a systemic bias towards the substitution of substantial production (constrained by space) for monetary circulation (constrained by time) wherever possible. Here, time-oriented symbolic commodities, such as money, debt, and speculative instruments, appear as the technical production and manipulation of probability spaces. The dominant forms of labor peculiar to such an economy—specialized conscious human activity—appears to lose its spatial character, its localized nature, and is expressed as amounts of time. This foregrounds the confused conceptual relationships between value, space, and time within a global knowledge economy and emphasizes the need to understand the specialized dialects that produce the financial abstractions that constitute the bulk of global economic activities, along with their legitimacy and perceived value.

Consequently a method for analyzing values in the specialized language of technology policy became necessary. I developed the method while analyzing a 1.3 million word corpus of knowledge economy policies from throughout the world. It became clear that the policy statements were primarily *axiological*; that is, the value systems that policy authors both propagate and draw upon provide the primary coherence for the texts. From a strictly logical perspective, the policy documents make very little sense for the most part. The axiological bias of policy was further emphasized to me when I tried to investigate the policy production process through a large corpus collected by researchers from the University of Vienna (Weiss and Wodak, 2001). There appeared, for instance, to be an almost complete disjunction between the values expressed by individual policy authors in personal interviews and those that were expressed in the policy statements they produced. The values expressed in policy are *institutional* values which are inherently constrained by the institutionalized rituals of production peculiar to the "specialist committee" project structure, an increasingly widespread organizational model for policy production (Wodak, 2002).

The role of legal language is to codify policy in order to define the meaning of particular spaces and to regulate human behavior within them. Current technology policy is directed towards the conscious aspects of human activity: art, language, music, education, financial exchanges, and practically all forms of interaction between people. The intrusiveness of current global legislation goes further to define the ownership of "well known marks"—configurations of colors, letters, images, sounds—and the value that knowledge of them is worth to their "owners." The genetic codes of whole nations are now being traded like so much sorghum. While "goods of the mind" and the "essence of life" have become the most talked-about of new commodities, relations between people are the primary focus for production in the "knowledge economy." Meanwhile, older forms of relatedness—family, neighborhood, and nationhood—are being transformed, not only by people's deployment and use of new media, but in the legal language produced by people who make international policy and international law. The implications are not at all clear. But the impetus of the current trajectory appears to be oriented towards the global enclosure, transformation, and commodification of social consciousness at every level of the human social and biological world.

Acknowledgements

This work began as doctoral research at the Queensland University of Technology. It is in no small way a product of fortunate social circumstances. Completing it would have been impossible without the support of family, friends, colleagues, and the many institutions that have graciously supported me.

My family, most especially Helen Dubois, Zara Graham, and Matthew Graham, have endured significant hardships and deprivations as a result of my choosing to undertake this work and all the work that has led to it.

No ideas are developed in a vacuum. I thank the friends and colleagues whose generosity with their time, wisdom, encouragement, and criticism has made the current work possible (of course the usual caveats apply). These include John Armitage, Gertraud Benke, Dominic Boyer, Victor Callan, Leigh Canny, Chris Clereigh, Norman Fairclough, Kevin Foster, Keith Hart, Greg Hearn, Greg Hoyle, Rick Iedema, Peter Isaacs, Peter Jones, Cushla Kapitzke, Mark Latonero, Allan Luke, Carmen Luke, Jim Martin, Bernard McKenna, Peter Muntigl, Jay Lemke, Anne Pisarski, Joanne Roberts, David Rooney, Nate Schmoltz, Roger Silverstone, Glenn Stillar, Paul Turpin, Art Schulman, Karin Tusting, Teun van Dijk, Gilbert Weiss, Ingrid Westhoff, and Ruth Wodak. I am bound to have forgotten one or more people in this long list, and my apologies if you are one of them.

I acknowledge a debt of gratitude to the various institutions and funding bodies that have supported my efforts over the long course of this work: The University of Waterloo; The Canada Research Chairs Program; The Australian Research Council; The Social Sciences and Humanities Research Council of Canada; The Wittgenstein Centre for Language (University of Vienna); The UQ Business School (University of Queensland); The Centre for Social Research in Communication (University of Queensland); and The Faculty of Business (Queensland University of Technology). To my editor, Steve Jones, and my publisher, Peter Lang, I owe special thanks for patience, encouragement, and under-standing. After having entirely lost one draft of this manuscript through theft, another partially finished draft through data loss, and having moved between countries and continents under less than favorable conditions, to say this manu-script is late to press is an understatement. Finally, to my colleague, friend, and life companion, Dr Naomi Sunderland, this work owes more than I can express in words. Through every draft and revision, every hardship and disruption, every idea and false start, she has been a guiding force, a relentless critic, an unwaver-ing supporter, and a penetrating intellect whose contribution to this work I cannot estimate. Thank you.

Related publications

Much of the work that provides detailed grounding for this book has been pub-lished in journals and collected volumes. Parts of these appear throughout the book in a substantially rewritten and updated form. Some of the data in Chapters 6 and 7 has been published, respectively, in *TEXT* (DeGruyter) and *Discourse & Society* (Sage), and I thank the publishers and editors for their support. There are many shorter works that relate directly to the larger purpose of the current work and I have listed some of these should the reader wish to pursue the data and ideas in more detail.

Fairclough, N. & Graham, P. (2002). Marx and discourse analysis: Genesis of a critical method. *Estudios de Sociolingüística 3*, (1): 185-230.

Graham, P. (2000). Hypercapitalism: A political economy of informational ideal-ism. *New Media and Society, 2*, (2): 131-156.

Graham, P. (2001). Space: Irrealis objects in technology policy and their role in the creation of a new political economy. *Discourse & Society, 12*, (6): 761-788.

Graham, P. (2002a). Predication and propagation: A method for analyzing evaluative meanings in technology policy. *TEXT, 22*, (2): 227-268.

Graham, P. (2002b). Hypercapitalism: New media, language, and social percep-tions of value. *Discourse & Society, 13*, (2): 227-249.

Graham, P. (2002c). Space and cyberspace: On the enclosure of consciousness. In J. Armitage and J. Roberts (Eds.), *Living With Cyberspace: Technology & Society in the 21st Century* (pp. 156-164). London: Continuum.

CHAPTER ONE

Introduction

One of the more questionable assumptions I make in this book is that the global political economic system we live in can still be described as some form of capitalism. I am inclined to think that it probably cannot. Nevertheless, whatever the character of the system in which we are presently situated, the fact remains that most people, whether "for" or "against" it, still refer to it as some form of capitalism. So in the spirit of dialectical enquiry I assume that we remain in capitalist social relations of production.

As I use it here, the term "hypercapitalism," has two distinct but closely related meanings. The first has to do with the propaganda function and refers quite literally to "hype" and those who disseminate it. The "dot com crash" or "tech wreck" that began in April 2001 has produced in its wake numerous but rather unsurprising accounts of market analysts who had artificially inflated technology stock prices by providing false research findings to investors (Lovink, 2002). Little has been said so far about the proliferation of the vast media spaces that were given over to expounding the utopian prospects of new information and communication technologies (ICTs). There is even more to be said about the role of more traditional institutions in disseminating the hype about new ICTs. Whole campuses, faculties, schools, and programs in universities and technical colleges have risen to meet the challenge of disseminating ICT hype and, simultaneously, to capitalize upon it. Even after "the crash," and despite an almost universal lack of evidence indicating how ICTs are an unmitigated benefit, policy initiatives continue to push the belief that governments, schools, businesses, and practically every kind of organization need to be "wired" into the new utopia of digital ICTs. The "hype" of hypercapitalism has been nothing short of a global propaganda campaign, and a very successful one.

The second sense in which I use the term hypercapitalism has to do with the speed of communication and refers to the prefix "hyper" (Armitage and Graham, 2001). If nothing else, digital ICTs have greatly increased the speed and extent of communication. In a purely commercial sense, the most significant effects of increased informational speed and mass have been realized in the realms of currency trading. We can leave aside arguments about the wisdom of buying and selling money for the moment merely to note that the largest part of the global economy is now, and has been for some years, the trade in currency, which outstrips the trade in tangible goods by multiples of 1000 (Saul, 1997; Hart, 1999). Stocks, bonds, futures, and all the multiple forms of money, along with currency, are traded around the clock at close to light speed in quantities that defy imagination and comprehension. The acceleration of social interaction associated with ICTs outside the realms of money trading also has significant implications for the character of our emergent social order. Formerly disparate and distant people, institutions, and cultures are coming into contact and beginning to relate in new, unfamiliar ways.

The character of work is changing as imperatives for "tech-savvy," "multitasking" staff who will work under part-time, "flexible" conditions have become the norm. The character of business is changing now that "departments" can be coordinated globally on a remote basis, allowing production to be carried on in, for example, Indonesia, while the marketing department is in Los Angeles, accounting is in New York, and head office is in the Cayman Islands where taxation regimes are more favorable. The character of personal relationships has also changed. People who previously might never have met have become fast friends or distant colleagues in a digitally revived flurry of letter writing via email. The character of political activity has changed. Today, a person can be charged with terrorism for manipulating restricted data or digital "frame-breaking." Whole political movements are mobilized across formerly intraversible spaces without the bulk of people involved ever having met in person. Quasi-governmental institutions, such as the World Trade Organization (WTO), the World Bank, and the International Monetary Fund (IMF), have extended their influence to the most micro levels of society, and they have done so on a global scale. The character of identity has changed. A person's identity can be stolen and their lives destroyed by the misappropriation of data. The character of crime has changed, and the largest robberies no longer involve the use of what would once have been called "force." Instead they involve the manipulation of digital data. Those charged with policing functions struggle to keep up with the changing nature of such crime. Consequently, surveillance has become pervasive to the point of being useful only in a forensic sense. In short, practically every aspect of our symbolic existence is undergoing transformations because of the greatly accelerated information exchanges made possible by digital ICTs. All of this has happened, and continues to happen, at a very fast rate over a very short period of time.

To understand the political economic implications of hypercapitalism, I take an approach derived primarily from Karl Marx. Given the many changes since Marx was writing, such an approach cannot proceed from the dogmatic or "automatic" Marxist principles developed and ossified under totalitarian Stalinist or Maoist regimes (Smythe, 1980; Poster, 2001). Yet I believe that Marx's approach still has much to offer to the project of uncovering the contradictions of our age and for understanding the historical significance of hypercapitalist relations. The basic assumptions of the perspective I present here are as follows:

1. *Acts of meaning-making are material processes.* Such a view is anathema to many Marxist scholars who believe that meaning is part of the "ideal" rather than the "real"; part of the cultural "superstructure" rather than the economic "base"; or part of immaterial rather than the material (cf. Jones, 2004). But such assumptions fail to acknowledge that an historical materialist perspective is not a matter of asking whether some aspect of human being is material or ideal, but is premised on the assumption that our existence is a function of historical development as wholly material beings. To say that meanings, including ideas, are immaterial is to mistake a process for a "thing"—it is literally a mistake of grammar. To say that "thoughts exist" or that "concepts exist" is also misleading. Thoughts do not exist in any objective sense. Nor do concepts. However, people undoubtedly think and conceptualize. Thinking and conceptualizing are material processes that are conditioned—historically, materially, and socially. In many respects, the approach I have taken here is a response to relativist, idealist "postmodern" philosophies propounding the idea that what we call reality and truth are merely discursive constructions, and to the positivist philosophies that draw a hard line between what counts as real and what does not. A mediation perspective provides a lens through which to view the materiality of meaning-making processes and their movement through space and time.

2. *All meanings are mediated.* To insist either that "the medium is the message" (McLuhan, 1964) or that "Content is King" (Gates, 1996) is to miss the point to some large extent. The medium is certainly *a* message—just as the "content" of any mediation is *a* message. Both perspectives are useful heuristics, but again they emerge from errors in grammar, again by presenting processes as things, but also by expressly or implicitly relying on the restrictive article "*the*." Silverstone (1999) presents a process view of *mediation* that sees the movement and transformation of meanings across times, spaces, and social contexts; which acknowledges that, yes, there are technological aspects of mediation that cannot be ignored, and there are substantial issues surrounding what is generally understood by the term "content." However, mediation is far more than either "content" or technology. It is a complex set of real, material, social processes facilitated by specific technological means.

Since Aristotle, and probably before, it has been recognized that no meanings are made as pure, unambiguous forms. All meanings are filtered through cultural, economic, social, historical, psychological, and institutional filters.

3. *The knowledge economy is an economy of meaning.* Political economy is the study of how values are produced, exchanged, distributed, and consumed (the economic), and how power is distributed, maintained, and exercised (the political) within particular social and historical contexts. The emergence of a "knowledge economy" in policy is nothing more than a political acknowledgement that certain classes of meaning are privileged; that there are more and less valuable meanings; that access to these meanings is restricted; and that meanings can in fact be owned and exchanged, if not entirely consumed. All the problems of Intellectual Property (IP) arise from the fact that the knowledge economy is about the production, distribution, ownership, and exchange (the commodification) of meanings. Under hypercapitalist relations, certain classes of meanings become "knowledge commodities." Among the problems of IP are the various difficulties in distinguishing between classes of knowledge commodities. IP generally makes few practical distinctions between different classes of meaning: a song, an academic research paper, a soap opera, a design for a nuclear missile, or the genetic properties of an edible plant may all be owned in essentially the same manner under existing IP laws. Issues of public and private values become paramount with the "official" emergence of an knowledge economy.

4. *What we call "value" is an inalienable part of all meanings.* Rather than speaking of "value" as an inherent part of some "thing" or other, I understand the term to refer to one aspect of meaning, and is therefore part of the same material processes of meaning-making more generally. Various schools of sociolinguistics, discourse analysis, anthropology, and semiotics have recognized this.[1] Throughout this book, I take Lemke's (1995) framework for discourse analysis as the basis for understanding how the evaluative dimension of meaning figures in any knowledge economy. Alongside the "aboutness" function of any given instance of meaning, and occurring at the same time, there is a texturing function (how meanings are expressed) and an evaluative, or attitudinal, function (the social attitudes expressed, established, and transformed by meanings). I expand upon these aspects later, in Chapters 5 and 6. For the moment, it will suffice to say that all meanings include an evaluative dimension. Hence, rather than understanding "value" as something that inheres in any particular thing, evaluation is meant here as an *active* term, and refers to the constant taking and retaking of stances towards aspects of the world. What we call "values" are more or less ephemeral products of evaluation. Like all aspects of meaning, evaluations are socially produced and mediated. Evaluations therefore tend to appear as cultural patterns (Firth,

1951). Patterns of evaluation are never quite stable, though some remain so for very long periods of time as, for example, in some religions.

5. *The perceived value of any given aspect of life shapes people's activities and relationships in respect of that aspect of life.* As it is most widely understood today, the study of economics focuses largely upon a single dimension of evaluation (price) and its expression (money). Innis (1942) foresaw that on this basis economics would decline into little more than "a higher branch of accounting." The continuing failure of mainstream economics—by which I mean the various econometric approaches that have Austrian and Chicago School roots, and which are most influential in contemporary policy decisions—to comprehend social interactions and motives beyond the price system has resulted in a general failure by economics to either predict or understand human behavior, even within the narrow confines of the price system. Most aspects of value lie outside the price system, but nevertheless affect it in significant ways. It is these aspects of value that I focus on throughout this book.

6. *To understand hypercapitalist relations, we must understand the relationships between meaning, mediation, and evaluation in political economic terms.* The production, exchange, and distribution of values is the central focus of any political economic understanding. Knowledge commodities are a very strange class of commodities: they conflate the problems of meaning (the production of socially exchangeable knowledge), mediation (the processes through which meanings are distributed and exchanged), and evaluation (the situation of various classes of meanings within hierarchies of social significance and desirability). To understand the implications of our knowledge economies we need to understand the processes by which meanings are produced, exchanged, and evaluated, and how such processes shape the political character of any given social system. Because they conflate three ostensibly separate moments of political economic analysis, knowledge commodities are rife with contradictions (Poster, 2001). They draw our attention simultaneously to the materiality and ephemerality of meanings. They draw attention to the false distinction between "facts" and "values," both of which collapse in acts of distinction (Bourdieu, 1998). They draw attention to the assertion that use-values and exchange-values are not necessarily separable in a knowledge economy. These are merely a few of the challenges presented by the emergence of a knowledge economy.

About the rest of the book

To address the challenges outlined above, I have organized the remainder of the book as follows. Chapter 2 details the method I have adopted and its relevance for understanding hypercapitalist political economic configurations. The chapter includes a history of "value" in studies of political economy. Chapter 2 emphasizes the gradual "linguistification of value" in theories of political economy—the theoretical movement from its assumed situation in objective substances, such as gold, silver, and land in mercantilist theory, to its overt situation in the discourses of specialized expertise, such as those of econometricians, politicians, central bankers, and so on. The trajectory I describe is closely related to the fracturing of the social sciences in Western societies, and to the proliferation of new media forms.

The gradual withering of mainstream political economy into a science of price left a rather large semantic residue of values unaccounted for—aesthetic, cognitive, social, and moral values, for example. These were taken up, in the first instance, by the newly emerging fields of sociology, psychology, anthropology, and by "the philosophers of value" (Graham, 2002). Later, after the first World War, the study of value fragments further into the fields of propaganda studies, political science, public opinion studies, public relations, "general semantics," cultural studies, and so forth (Graham, 2003).

Historical research into value as a technical device in political economy underpins my approach to understanding how evaluative patterns are propagated from within the specialized intellectual silos that have developed over the last 150 years or so, and which now inform policy. The history of value I present shows how official designations of value have moved from objective, exogenous objects, such as precious metals and land, to manual labor, to the linguistic domains of specialized knowledge production. These movements have reached the point at which the value of whole nations can literally be "talked up" or "talked down" by people in privileged positions. This, I argue, is also a function of new media and the modes of association they facilitate. The second part of Chapter 2 explains the relevance of Marx's method for understanding these associated historical trajectories. Fairclough and I (2002) have argued that Marx engages in a form of critical linguistic analysis, known in classical scholarship as Dialectics, to arrive at his *magnum opus*. In Chapter 2, I briefly detail the links between classical Dialectics and contemporary discourse analytical methods and how the principles of these methods can be applied to understand the significance of the current political economic system.

Chapter 3 presents a theoretical framework comprised of critical social theory, studies of language, and new media technologies in the context of a knowledge economy. It is the social theory underpinning the book, and shows that Marx's critique of political economy, and contemporary sociolinguistic and media perspectives, are both complementary and relevant for understanding the nature of hypercapitalism. It synthesizes these social systemic perspectives to demonstrate that any knowledge economy is necessarily a political economy of language, thought, and technology. I emphasize the need for a new and comprehensive critical approach to grasping emergent political economic formations, and the considerable gap between hyperbolic claims of vested interests and the social realities of an allegedly "globalized" humanity. In doing so, I foreground the necessity of understanding how language practices and the relatedness of people via new mediations define current political economic circumstances. As a direct result of a need to understand ourselves and the changes we are undergoing, a comprehensive reformulation of political economy, social theory, and linguistic, institutional, and technological mediations has become necessary to grasp the implications of our current modes of association.

Chapter 4 is concerned specifically with the functional convergence of language and new media as it is realized in accelerated systems of exchange. Facilitated by new global media networks, trillions of dollars swirl around the globe at the speed of light every day. Marx recognizes in the *Grundrisse* that a relationship exists whereby "the velocity of turnover ... substitutes for the volume of capital" at least for a short time (1973, p. 518). To confound matters further, the bulk of commodity forms traded today are forms of money or, more specifically, financial abstractions contrived in the expert dialects of finance, politics, and econometrics. In hypercapitalism, the strange and contradictory set of relationships embedded in the logic of capital—those between production, circulation speed (or the speed of mediation), wealth, legitimacy, power, language, and value—are fully expressed. These aspects seem inseparable from each other in the current system. The products of powerful and "sacred" dialects are rendered digital and propagated globally as binary bits representing numerical measures of economic wealth, or money (itself a mode of meaning), increasing and decreasing in value with each revolution.

Political economic trajectories are directly contingent upon the deployment and use of new ICTs, but are actually hidden by a focus on the purely technological. Such a focus hides the more significant trajectories that underpin hypercapitalism: the increasingly abstract and alien character of economic value; the subsumption of all forms of labor under the systemic logic of capital; and the convergence of formerly distinct spheres of analysis—production, distribution, circulation, and consumption. Each of these trajectories is in a relationship of interdependence with the others and cannot be considered in isolation. In practice, they have become blurred because they appear to be contingent upon a broader, more invisible, more important convergence: a convergence in the social functions of new media, language, and consequent perceptions of value.

A corollary to characterizing new political economic relations in these terms is the characterization of contemporary political economic conditions in terms of speed. In a technologically mediated global economy, the largest sector of which produces financial abstractions designed to be continually exchanged but never "consumed," questions about precisely what is being produced and consumed, and by whom, become quite difficult to answer. The "knowledge economy," as it is currently conceived of, implies that the light-speed production of particular mental predispositions has become a central focus for globalized productive processes. In a system with such a singular and ephemeral focus, production, consumption, and circulation converge to form a temporally inseparable moment, and "value creation" becomes an immediate, continuous process that analytically collapses the formerly separable spheres of production, distribution, exchange, and circulation. I argue that there can be no analytical usefulness in separating these spheres within hypercapitalist political economy because the boundaries—conceptual, practical, and temporal—between them are dissolved by new media's ubiquity; by the work habits engendered by new mediations; and by the mass, and more importantly, the speed of hypercapitalist exchanges as they expand to encompass a global totality.

Chapter 5 focuses more closely on the links between emerging evaluative biases and attitudes towards time and space engendered by new patterns of mediation. I extend the argument in Chapter 4 by using approaches developed by Harold Innis to consider the different character of knowledge monopolies throughout recent history and their influence on current trends. The chapter lays out the fundamental paradoxes that any account of our current knowledge economy needs to consider: namely meanings of time and space in everyday life as they are affected by new mediations.

Technologies of mediation are the means by which we move, produce, store, transform, and distribute meanings through space and time. They are the means by which we organize, delineate, link, and de-link people, places, and institutions. Seen from the perspective of political economy, new mediations are problems that turn on relative evaluations of space and time. The currently emergent knowledge monopolies are clearly biased towards disruptions in social meanings of space because of their extreme prejudice against time and memory: time between people and places is actively destroyed, and social memory is inhibited by a systemic bias towards the future. History is consequently rendered irrelevant.

The circulation time of symbolic commodities is at the heart of these developments. According to the logic of capitalist acquisition, an increase in the circulation rate of money can substitute for massive capital, capital welded to space, at least temporarily. The logic of a system oriented towards circulation favors kinds of mediation that span the entire planet, and which facilitate massive, continuous, light-speed transactions of symbolic commodities, especially forms of money. In hypercapitalism, social meanings of time and space become problematic. With its bias towards circulation of exchange-values, the "knowledge economy" can be seen as the ultimate expression of capital's systemic bias against space and in favor of time. Put simply, the knowledge economy is a globally mediated expression of the confused dictum that says "time is money." In the current context, the dominant forms of labor peculiar to any knowledge economy—specialized intellectual activity—loses its spatial aspect, its local character, and is expressed as amounts of time measured in universal units against universal standards. This focus foregrounds the confusing relationships between value, space, and time within a global knowledge economy and further foregrounds the need to understand the specialized dialects and networks of mediation through which the bulk of global economic activities, along with their legitimacy and perceived value, are produced.

Chapter 6 presents a specific method for understanding how "official" patterns of evaluation impact upon everyday life. People produce, reproduce, and transform culturally specific evaluative patterns (axiologies) in the meanings they make. Because the largest part of hypercapitalist economy is comprised of the products of expert dialects, a method for analyzing the axiological aspects of "expert" meanings is essential. I show how these patterns are infused into everyday life, and speculate upon the implications of newly emerging axiologies being produced by experts in the development of a "global knowledge economy" driven by new ICTs.

The method I present is developed with a sensitivity to historically infused axiologies inherited by contemporary experts. The contradictory and conflicting axiologies of contemporary expertise have their origin in the various institutions which have been past holders of knowledge monopolies, such as the church, monarchies, and guilds of the past. Such an approach to analysis is necessary because the evaluative biases that people express in the meanings they make are only ever partially overt—they are surface expressions of much larger and longer relationships, the product of historical and institutional substrata, and are far more elusive than any analysis of lexis or grammar alone can reveal. At any given time, social perceptions of value are shaped by the axiological biases of dominant institutions, particular groups of people, and specific individuals.

In demonstrating the analytical method in Chapter 6, I focus on policy texts. From the analytical approach I take, it becomes clear that the production of policy is primarily axiological—that is to say, the coherence of policy is derived from the value systems that various policy authors simultaneously propagate and draw upon. Upon close analysis, at least from a strictly logical perspective, many of the policy texts that propound the virtues of "the global knowledge economy" make very little sense (Graham and McKenna, 2000). This is somewhat anathema to "post-enlightenment" legislative environments that claim truth, objectivity, and rationality as their foundational principles. The axiological biases of policy texts are a function of the institutionalized rituals of production peculiar to contemporary policy structures. While contemporary policy claims to be "evidence based," rational, objective, and so on, according to the post-enlightenment principles of scientifically informed decision making, there is very little evidence to suggest that this is the case (Luke, 2002). It appears, rather, that policy decisions are made primarily along axiological lines *other than those associated with truth.*

Some rationale for a focus on policy is necessary at this stage. The original impetus for this work sprang from the high levels of financial speculation that fuel "the global economy." I became further fascinated by the incredibly abstract nature of the commodities that are traded within this system. Such commodities do not appear from nowhere, newly hatched with a determinate value stamped on them. They firstly require some official legitimacy to be traded with any openness, or to any great extent. This can only be established in legislation, and thus within the realm of policy production, at both national and supranational levels. New instruments of financial abstraction then need to be accepted as formally legal commodities within the realms in which they are traded. That much is clear.

But most financial commodities are traded in rarefied realms that the majority of people will never have access to, at least not directly. On the whole, policy remains largely uninterested in the arcane formulations that underpin the proliferating speculative instruments of hypercapitalism. The overt focus of knowledge economy policies is to promote the use of new ICTs in every possible realm of human activity. Anything that can be digitized and traded will be, at least according to the authors of policy. Whether or not this becomes the case remains to be seen. But that is not the point. The point is that policy is the source of legality and formal legitimacy in most "advanced" contemporary societies.

Policy is the official means by which public resources are allocated; by which certain actors are designated as powerful and authoritative within given social domains; by which conceptions of the common wealth are developed, transformed, and enacted; and by which notions of property are developed and formalized. One need not assume that what people say in policy will happen as decreed. However, the policy field is the discursive edifice that expresses the methods, means, modes, and principles by which economic resources and power are distributed throughout societies—it is the practical expression of political economic principles. It is in policy that relationships between people are formalized, transformed, and given legal expression. The axiologies expressed in policy are those that inform decisions about the legal principles, methods, means, and modes by which people interact; by which legitimacy is distributed; by which resources are distributed; and by which political and legal power are delegated.

The method in Chapter 6 is developed with a particular sensitivity to the policy genre, but its ramifications extend well beyond that field. I emphasize the need to distinguish between the different kinds of evaluations which are possible for *Substances* and *Processes*; between spatially oriented and time-based elements of political economy; between the "things" of policy and the potential outcomes of *Processes* that causally relate such "things"; and between the factual (or propositional) content and the essentially hortatory function of policy, which is realized in overt or implied proposals for particular sorts of actions and attitudes. Distinguishing between these aspects is difficult because of the highly condensed language peculiar to the contemporary policy genre, and because of social, historical, and institutional pressures on policy writers that tend to present "instructions for action" as "matters of fact."

Policy evaluations are actualized at four distinct levels of abstraction, extending from the predicates inscribed in policy texts to the propagation of cultural attitudes on a global scale. Often, again because of the condensed nature of policy language, the kinds of evaluations made are the sole means by which *Substance-Process* distinctions can be made. The method also emphasizes the historical nature of perceived value by emphasizing the axiological resources that institutions of power have developed over many hundreds of years. I relate these historical infusions to mediation processes, seeing the evaluative resources of policy as a) the most thoroughly mediated and inculcated evaluative resources we have, and b) resources that are overlaid historically upon each other by virtue of their institutionally and technologically mediated nature. In Chapter 6, I draw together the relationships between the languages of public policy, their mediation processes, their processes of production, official systems of value, and their impact on everyday life. The objective is to provide an understanding of how value systems are expressed, actualized, codified, and propagated in and for "the knowledge economy."

Chapter 7 describes a significant rhetorical device of policy—the creation of utopian futures and how this is done in contemporary policy texts. The utopias of any age are its most powerful illusions. From "the next world" described by Plato to the gold-fields of the nineteenth century in Australia and California, utopian futures have remained a feature of political strategies since the beginnings of recorded history. Our official "utopias" have been perennial "places" to aspire to, places where life will be better, where we will finally realize our dreams, whatever they might be.

Today's official utopia is said to be located in "cyberspace." Like the "new world" of the late fifteenth century, it is a space being aggressively colonized to expand existing interests. In Chapter 7, I show how new media have been historically central to the development and character of new utopias. When new media emerge, the character of official utopias changes. This has a consequent impact on perceptions about the value and meaning of space and time. Periods during which new media emerge, by definition, coincide with extensions and transformations in human relationships. They change the scale and character of human relationships, often irreversibly. At such times, previously informal relationships get formalized; social relations are entirely transformed; and qualitatively different epochs come into being. Examples include the formalization of feudal relationships in late twelfth-century Europe, the enclosures movement that prefigured industrial capitalism, and the colonization of the electromagnetic spectrum beginning in the early twentieth century. All of these movements were directly related to the emergence of new media technologies: the widespread availability of paper in the twelfth century; movable type in the fifteenth; and radio in the early twentieth. Our current period is undoubtedly of similar significance.

Chapter 8 identifies the concrete character of "cyberspace." A central problem addressed in this chapter is the political economic nature of cyberspace—literally, the economic characteristics of global bandwidth. I argue that this space has been largely misunderstood, especially in recent times. It has, for the most part, been treated in political economy as a commodity rather than a form of real estate or property. The "enclosure" of this property has ramifications for human relatedness which are yet to be widely understood. It is a global decision-making space. As such, it is perhaps the most important common property for a "globalized" humanity.

Chapter 9 is where a conclusion would usually be. The object of this book—understanding what a "knowledge economy" might mean under current circumstances—first appeared to me to be an enterprise tied exclusively to the logic of capitalism. I no longer believe this to be the case. A common mistake, which is perhaps a characteristic of formulations in political economy, is to assume that the logic of the commodity—essentially a capitalist form—would prevail in any political economic form that emerged from capitalism. In other words, the tendency is to approach the problems of a knowledge economy using concepts and categories that are more than three centuries old to describe phenomena that are qualitatively—in many significant respects—less than forty years old.

Seen from the perspective I present here, the core phenomena of the knowledge economy appear to be very ancient. It seems characteristic of transitional periods in human history that we find ourselves driven back upon two of the most ineffable concepts in the human constellation: time and space. Consequently, new conceptual formulations of political economy tend towards vagueness, serving firstly as indicators of possible directions in which theory might move in order to conceptualize the nature of an emergent system. Any conceptual reformulation in such a period must remain both incipient and tentative.

Not surprisingly, then, the material I present throughout this book suffers from the problems of generality. But the subject of a global economy—in fact, any aspect of global relatedness—will tend towards "grand" theorizing at the expense of a focus on individual agency. However, and this is important in the context of what I am attempting here, historical contextualization of our global political economic system is both necessary and important, not merely because a global political economic system *does* exist, but because it has become a central focus and rationale for policy decisions at all levels of government.

The logic and values of global political economy, which actually take the form of a belief system, have become the basis for political decisions that directly influence the distribution of resources and power throughout humanity. The system therefore urgently requires understanding, however vaguely and generally to begin with. Specificity and precision are neither feasible nor practical in transitionary and unstable states of human change. New media are, by definition and primarily, new ways of relating. New forms of relatedness are necessarily overlaid upon older forms, giving rise to conflicts and crises of understanding. This is most obvious when the new medium is oriented towards control over the spatial aspect of relatedness. Those using a new medium to propagate ideas and direct action across vast geographical spaces will invariably encounter cultural resistance. Cultural resistance is firstly axiological—it is based in conflicting value systems. Human resistance is a function of a felt need for cultural autonomy, or justice, or social equilibrium, or all of these. Cultural disruptions arising from new media use are manifestations of perceived threats to cultural autonomy in the determination of values; of a sense of justice in the formal and informal relationships between people; and of a clear historical tendency in social systems towards a social equilibrium between the separate and interdependent social values peculiar to space and time. A medium oriented towards political control across vast spaces will firstly seem as if it is oriented towards the elimination of the time element. That is a perceptual illusion. Large social spaces are created at the expense of time between people. Hence the destruction of time appears to be the primary object for new mediations rather than the means by which larger, less stable social spaces are created. This relationship will necessarily be confusing. Since the advent of electronic media, the maximum speed at which content moves has been fairly stable. This might lead one to suspect that time has been steadily diminishing in importance since electric media. This is not actually the case, but it points to the very definition of the word "media." It suggests that an historical orientation for research into the political-economic dimensions of new media is an imperative if we are to have any sense of our present and, more importantly, our future.

CHAPTER TWO

Value in history

*A*s capital progresses as a system of social relationships, more intimate and intricate facets of human activity have become formally com- modified. They have been incorporated into the logic of commodity production as saleable aspects of human activity, or what is commonly called *labor* under capitalist relations. This general tendency is exemplified in terms like "knowledge worker," "knowledge economy," and "information econ- omy." Such terms presuppose forms of labor that can be bought and sold in order to produce commodified artifacts of conscious activity—or what can be called "knowledge commodities." Like all commodities, there is a presuppo- sition that knowledge commodities can be alienated from their source (conscious human activity), technologically objectified, and then traded in global markets. This emergent economy is organized primarily around the production of symbolic artifacts and is facilitated by new ICTs. With this progression, new and more abstract forms of value have developed which correspond to the newly formalized "labors of abstraction" that a knowledge economy entails. Although there are connections between these two historical trends—the commodification of more intimate aspects of human activity and the development of more abstract forms of value—they are neither obvious nor direct. They are expressions of the relationships that exist between mean- ing; its processes of mediation; technical development in general; and the systemic logics of production, reproduction, and transformation peculiar to specific periods in human history.

Put simply I am concerned in this chapter with describing the linguistifica- tion of economic value—that is, its movement from a category pertaining specifically to certain substances (for instance, precious metals, factories, or land) to a category that pertains entirely to the products of those who "legiti- mately" speak expert dialects. The historical shift in value-relations and concomitant perceptions of value—which, although interdependent, are not the same "thing"—has led to the situation of economic value in institutionalized expertise. That shift can be traced through the fragmenting and increasingly specialized disciplines of social sciences since the mid-nineteenth century. But the trajectory cannot be understood by way of describing that disciplinary fragmentation. To explain it requires a return to the foundational categories and assumptions of political economy in order to question their relevance, and where they are found lacking in this respect, to propose new ways of grasping their meaning in the context of recent developments.

This has become especially important since the emergence of a new and dominant form of political economic organization on a global scale. Among its more definitive characteristics are the importance of international and global institutions, and the ways in which the actions of such institutions are integrated at national, regional and local levels. More particularly, there has been a systemic emphasis throughout the twentieth century on commodifying and controlling the most intimate aspects of human existence, especially thought, language, attitudes, and opinions. The overall task of this book is to identify the parameters of an emergent system of political economy and to propose an analytical approach that operates at the most fundamental level of political economy: namely the formation of evaluative patterns, or axiologies, in human societies. This chapter is oriented towards identifying the historical and philosophical foundations necessary to achieve those tasks. In the broadest sense, these foundations are organized around the abstract and concrete realities of space and time (meant here as plural and plastic concepts), the ownership and meaning of which define any form of political economy.

History, value, language, and theories of social change

The term "new" in the title of this book preempts an historical orientation. A theory of social change is implied. This raises problems in the current intellectual climate of specialized "disciplines" within social science, a relatively recent development. Prior to the nineteenth century,

> the theory of society ... was an integral part of philosophy or of those sciences (such as the economic or the juristic), the conceptual structure of which was to a large extent based upon specific philosophical doctrines. The intrinsic connection between philosophy and the theory of society ... formulates the pattern of all particular theories of social change occurring in the ancient world, in the middle ages, and on the commencement of modern times. One decisive result is the emphasis on the fact that social change cannot be interpreted within a particular social science, but must be understood within the social and natural totality of human life. (Marcuse and Neumann, 1942/1998, p. 95)

Not only can the many sub-disciplines of social science today be seen as "fractured" social theory, but as social theory fractured along the lines of specific aspects of value; or, as society evaluated and reconstrued according to certain categories and methods of measurement which are peculiar to the sub-disciplines of social science.[2] Disciplinary categories, including methods of measurement, are presented as social facts when they are really academic evaluations of a particular kind. A critical theory of the social, though, integrates these fractured aspects of social science and must therefore begin with an integrated understanding and formulation of value (Marx, 1973, p. 259). As I will argue here and in later chapters, what we call *value* is a function of the perceived desirability of any given aspect of our existence.[3] But the perceived desirability of anything is socially, institutionally, linguistically, and technologically mediated. As political economy has asserted for centuries, values are produced by people. To put it more correctly, social systemic patterns of evaluation are products of social relations of production.

My approach to the problems addressed here is informed largely by Marx's critique of classical political economy, which also takes the notion of value as its starting point, and by the critical perspective of Adorno, who reinterprets Marx in the context of a more thoroughly mediated society.[4] A distinguishing feature of this approach is that it does not separate history or philosophy from method (cf. Harvey, 1973, pp. 14-15). Nor can such an approach separate perceptions of value from language, "fact," and historical context (pp. 154-155). Focused as I am on the interrelationship between meaning, mediation, and evaluation, operationalizing a meaning-based perspective informed by Marx becomes somewhat problematic in the context of twentieth-century scholarship.

Marx and language

Apart from dogmatic Marxist arguments that meaning is part of the "ideal" rather than the real, various critiques of Marx include the suggestion that he lacked any systematic "theory of language" (e.g., Cook, 1982, p. 530; Lepschy, 1985). But to assert that is to overlook the nature of nineteenth-century scholarship. While much attention has been directed towards understanding the historical and intellectual links between Kant, Hegel, and Marx, little attention has been given to the broader context in which these writers appear as pivotal figures in the history of Western thought.[5] Their contributions cannot be understood without taking into account the influence of classical scholarship during the period in which they wrote (Bloom, 1943). Nor can we grasp the centrality of language critique to Marx's method without taking into account nineteenth-century scholarship in general, and in particular, Marx's philosophical and juridical education in Germany at a time when Hegel's philosophy was considered to be a revolutionary intellectual force. An understanding of language was central to scholarship during the time Marx studied and wrote, with studies of grammar being the foundation of scholarship.[6]

In the following section, I briefly outline some important linguistic aspects of Marx's critical method that are implied in the nineteenth-century context of his scholarship and which are also expressed overtly in his writing. I also show the relevance of such an approach to understanding the changes that are currently happening on a global scale. In this context, I then outline the significance of new media—the means of production, distribution, exchange, and circulation of knowledge commodities—and their institutional origins for understanding value-relations. Then I detail the institutional fragmentation of value as a technical idea, thus laying categorical bases for a method suited to analyzing value-relations and perceptions of value in the contemporary global milieu.

Language and political economic change

Norman Fairclough and I (2002) have detailed elsewhere the very powerful, but largely ignored or misunderstood, linguistic aspects of Marx's critical method. Marx's remains an approach through which we can comprehend the form of political economy currently emerging on a global scale. Inherent in his method of analysis are assumptions about the relationship between time, space, meaning, value, and human relationships. In the following section, I outline what I see as the most relevant aspects of Marx's method for the study of an "informational" mode of political economy, especially in respect of how axiologies are changing. Marx's method of discovery, especially evident in his early writings, is significant for its understanding of how language figures *as* political economic activity in the broadest sense. It also provides a sound basis for developing the foundations of a relational and dynamic approach that considers language, or more generally, meaning making, as networks of material, social *praxis*, as an important part of social production processes—as an integral part of the processes that produce, reproduce, and transform human social organizations at every level.

Harvey (1973) notes the necessity, but also the difficulty, of understanding Marx's use of language, especially where his reframing of Aristotelian concept of value is concerned:

> Part of the difficulty posed by Marx's analysis lies in his highly original way of using words. ... Marx uses words in a relational and dialectic way. Use value and exchange have no use in and of themselves ... . The term "use value" can thus be applied to all manner of objects, activities and events in particular social and natural settings. It can refer to religious ideology, social institutions, work, language, commodities, recreation, and so on. It is even reasonable to consider the use value of the term "use value" ... . (p. 154)

A further difficulty that arises from using an approach informed by Marx, especially in light of contemporary scholarship, is that the contemporary "view of theory stems from an artificial separation of methodology from philosophy" (1973, p. 11). The pressure on scholars to separate and clarify the relationship between their theoretical and methodological approaches is, in the first place, "a matter of convenience, but it is amazing how far conven-ience can lure" (p. 11):

> From this separation flows a tendency to regard facts as separate from values, ob-jects as independent of subjects, "things" as possessing an identity independent of human perception and action, and the "private" process of discovery as separate from the "public" process of communicating the result. (pp. 11-12)

That is my rationale for using an approach informed by Marx's critique of political economy. The artificiality of such separations is in large part dis-solved by understanding his critique of political economy as a critique of the *language* of political economists (cf. Fairclough and Graham, 2002; Harvey, 1973, pp. 154-155).

As I show in Chapter 4, the emergent "knowledge economy" is a political economy of language, thought, and technology. But to some extent this has always been the case (Marx and Engels, 1846/1972):

> the class which is the ruling *material* force of society, is at the same time its ruling *intellectual* force. The class which has the means of material production at its dis-posal, has control at the same time over the means of mental production, so that thereby, generally speaking, the ideas of those who lack the means of mental pro-duction are subject to it. (Marx and Engels, 1846/1972, p. 136)

Which is also to say the dominant discourses that define "value" in political economy are as much socially situated products as the latest jet engine or mass-production factory, with identifiable (if not determinative) social con-texts of production and *very real social effects*. The linguistification of value, and its division into conceptually and institutionally isolated "species" of value studies, is central to understanding the historical fragmentation of the social sciences into narrow and specialized disciplines. In a global social sys-tem dominated by the language of intellectually specialized elites (Saul, 1992, 1997), any contemporary political economy must engage with these discourses *as* political-economic products, as well as processes, conditions, and technologies of production. In this sense, a critical engagement with the discourses of, by, and about contemporary political economy is also political economic activity. My focus on policy is an engagement with the axiological underpinnings of such discourses. It is also an analysis of the social condi-tions in which these discourse-based commodities are produced—it is an engagement not merely with "words," but with the historically specific cir-cumstances and conditions that make contemporary discourses about a knowledge economy possible.

To comprehend changes in our political economic circumstances from a critical standpoint it is therefore essential to avoid artificially separating the-ory from method. Such separations are nevertheless evident in places, if only to meet the normative demands of contemporary scholarship, and because of my situation within contemporary scholarship. In any case, Marx makes quite clear that the relationship between investigation and presentation, between the method of analysis and presentation of findings, between thought and language, is problematic because:

> the method of presentation must differ in form from that of inquiry. The latter has to appropriate the material in detail, to analyse its different forms of development and to track down their inner connection. Only after this work has been done can the real movement be appropriately presented. If this is done successfully, if the life of the subject-matter is reflected back in the ideas, then it may appear as if we have before us an *a priori* construction.

> My dialectical method is, in its foundations, not only different from the Hegelian, but exactly opposite to it. For Hegel, the process of thinking, which even he trans-forms into an independent subject, under the name of 'the Idea,' is the creator of the real world, and the real world is only the external appearance of the idea. With me, the reverse is true: the ideal is nothing but the material world reflected in the mind of man and translated into forms of thought. (Marx, 1976, p. 102)

I have tried throughout the present work to foreground a dialectical method of analysis wherever possible, and to foreground the distinction between method and "theory" only wherever necessary.

Marx's method has come to be most readily identifiable with the term "historical materialism" (Jarvis, 1998, p. 98; Marx, 1976, pp. 100-103). But the deployment of that term has often fallen victim to, and consequently rein-forced, the dualism it sets out to dispel: that between idealism and materialism, which is among the oldest of philosophical contentions in hu-man history (Aristotle, 1999, p. 452). At the foundations of any form of political economy are conceptions about the definition, use, and meaning of space (geotechnical, social, and symbolic), time (the tempo and measurement of human activity), and value in all its forms.[7]

With these elements foremost in mind, I now briefly outline the aspects of Marx's approach that situate his method of inquiry in the history of linguisti-cally focused critical scholarship. Marx's is a form of critique that can cope with the social power of language in the context of an emergent form of po-litical economy without reducing social life to language and without removing language from material existence (Fairclough and Graham, 2002). Furthermore, realizing the historical and intellectual currents that shaped Marx's thought is to realize that he necessarily had an acute sensitivity to the significance of language and history, and recognized the primacy of social relationships in any assessment of political economy.

Marx: language, philosophy, and method

Abstraction and materialism

> Hegel substitutes the act of abstraction revolving within itself for these fixed ab-stractions; in so doing he has the merit, first of all, of having revealed the source

of all these inappropriate concepts which originally belonged to separate philosophers, of having combined them and of having created as the object of criticism
the exhaustive range of abstraction rather than one particular abstraction. We shall
later see why Hegel separates thought from the subject; but it is already clear that
if man is not human, then the expression of his essential nature cannot be human,
and therefore that thought itself could not be conceived as an expression of man's
being, of man as a human and natural subject, with eyes, ears, etc., living in society, in the world, and in nature. (Marx, 1844/1975a, p. 398)

While much is made of Feurbach's materialist influence on Marx, Colletti
argues that it is "naïve" to overstate it (1975, p. 24). Marx was essentially
Aristotelian in his approach, and was thoroughly familiar with the ancient
Greeks in general (Fenves, 1986, p. 433). Feurbach's materialist move, while
clearly approved of by Marx, was merely another variation on "one of the
most profound and ancient themes in philosophical history, and recurs constantly in the debate between Idealism and Materialism" (Colletti, 1975, p.
24). We can comfortably assume that Marx was quite aware of the debate,
well before Feurbach formulated his abstract materialist theses against the
neo-Hegelian school.

Aristotle's formulation, as developed by the scholastics, remained largely
intact until Hegel reshaped it in one very specific sense. The scholastic tradi-
tion was concerned with the immutable and Universal attributes of isolated
things—the Universal and essential characteristics of objective, static
forms—regardless of whether one understands matter as being in flux or in
stasis. Hegel's contribution was to add the dimension of time—History—and
formulated a theory of abstraction that assumed opposing dynamic forces as
the transforming impetus of history (Hook, 1928a, p. 117; McTaggart, 1893).
Hegel's contribution to philosophy is closely related to Charles Darwin's
contribution to biology—it is incipient "evolutionism."

In his critique of Hegel's concept of abstraction, Marx develops many of
the concepts later deployed in his critique of political economy: alienation;
conceptual fetishism; objectification and reification; the labor process; labor
as an all-embracing conception of human activity; and the primacy of material reality, including social reality, in determining consciousness. All of these
aspects can be identified in Marx's early engagement with Hegel's historically motivated Idealism (Marx, 1843/1975). However, to elucidate what
would be recognizable as a method for the critical analysis of language,
Marx's approach to the dialectic, another legacy of the Greeks, needs consideration. Marx, Hegel, Kant, and all of the best-remembered scholastics
deployed dialectic argumentation as a way of challenging the "first principles" of knowledge about any given subject, with the purpose of formulating
new understandings (Makdisi, 1974).

Dialectics: Outlines of a critical method

> Dialectics—literally: language as the organon of thought— would mean to attempt
> a critical rescue of the rhetorical element, a mutual approximation of thing and ex-
> pression, to the point where the difference fades. Dialectics appropriates for the
> power of thought what historically seemed to be a flaw in thinking: its link with
> language, which nothing can wholly break [...]. Dialectics seeks to mediate be-
> tween random views and unessential accuracy, to master this dilemma by way of
> the formal, logical dilemma. But dialectic inclines to content because content is
> not closed, not predetermined by a skeleton; it is a protest against mythology.
> (Adorno, 1964/1973, p. 56)

Marx cannot be fully understood without taking into account the contribution
of classical scholarship to the development of dialectical methods.[8] Throughout the early works of Marx (e.g., 1843/1975, 1844/1975a,b), through to the
Grundrisse (1973), elements of a classical Aristotelian dialectics are quite
overt. Terms such as "subjects and predicates"; "Ens," "genus," and "species"; "differentia and semblances"; "accidents and errors in language" and
so on, pervade the texts. These are the terms of classical dialectics (Grote,
1872).

As developed in the classical system, dialectical arguments have "for their
province words and discourse; they are ... powers or accomplishments of
discourse" (Grote, 1872, p. 384). Dialectic focuses on *Endoxa*, "premises,
propositions and problems" which are "borrowed from some one among the
varieties of accredited or authoritative opinions", from "a particular country,"
"an intelligent majority", or from "a particular school of philosophers or wise
individuals" (p. 383). In Lemke's method of discourse analysis, Endoxa are
the "thematic patterns" of a *discourse community* (Lemke, 1995, p. 42). Endoxa are found "exclusively in the regions of ... received opinions," and
dialectical argumentation proceeds upon the assumption that in "every society there are floating beliefs, each carrying with it a certain measure of
authority" (Grote, 1872, pp. 385-386). Dialectics assumes that the beliefs and
propositions about a given aspect of the world common to any given community will often contradict each other. But they are an important focus for
precisely this reason—they form the basis of what we call "common sense."
Each individual, as they mature, "imbibes of these opinions and beliefs in-
sensibly and without special or professional teaching" (1872, p. 385).
Consequently, they "carry with them more or less authority, and it is from
them that the reasonings of common life ... are supplied" (p. 385).

Endoxa typically carry with them an evaluation of "probability," precisely
because of their status as authoritatively received or accepted opinion (Grote,
1872, pp. 389-390). They are supported by "the mass of opinions and beliefs
floating and carrying authority at the same time," and dialectical analysis "is

carried on within this wide field of floating opinions" (pp. 389-390). Dialectics "searches for a 'counter syllogism' of which the conclusion is contradictory" to the Endoxa it is investigating (p. 390). It does not proceed from first principles; it aims to provide new ways of developing them, and the primary purpose of deploying dialectics is to "open a new road to the first *principia* of each separate science" (p. 391). In any case, first principles "can never be scrutinized through the truths of the science itself, which *presuppose them and are deduced from them*" (p. 391, emphasis added). Such principles can only be challenged from outside a particular science, and dialectical argumentation is designed precisely for this purpose. Its most useful function is that of "dissipating the false persuasions of knowledge" based on contradictory principles or taken-for-granted, common sense beliefs and assumptions (p. 391).

The primary category of classical dialectics is *Relation*. Considered in the most comprehensive sense, all the dialectical categories "are implicated and subordinated to Relation" (Grote, 1872, pp. 115-120). Relation, "understood in the large sense which really belongs to it, ought to be considered as an Universal, comprehending and pervading all the Categories" (p. 120). Consequently, "[n]ew Relations may become predicable of a thing, without any change in the thing itself, but simply by changes in other things" (p. 122). As a method of inquiry dialectics can be described as a *relational* and *social* theory of language, a theory of *language in use* that is drawn from "common speech," and which is inalienably bound up with social consciousness and relationships in a world which is assumed to be wholly social and material in its constitution. The relational aspect of dialectical categories (*ad aliquid*) is thus most important for my purposes here. That is no selective contrivance. The relational aspect of dialectic is seen "not as one amongst many distinct Categories, but as implicated with all the Categories" (p. 126).

The primacy of the relational in classical dialectics can be seen throughout Marx's early texts. The relational aspect of classical scholarship is organized around the concept of *Relata* (Grote, 1872, pp. 100-104). *Relata* are "said to be *of other things*, or are said to be in some manner *towards something else*" (p. 100). Thus, *Relata* are "so designated in virtue of their relation to another *Correlata*; the master is master *of a servant*—the servant is servant *of a master*" (p. 101; see also Hegel, 1807/1966, pp. 228-240). Therefore "the *Relatum* and its Correlate seem to be *simul naturâ*. If you suppress one of the pair, the other vanishes" (Grote, 1872, p. 102): no servant, no master; no master, no servant.

There are four protocols for engaging in dialectic. The dialectician must: i) "have a large collection of propositions" on the subject; ii) "study and discriminate the different senses in which the Terms of these proposition are used"; iii) "detect and note Differences"; and iv) "investigate Resemblances" (Grote, 1872, p. 401). These protocols of dialectic are also common to what is called the "corpus linguistics" approach to discourse analysis (Fairclough, 1992, pp. 228-230). They are also common (for already obvious reasons) to the method I demonstrate in Chapter 6, and to contemporary sociolinguistics more generally.

In Dialectics, propositions may be collected "out of written treatises as well as from personal enquiry." If a proposition is "currently admitted as true in general or in most cases, it must be tendered ... as a universal principle" (Grote, 1872, p. 401). In the conduct of dialectical enquiry, "[a]ll propositions must be registered in the most general terms possible, and must then be resolved into their subordinate constitute particulars, as far as the process of subdivision can be carried" (p. 402). On the second protocol, terms must be investigated for "Equivocation" because, often, they have different, double, or multiple meanings in common usage; their usage and therefore their predicates may differ vastly (p. 402). On the third and fourth protocols, terms must be studied for Differences and Resemblances because terms that seem closely allied may, because of their usage or equivocation, have vastly different meanings in different contexts. Conversely, "subjects of great apparent difference" may bear resemblance for precisely the same reason: context of usage; if the different meanings of terms are not known, then dialecticians "cannot know clearly" what is being (p. 406).

Dialectic method is not concerned with discovering or prescribing truths, but rather with identifying contradictions and inconsistencies from which new understandings can be synthesized (Grote, 1872, p. 385). The method is for investigating the common meanings—the accepted assumptions, definitions, and understandings—of a given subject matter by way of investigating the received, authoritative statements about these. This is also in common with contemporary critical approaches to language analysis (Lemke, 1995, p. 42). Dialectical method proceeds by laying out the *doxa* of, for instance, political economy, into its accepted propositions; differentiating between the various uses and meanings of these; and showing the relationships of these parts to the whole of the subject matter. The form of the dialectic that Marx deploys cannot be confused with the *reductio ad absurdum* carried on by the late scholasticism of the counter-reformation (McKeon, 1928; Saul, 1992, 1997). Rather, it can be considered as an expression of centuries in the critical development of what we now know as "scientific method":

> From the beginning of the fourteenth century ... there set in a persistent and searching reconstruction of the Aristotelian tradition, which, when directed to the Physics, led by gradual stages to the mechanical and mathematical problems of the Galilean age, and when directed to the Logic led to the precise formulation of the method and structure of science acclaimed by all the seventeenth century scien-

tists. (Randall, 1940, p. 180)

And, when directed to political economy, it led to the formulations of Adam Smith and Marx, among others. The "free thinkers" among the scholastics, particularly those in the school of Padua, developed through dialectic, a scientific method based on the "careful analysis of experience" that "left their hands with a refinement and precision … which the seventeenth century scientists who used it did not surpass in all their careful investigation of method" (Randall, 1940, p. 178). Thus we find in general usage during Marx's time a refined classical method—refined by centuries of application by the Paduan scholars in the first instance, and modified by the introduction of the *time* relation by Hegel later on. Marx's dialectic analysis underpins much of contemporary discourse analysis, and it informs my method of analysis throughout this book.

Throughout Marx's work, he is concerned with investigating "both consciousness *and* life and the 'relation' between them" (Warminski, 1995, p. 120). But Marx does not see language, consciousness, and life as separate "things," even though they may be seen as different aspects of human activity. This can be seen most clearly in *The German Ideology* (1846/1972), wherein Marx and Engels describe "the language of real life" as "the material activity and the material intercourse of men [*sic*]" (1846/1972, p. 118). For Marx, life, language, social activity, and consciousness are essential and inseparable aspects of humanity which are socially produced in relation to the rest of nature. Specifying relations in terms of "subjects," "predicates," and so on is, for Marx, the act of asserting dynamic, causal, reciprocal, co-extensive, paratactic, and hypotactic relations amongst elements referred to in language and amongst the elements of human life itself, which is in the end nothing other than human interactivity, "the language of real life" (p. 118).

Permeating that language is an organizing system of values that gets expressed in words, narratives, arguments, and actions of all kinds. To understand how the current system got the way it has, we must turn to the realm of values. Of particular interest is the price system, the system of value that seems to so thoroughly dominate everything from political decisions to personal choices. So let us turn our attention to the *doxa* of recent political economic thought to show how "official" construals of value that prevail in the current climate have emerged from a systematic, long-term intellectual effort to extract money values from their connection with all other aspects of life. This has been an achievement of discourse and is therefore amenable to dialectical enquiry.

A brief history of value as a technical concept

To develop the concept of capital it is necessary to begin not with labour but with value, and, precisely, with exchange value in an already developed movement of circulation. It is just as impossible to make the transition directly from labour to

> capital as it is to go from the different human races directly to the banker, or from nature to the steam engine. (Marx, 1973, p. 259)

> Labour was the first price, the original purchase money paid for all things. It was not by gold or silver, but by labour, that all the wealth of the world was originally purchased; and its value, to those who possess it, and who want to exchange it for some new productions, is precisely equal to the quantity of labour which it can enable them to command. *Wealth, as Mr Hobbes says, is power.* (Smith, 1776/1997, pp. 133-134, emphasis added)

The term "value" has come to be typically identified with "price" in studies of political economy. But people seem easily to ignore that money is at the same time an idea, an agreement, a form of communication, and merely one expression of value. Social perceptions of value shape, and are shaped by, the normative practices of dominant institutions; of particular groups of people, such as the family; and of course those of specific individuals. The current tendency in public discourse to reduce all values to an expression of price makes the crudest of value-statements possible: "Some people are more valuable than others" (ABC, 1978 in Bagdikian, 1997, p. 114). It would appear that the concept of "more and less valuable people" has become as institutionalized as the price system itself, thus giving rise to the most dramatic increase in slavery since its peak in the US during the nineteenth century (Bales, 1999). It is from *inside* a globally mediated social system, in which the price system of money-values has come to dominate social perceptions of value on a global scale, that I attempt to trace the outlines of "economic" value as a technical device that has been shaped by, and given social force through, the normative work of people and institutions delegated with the authority to define its various meanings.

Values, whether monetary or otherwise, as they are expressed in the language that people speak and write, are only ever partially overt—mere surface expressions of much larger and longer sets of relationships. Underneath such expressions lies historical infusions of conflicting and contradictory value systems that are far more elusive than lexis or grammar. They are evident in the shape of our cities, the ways we work and travel, how we relate to people in our families, the way we pray, the way we talk about our environment, and the ways in which we relate with the rest of nature. My focus here is on how the character of value has changed in studies of political economy over the last century and a half.

While I have traced out dominant trajectories in the development and fragmenting of value studies in political economy, I have left out much historical context, and practically all reference to particular personal histories for the people who have been key in developing different understandings of value in this field. Apart from the usual constraints of space and time, I have taken such an approach for a number of reasons. First, I do not assume that the following history, in any significant way, captures the wider social dynamics from within which each fragmenting moment took its impetus. Rather, I have emphasized the contextual aspects of the media environment wherever appropriate, obviously for reasons to do with the overall purpose of this book. Second, I assume that the disciplinary and institutional value-fragmentations I describe here were more or less violently contested moments, both by individuals within the fields concerned and, in many cases, by whole classes of people within the populations affected by shifting "official" conceptions of value. Finally, I assume that in the fragmentation and *linguistification* of value, the institutions and persons recognized as central to the historical trajectory I describe will, to misquote an Arab proverb, "resemble their own times" more than they will their own "parents" (Bloch, 1940/1961, p. 148).

Tracing the movement of value as an object of intellectual and institutional contention is of fourfold analytical importance to this book: i) it shows what kinds of values and related forms of expertise are and have been possible as a direct result of understandings about what value *means*; ii) it also shows that forms of value and forms of authority are entirely connected, perhaps even mutually defining; iii) it emphasizes the institutional, and therefore institutionally mediated, nature of value; and iv) it shows how new media relationships changed understandings of value systems and thus perceptions of value, worldwide.

Classical political economy: Liberalism and the rational death of God

> The 'Enlightenment' drew its strength primarily from the evident progress of production, trade, and the economic and scientific rationality believed to be associated inevitably with both. And its greatest champions were the economically most progressive classes, those most directly involved in the tangible advances of the time: the mercantile circles and economically minded landlords, financiers, scientifically-minded economic and social administrators, the educated middle class, manufacturers and entrepreneurs. (Hobsbawm, 1962, p. 34)

Classical political economy was the first field in which "'value' became a technical term" (Langworthy Taylor, 1895, p. 414). Technicalization notwithstanding, "the term 'value' is intimately associated with the most remote experiences of the human race. Ever since it has been possible to predicate desirability of anything, have values existed" (p. 414). That is my working definition of "value" in the broadest and most abstract terms possible: the predication of *Desirability* for any given aspect of life.

Prior to classical political economy, "economics" was merely part of a wider system of philosophical scholarship in the scholastic institutions of the

Church (Neill, 1949). Here, as with the rest of social science, economics was "generally treated as a branch of ethics or of politics" (Neill, 1949, p. 532; see also Aristotle, 1961/1987). The emergence of liberalism undermined the authority of the Church, first in the field of economic values, and soon thereafter in the field of moral values (Neill, 1949, pp. 532-534).

In both England and France, liberal formulations of political economy initially retained the expansive scope of the scholastic enterprise. Economics, morality, and science were melded into a "natural law of justice in its essence" (Daire, 1846 in Neill, 1949, p. 535). Economics, the "moral economy," and "civil society" shared an assumed identity because of historical conventions in social scholarship:

> The Physiocrats … thought that they had discovered a new science, that it was an elucidation of natural law, and that its scope extended to all of man's dealing with man and nature. It was therefore a moral science governing man's social activity, much the sort of thing that John Locke once hoped to achieve for ethics by applying to that subject the laws discovered by his friend Newton. (Neill, 1949, p. 537)

Destutt de Tracy is exemplary of the expansive character of late eighteenth- to early nineteenth-century political economy. He hoped for a literal "ideology," a "science of ideas" that would "establish a sound 'theory of the moral and political sciences,'" one that embraced "grammar, logic, education, morality, and finally the greatest of arts, for whose success all the others must cooperate, that of regulating society" (Kennedy, 1979, p. 355). It quickly became clear to vested interests that such an endeavor aimed at supplanting the authority of the Church by replicating the full extent of its authority. The resultant attacks upon classical political economy's expansive ambitions was a fragmenting of the "value sciences."

This rapid fragmentation, most evident during the late nineteenth century, coincides with the social and intellectual transition from a Newtonian age of "Natural Order," in which an all-seeing God ruled over a clockwork Universe, to the feverish Social Darwinism of the late nineteenth century in which the whole of life was viewed as a struggle for survival: "the Natural Order was for the eighteenth century what evolution became for the nineteenth, the common concept into which every generalization was thrown" (Ware, 1931, p. 619). Of course, the latter worldview did not supplant the former. The assumptions of social Darwinism were merely overlaid upon those of the "Natural Order," augmenting them and giving the "Order" a dynamic, scientific, and historical explanation. The "Natural Order" arose not from the design of a clockmaker God but from all-out, constant competition on the part of every living thing for the necessities of life (cf. Tylor, 1877; Ware, 1931).

Changes in the most basic assumptions about the nature of value closely resemble those of the whole Western intellectual enterprise. That is not surprising. The fragmenting of "value" scholarship into the many "disciplines" of social science we know today is an artifact of intellectual specialization and fragmentation in general. The close connection between theories of value and the rest of scholarship cannot be overstated, if only because it appears to be so well hidden in the obfuscating contemporary milieu of specialized, elite dialects (Saul, 1992, 1997). With this sense of institutionally generated separation in mind, we can see in historical discussions about value the various and perennial antagonisms that have led to differentiated ways of understanding the world. More especially, we can see the antagonistic assumptions about *how* we come to understand our world in these arguments.

The core antagonisms in this long debate can be generally grouped under subjective versus objective; static versus dynamic; exogenous versus endogenous; and social versus individual assumptions about the source, meaning, and nature of human understandings. These broadest and most basic assumptions are evident throughout the history of value as a technical idea, just as they are in assumptions about the social world more generally.

Objective versus subjective conceptions of value

Seen from one perspective, "the historical evolution of the value debate became locked into a centuries old dialectical conflict between the objective and subjective approaches" (Fogarty, 1996).[9] Once assumptions about objective and subjective value are examined, some logical corollaries become apparent. The assumptions of subjective value implicates people's activity as the source of value: subjective value is a measure of activity and is therefore time-based. Assumptions that value is an objective category implicates non-human "things" (gold or real estate for instance) as the bearers of value: it is therefore a measure of substance or space, and we should expect that incommensurate forms of expression are used to describe these different perspectives on value. If we assume that value is entirely objective, we must assume that value is external to what people are and do—that value is an extrinsic, *a priori* quality with an independent existence. Further, we must assume that value resides neither in social nor individual aspects of human activity—in the objective view, people are unnecessary for value to exist. Conversely, if we assume that value is entirely subjective, we must assume that no objective, *a priori* values can exist independently of humans, either as individuals or societies. Therefore, in its extreme form, subjective value is entirely relativist. So assumptions about objectivity and subjectivity have clear implications for the direction of the value debate in political economy. For perhaps obvious reasons, the general direction of the debate has been towards an increasingly subjective account of value, or so it would appear.

The first elements of subjectivity in the modern theories of economic value enter at the end of the mercantilist era. The mercantilist theorists held an objective view of value—it was an intrinsic property of precious metals (Locke, 1696). Furthermore, value and power were identical to the mercantilist economic mind (Viner, 1948). This was the period during which "the serviceability to power of economic warfare, the possibility of using military power to achieve immediate economic ends, and the possibilities of substituting economic power for military power" were developed for the first time in an elaborate and systematic manner (Viner, 1948, p. 8). This was reflected in the prevailing attitudes to people and the world in general at the peak of mercantilist political economy:

> For, since the introduction of the new artillery of powder guns, &c., and the discovery of wealth in the Indies, &c. war is become rather an expense of money than men, and success attends those that can most and longest spend money: whence it is that prince's [*sic*] armies in Europe are become more proportionable to their purses than to the number of their people; so that it uncontrollably follows that a foreign trade managed to best advantage, will make our country so strong and rich, that we may command the trade of the world, the riches of it, and consequently the world itself. (Bolingbroke, 1752 in Viner, 1948)

Lord Bolingbroke's statement captures the excesses of hard-line mercantilist hyperbole quite succinctly: people are merely an object of wealth; wealth exists externally to people and to whole nations. Wealth is both the fulcrum and lever by which the whole world might be moved. Further, the intrinsic value of particular classes of people were immutable, and their purpose was seen to be collectively oriented:

> In this view, members of society did not interact with each other, but rather participated, one with another, in England's collective enterprise of selling surplus goods abroad. As in a company, the administration was formal. There was little of Adam Smith's awareness of individuals with personal motives working purposively on their own. Rather economic writers approached the problem of promoting national growth much as a factory foreman might view meeting a production quota. (Appleby, 1976, p. 501)

The social expression of the mercantilist mindset was quite straightforward:

> The rich were expected to buy their luxuries, the poor to have enough to subsist [...] With such a model at the back of their heads, these writers elaborated schemes for putting the poor to work. Houses for the "orderly management of the poor" was a favorite theme. (Appleby, 1976, p. 501)

The possibility of rising levels of equality and wealth was "unthought of, if not unthinkable" (Marx, 1976, p. 501). Two readily identifiable pressures combined to bring the mercantilist worldview to an ostensible end: rising costs in maintaining a colonial military presence on the part of mercantilist nations (Smith, 1776/1999, pp. 550-551) and the rising tide of a political and economic liberalism which, not coincidentally, rose on a flood of printed paper (Thompson, 1980, chap. 5). The popular values of liberalism were freedom and equality for all people and an increased emphasis on the rights of the individual (Appleby, 1976, p. 515).

Lost to antiquity, subjective conception of value first enters post-enlightenment economic thought with Adam Smith (1776/1997, 1776/1999) in England and the Physiocratic school in France. This is the period in history where the tension between objective and subjective understandings of value re-emerges in a formal sense. The Physiocrats, while accepting that human activity adds value in some way, assumed that value inhered primarily in "land and land rents" (Hobsbawm, 1962, p. 26). The early English theorists of mercantilist manufacturing, eventually attacked and briefly superseded by Smith and his followers, assumed that labor acted as a catalyst to release the value which inhered objectively in raw materials and manufacturing equipment. This view led to some of the complex problems that still remain for political economy to comprehend:

> Labour seems to be a very simple category. The notion of labour in this universal form, as labour in general, is … extremely old. Nevertheless "labour" in this simplicity is economically considered just as modern a category as the relations which give rise to this modern abstraction. The Monetary System, for example, still regards wealth quite objectively as a thing existing independently in the shape of money. Compared with this standpoint, it was a substantial advance when the Manufacturing or Mercantile system transferred the source of wealth from the object to subjective activity—mercantile or industrial labour—but it still considered that only this circumscribed activity itself produced money. In contrast to this system, the Physiocrats assume that a specific form of labour—agriculture—creates wealth, and they see the object no longer in the guise of money, but as a product in general, as the result of universal labour …
>
> It was an immense advance when Adam Smith rejected all restrictions with regard to the activity that produces wealth—for him it was all labour as such, neither manufacturing, nor commercial, nor agricultural labour, but all types of labour. (Marx, 1970, p. 209)

With Adam Smith, an expression of purely subjective value emerges for the first time: "the wealth of nations" is the work of people, and labor is the "original money paid for all things" (1776/1997, p. 134).

Marx's approach to value remains unique in political economy for its attempt to reconcile objective and subjective aspects of value without reducing the assumptions of one to the other in order to explain them. Surprisingly, Marx is often attributed as the author of the labor theory of value, but that is not at all accurate: "Labour is *not the source* of all wealth. *Nature* is just as much the source of use values (and it is surely of such that material wealth consists!) as labour, which itself is only the manifestation of a force of nature, human labour power" (Marx, 1875/1972, p. 382). For the purposes of this book, Marx's key comments about value are these:

Value ... does not have its description branded on its forehead; it rather transforms
every product of labour into a social hieroglyphic. Later on, men try to decipher
the hieroglyphic, to get behind the secret of their own social product: for the characteristic which objects of utility have of being values is as much men's social
product as is their language. The belated scientific discovery that the products of
labour, in so far as they are values, are merely the material expressions of the human labour expended to produce them, marks an epoch in the history of
mankind's development, but by no means banishes the objectivity possessed by
the social characteristics of labour. (1976, p. 167)

In other words, new understandings about the source and nature of value
change perceptions of what it means to be human.

According to Marx, what we call "value" is the product of interaction between subjective and objective aspects of our existence, mediated and
refracted through the normative frameworks of the social world, and expressed as "social hieroglyphics," as "things" socially imbued with a certain
significance in relation to others. Humans, he argues, tend to obscure and
objectify their interactions with each other and the rest of nature where values
are concerned, whether economic or otherwise:

The production of ideas, of conceptions, of consciousness, is at first directly in-
terwoven with the material activity and the material intercourses of men, the
language of real life. Conceiving, thinking, the mental intercourse of men, appear
at this stage as the direct efflux of their material behaviour. The same applies to
mental production as expressed in the language of politics, laws, morality, religion, metaphysics etc. of a people. Men are the producers of their conceptions,
ideas, etc.—real, active men as they are conditioned by a definite development of
their productive forces and the intercourse corresponding to these, up to its fur-
thest form. ... If in all ideology men and their circumstances appear upside-down
as in a *camera obscura*, this phenomenon arises just as much from their historical
life-process as the inversion of objects on the retina does from their physical life-
process. (Marx and Engels, 1846/1972, p. 118)

Marx and Engels extend the purview of political economy to include the production of *all* social phenomena, including individual and social
consciousness (1846/1972, p. 122). Not since Marx (perhaps with the exception of Freud, some Frankfurt School writers, and Lewis Mumford) has any
social science embraced such expansive aspects of the human condition: that
is to say, as a social totality. Nor has the concept of labor and production been
inscribed so broadly. Political economy has instead become economics,
which in turn has to some significant degree become "a branch of higher ac-
countancy" because of its narrowed scope and an adherence to a perceived
identity between value and price (Innis, 1944, p. 82).

While it has never been equaled in political economy since Marx, the expansive scope of classical political economy was not abandoned all at once.
Although the "utility curves" of the Austrian school of economics appear as
early as 1893, the debate as to the source and nature of value, though increas-

ingly narrow in scope, extended beyond what today is considered to be the "economic" field. For Marx, political economy is merely social activity viewed from a certain perspective—that of production (1981, p. 957). The classical categories of value, production, labor, commodities, and exchange formed the basis of Marx's discussions. But in Marx they do not obscure political economy's foundations: historically determined social interactions.

Individual psychology and the triumph of price in economic theory

The tendency of political economy to offer an exhaustive, socially grounded account of value collapsed after the pressure applied by Smith, Marx, and the European socialists to the very concept of value. Consequently, the journey towards a wholly subjective formulation of value has fairly much remained in dominance throughout the West since the late nineteenth century, especially in the realms of policy. The "Austrian school" remain the most influential originators of "subjective value theory" (Bonar, 1888; Sweezy, 1934).[10] Members of this school are also called "utility theorists" because they explain exchange-value—or rather its epiphenomenon, price—in terms of use-value, or "utility" (Langworthy Taylor, 1895; Sweezy, 1934). A corollary of, and indeed a catalyst for, this approach was the emergent discipline of psychology, with a heightened emphasis on psychological theories of pain, sacrifice, desire, and pleasure being introduced into studies of value (Sweezy, 1934, p. 177). The main assumptions of subjective value theory are: i) that the focus for economic studies of value is the individual; ii) that the individual will always choose "correctly" in terms of his or her satisfaction, "correctly" not being understood here "ethically," but rather "economically" (1934, p. 178); iii) that an individual "carries his pleasures and his exertions to the point where the margins of pleasure and of sacrifice correspond, so that the last increment of pleasure exactly repays the last dose of labour" (Langworthy Taylor, 1895, p. 419); and iv) that labor is always a measure of pain and sacrifice, and purchases are always an expression of the pleasurable satisfaction of desires (Langworthy Taylor, 1895; Sweezy, 1934).[11]

At this point in the development of political economy, the effects of social factors—along with all ethical and other apparently non-economic factors— are almost entirely elided. Nevertheless economic studies still claimed, and continue to claim, to explain the actions of whole societies, along with the actions of the "ordinary mind" (Sweezy, 1934, p. 179).[12] That this school of economics has proven to be almost unerringly wrong in their most important predictions for over a century has not dampened their enthusiasm for individualistic, mathematical "models" of society (Sherden, 1998; Saul, 1997). This branch of economics, from the outset, resembles the Physiocrats in levels of dogmatism and abstraction. Evidence contrary to theory was, and still is, dismissed as "irrational." The answer? A purely Hegelian "so much the worse for the facts!":

> Professor Strigl's basic device for freeing economics from the embarrassments of psychological and other kinds of empirical investigation is to be found in his distinction between the categories and the data of economic science. The categories are derived from the very fundamental fact of economics, or rather of economising, itself. Their validity is as general ... as any sort of human life we know about. From these categories, all the laws of pure economics can be deduced. (Sweezy, 1934, p. 180)

A reliance on deductive relationships between abstract categories, construed as immutable, *a priori*, universal economic laws produced an increasingly one-sided, reductionism. Recognizing the one-sidedness of the subjective value theorists, Schumpeter (1909), most notably amongst others, put forward a conception of "social value," seemingly to dismiss its validity.

Social versus individual formulations of value

At this point, arguments about the nature of value in political economy, which were becoming increasingly entangled in the apparently objective identity between price and value (the paradoxical result of subjective value theory), become focused on the tension between social and individual sources of value. Schumpeter is clear that his formulation has "nothing whatsoever to do with the great problems of individualism and collectivism," and that his concerns are "purely methodological" (1909, p. 213). In his investigation of "social value" as a concept, Schumpeter acknowledges that utility theory "never spoke of social, but only of individual value" (1909, p. 213). But individualism, he argues, is the correct mode of economic investigation: "we have to start with the individual" because the reasoning of marginal utility "cannot be directly applied to society as a whole" (p. 215).

While Schumpeter concludes that social wants exist (such as the communal need for such things as "battleships"), because it cannot by definition be subject to study through the methods of subjective value theory, social value is at best a useful metaphor. Again, the uncomfortable fact that individualistic theory does not and cannot explain phenomena that are social in origin is used to rationalize the ultimate invalidity of social theory *tout court* (1909, pp. 231-232). This is all the more remarkable because Schumpeter is recognized among his later followers as a superlative sociologist as well as an economist (Taylor, 1951). The circularity of subjective value theory, whether exclusively individualistic or metaphorically social, along with its paradoxical focus on objectified abstract "things" ("price," "demand," "supply"), appears to escape the early Schumpeter and the latter day adherents to extreme versions of subjective value theory.

The circularity of subjective (or "marginal" or "utility") value theory boils down to this: all values are the expressions of felt needs of some sort. These needs are measured against the pain of acquiring the means of their satisfaction and extinguishment. The resultant psychological predispositions of such interactions is "value," or to be precise, "marginal value." Whereas people can feel needs, society, having no psychology, nervous system, or any other parts of human anatomy, cannot. Thus, society can have no needs, and *therefore no values*. The intractable logical difficulty with the marginal value theory, then, is the problems created by an extremely *subjective* set of assumptions about value mixed with an extremely *individualistic* set of assumptions about the nature of society. If all values are expressions of individual needs, then society can have no needs and no values. Therefore, for a wholly subjective value theory there can be no such thing as social value systems, even when these clearly exist. History, culture, and other conditions of production are excluded from economic theory based on such assumptions. Society appears as a mere abstraction, as nothing more than the sum of subjective individual desires.

The semantic turn: Philosophers of value

The increasing emphasis on price and money in mainstream economics, well noted by Harold Innis, left somewhat of a problem for economics, namely a semantic residue. Smith, Ricardo, Marx, and the Physiocrats had all attempted, with varying degrees of success, to develop a science of society as a whole, recognizing the very real effects of all those aspects which were later to be excluded from the determination and meaning of value in political economy. An intellectual struggle ensued over the scope and meaning of value, and of what was to be done with its semantic byproducts. To see how arguments about the nature of value developed, it is worth looking to Ralph Barton Perry (1914, 1916), an exemplar of the philosophers of subjective value, who stepped in to the void left by narrowly subjective theories of value in political economy. In a very real sense, the formalizing of philosophies of value decisively pronounces the death of a broadly conceived conception of value in political economy. In doing so, it consigned the residue of "uneconomic" values to other realms of enquiry.

In 1916, economics and the philosophy of value meet formally for the first time in the *Quarterly Journal of Economics*, ostensibly to identify potential commonalities. The effect was rather to define boundaries between "recently conventionalized," "technical" understandings of value in economics and value more generally:

> I am certainly not using the term "value" in the sense which has recently been conventionalized for purposes of economics [as "wealth"]—and do not mean to. That sense is purely technical. … As respects terms, the situation is simply this. The term "value" is a more general term than "worth" or "good." Such a term is

indispensable if we are to disengage a generic idea or principle from the over-
whelming variety and confusion of our world of praise and disparagement.
Consider the ways in which a single object such as a book may be praised or dis-
paraged. ... These various properties "cheap," "mendacious," "ignorant,"
"edifying" and "crude," differ characteristically as a group, from such other properties as the book's color, weight, and size. They are the terms in which the book
may be estimated, the predicates of *critical* judgment that may be pronounced
upon it. We need the term "value" as a term to apply to all the predicates of this
group. We may then speak of economic values, moral values, cognitive values, religious values and aesthetic values as various species of one genus. It follows that
we should no longer speak of economics, after the manner of von Weiser as "treat-
ing the entire sphere of value phenomena"; but as one of the group of value
sciences, having certain peculiar varieties of value as its province, and enjoying
critical competence or authority only in its own restricted terms. (Perry, 1916, pp.
445-446)

Perry is clear that the various "species" of values do not exist in isolation
from each other, and that the "fruitfulness of grouping them together lies in
the fact that there are fundamental principles common to them all, and in the
fact that they perpetually interact" (p. 446). However, he argues, even though
the many species of value are "all functions of life," and have "both a common source and innumerable threads of cross-connection," certain of them
are nevertheless "mutually independent in that there is no constant relation
between them, either in quantity or in sign" (p. 446). This is self-evident to
Perry because "the same object may possess positive value in one sense, and
negative value in another" (p. 446). For instance, a "drug may increase in
price at the same time that it grows more injurious to health" (p. 446). And,
"if economic commendation implied ethical commendation and in the same
proportion, we should be dealing with only one type of value; but in as much
as what is commended economically *may* be condemned ethically, there are,
evidently, as we say, two standards" (p. 446).

Perry is also aware of how historically significant is the shift to a subjective view of value in economics. But his enthusiasm for the move comes at
the price of a serious omission:

Economic theory has steadily grown more psychological. It has long abandoned
the naïve view that economic value is an inherent property of gold and silver.
More recently it has abandoned the view that economic value is a sort of stamp or
coating that things acquire in the course of their production, whether by agriculture or any form of labor. (p. 447, emphasis added)

This leaves a single realm of investigation, a point of "widespread agreement" among economists and philosophers of value, "namely that values
arise and have their being in the realm of emotion, desire, and will" (p. 448).
Here, Perry's omission, indeed that of the whole subjective school, becomes
apparent: it is the entire social production process, the entire network of activities and artifacts through which societies reproduce themselves from

every perspective and at every level: materially, socially, relationally, mentally, and economically.

While non-economic aspects of value seem to Perry to be somehow related to economic value, he claims that they belong to separate realms of inquiry: "the philosopher of value, like the economic theorist, must carry his distinctions and his laws back in the last analysis to the dynamic aspect of mind, to that part of man, individual and social, with which he feels and acts" (Perry, 1916, p. 448). What Perry forestalls here, and has been constantly suspended ever since in the history of value in mainstream political economy became increasingly "subjective," is that "that part of man, individual and social, with which he feels and acts," an individual's realm of "emotion, desire, and will" is as much a social product as factories, cities, money, and language (Marx, 1846/1972, pp. 122-123).

That is meant neither as a mechanical assertion of social predetermination nor an assertion of economic determinism. It is a rather simple statement of a self-evident, historical fact. Even a psychological touchstone of subjective value theorists, Sigmund Freud, would "scorn to distinguish between culture and civilization":

> Human civilization includes … all the knowledge and capacity that men have acquired in order to control the forces of nature and extract its wealth for the satisfaction of human needs and … all the regulations necessary in order to adjust the relations of men to one another and especially the distribution of available wealth. (1928/1991, p. 184)

The conditions into which humans are born, including the categories of thought in widespread use; the social universe of education, work, entertainment, culture, and beliefs; normative standards of behavior including laws, and so on—as they exist in socially mediated reality, and as they are defined and expressed in language—*precede* each individual as much as they *produce* them as individuals, along with their dynamic and context-bound axiologies. Individuals can do no more than shape materials which they find ready to hand in the world, materials of varying levels of abstraction, and they can only do so with the stuff from which they are made (Marx and Engels, 1846/1972, pp. 118-122). These materials include, are motivated by, and result in, evaluations, or expressions of value.

Philosophical nuances aside, Perry's sojourn into political economy leads inexorably towards one conclusion: the necessity for a division of intellectual labor in understanding value. After defining the juncture at which moral and economic values meet, Perry then explains why the economists ought not trouble themselves with moral issues. While Perry allows that "the economist is welcome to discuss them," he argues that all issues of value not concerned with the subjective determination of prices lie outside the sphere of political economy, including alternative models of distribution, production, and exchange, and are best dealt with by "philosophical ethics" (Perry, 1916, p. 485). Thus, "the most valuable work of the economist will be in the more restricted field," and the "higher" and more "generic" values, those with moral consequences, ought to be left to the philosophical specialist (p. 485).

By 1916 psychologically-based theories of value dominated political economy and moral philosophy. The movement achieved not only the intellectual separation of value studies into economic, philosophic, and semantic disciplines, but also the hard distinction between the individual from society in mainstream political economy. And, as economics withered to a study of price, another major axiological developed at the same time—the field of eugenic sociology.

"Normal" people: Statists, statistics, and the "nature" of inequality

Normativity is a strictly social and subjective category of value: it refers to a particular kind of social work done in institutions which has the effect of producing and reproducing certain ways and forms of being, seeing, speaking, and acting within those institutions. *Normality*, on the other hand, is a concept that first emerges in a technical form in the study of "eugenics" (Hacking, 1996). Meaning, literally, "good origins," eugenics was the invention of Francis Galton and is notable as the first post-Enlightenment effort to institutionalize, quantify, and thus make scientific the money-value of specific "types" of people.[13] At first, eugenics emerged from within the rupturing fields of economics, anthropology, statics (now statistics), biology, and in particular, their admixture with the evolutionary perspective elaborated in Darwin's (1865) *The Origin of The Species* (Field, 1911, p. 4). Social Darwinism and "Evolutionary Philosophy" combined in eugenics to become the foundations of late nineteenth-century sociology (Ford, 1909; Galton, 1887; Spencer, 1876 in Tylor, 1877). It incorporated the strong Darwinism of the time, which was an enormous value disruption in itself, challenging as it did the creationist doctrines of the Church (White, 1896/1960, chap. 1). Galton's sociology added interventionist aspects of biological control to social sciences and politics (Field, 1911; Galton, 1901, 1904; Hacking, 1996).

Galton's original framework seems somewhat crude and simplistic by today's standards:

> The main book, that great ability is hereditary, is here substantially unaltered; supported, now, by abundant genealogical material, which nearly fills the book with pedigrees of judges, statesmen, the English peerage, commanders, literary men, men of science, poets, musicians, painters, divines, the senior classics of Cambridge, —even oarsmen and wrestlers, as examples of the ability of the muscles rather than of the mind. But if the theme is in the main the same, the manner of presentation is notably changed. Galton's characteristic originality of thought is

reinforced by his equally characteristic attention to scrupulous precision of method. (Field, 1911, p. 6)

Despite the rather obvious flaws in its theoretical origins, the assumptions of eugenics remain a pervasive influence today (Hacking, 1996).

Galton was firstly a student of *statistics*, a field of study which arose as an emergent scientific, and inherently adverse reaction to "divine right and royal prerogative" (Ranney, 1976, p. 143), an outlook that:

was challenged in the late sixteenth and seventeenth century by what Greenleaf calls the theory of empiricism. This new way of looking at things was first advanced by Francis Bacon and later by James Harrington, Sir William Temple, and Sir William Petty. It was based on the inductive analysis of facts observed from both history and the experience of contemporary governments …

As one of their principle tools the English empiricists developed "statistics" in the original meaning of the word. The point is worth noting briefly. The empiricists sought to foster what they called "statists"—that is, men who had wide personal experience in and knowledge of political affairs and had, as a result, gained skill in management. (Ranney, 1976, p. 143)

Statistics (then "statics") was thus to be the statists' rigorous collection and comparison of mathematically verifiable facts about society and its control— the tools for a science of quantitatively defined bio-social management system (Ward, 1895).

Enthusiasm for eugenics, combined with the widely felt panic of *fin de siecle* imperialism throughout western Europe, prompted George Bernard Shaw to say "nothing but a eugenic religion can save our civilization from the fate that has overtaken all previous civilizations" (1904 in Galton, 1904, p. 21). For liberal socialists, most notably the Fabianists, who believed that "the causes of science and socialism were inextricably linked," eugenics provided a scientific sociological method through which the quality of "social stocks" would be improved (Paul, 1984, p. 574; Galton, 1904).

Galton believed that "natural selection" had failed in the case of the human race, mostly because human laws and sympathies led us to support an ever growing underclass of poor and therefore inferior people who would continue to reproduce at a far greater rate than the rich, if only by sheer weight of numbers (Galton, 1901, p. 132). To illustrate how the sealed logic of Galton's theory operated, here is how he speaks about the value of specific types of people and how these are best determined:

Dr Farr calculated the value at its birth of a baby born of the wife of an Essex labourer, supposing it to be an average specimen of its class in length of life, in cost of maintenance while a child and in old age, and in earnings during youth and manhood. He capitalized with actuarial skill the prospective values at the time of birth, of the outgoings and the incoming, and on balancing the items found the newly born infant to be worth 5*l*. A similar process would conceivably bring out the money of value at birth of children destined when they grew up to fall into

each of the several classes, and by a different method of appraisement to discover
their moral and social worth. As regards the money value of men of the highest
class, many found great industries, establish vast undertakings, increase the wealth
of multitudes and amass large fortunes for themselves. Others, whether rich or
poor, are the guides and light of the nation, raising its tone, enlightening the difficulties and imposing its ideals. The most gifted of these men, members of our yet
undefined X class, would each be worth thousands of pounds to the nation at the
moment of their birth. (1901, p. 132)

Galton and his five-shilling babies ought hardly be worth mentioning. And
were it not for the enormity and duration of the movement Galton inspired,
he could be ignored. As it happened, though, eugenics underpinned dominant
thought for the "left" and "right" in interventionist policy throughout the
West until at least 1940 (Paul, 1984).[14] This was most overtly the case between 1901 and 1940, during which time Hitler and his Third Reich,
possessed of perverse notions of "race hygiene," had developed a mechanical
and systematic method for annihilating the least "valuable," most "abnormal"
and "burdensome" people in society. The intrinsic value of people had become objectified in policy. Many millions of those found lacking would be
subjected to mechanical and efficient systems of eradication.

    The eugenics movement provided the basis upon which the conception of
objective, "value-free" *Normality* was built—the now mythical "normal person" became a socially ratified, empirically verifiable "fact" (Hacking, 1996,
pp. 59-61). It was this concept, combined with more racially motivated literature of the day, that paved the way for allegedly scientific and rational
assumptions about the inherent inequality of whole classes, races, and
"types" of people (Graham, 1977; Paul, 1984). Notions of *Normality* became
a part of *Normative* evaluations throughout whole societies. What happened
as a consequence of such values being propagated *en masse* were the mass
murders in Stalin's USSR and Hitler's Germany (Bullock, 1991). At the
height of the eugenics movement, between 1934 and 1938, the predominance
of actuarial statistics, combined with the economic emphasis on cost and
price, pushed jurisprudence to place a precise average monetary figure on
"the value of life" (Symmons, 1938).[15]

Social anthropology, sociolinguistics, and symbolic value

Other important contributions to the technical study of social perceptions of
value can be found in social anthropology. Early ethnographic work by
Mauss (1925/1990), Durkheim (1933/1960), and Malinowski (1921) on symbolic value forms the basis of this school of thought (Firth, 1953; Hart, 2000,
pp. 19-20). Social anthropology was developed as a conscious and critical
response to Spencerian and Galtonian social Darwinism, and to the extreme
individualism of subjective value theories in political economy (Hart, 2000,
p. 186). As concrete as social anthropology's object might be, the study of

values in this field has never been treated as unproblematic (Firth, 1953). Various recent perspectives, such as those drawing on the work of Kuhn (1962), claim new insight into the value-laden nature of scientific practices. But since at least 1908, it has been recognized that, both in the "physical and natural sciences," perhaps more so in the social sciences, there exists a slippery relationship (if any) between "fact and value, or, more generally, science and value" (Urban, 1908, p. 291). Social science had always been somewhat more suspect to charges of privileging value judgments over facts because "these sciences, or this part of science, unlike the physical sciences, contains value judgments or propositions as part of the very material of science itself" (p. 292). It has long been recognized that "truth" is a certain kind of evaluation (Aristotle, 1999, pp. 4-5; Lemke, 1995, p. 43); that "every attempt to describe truth value and to discriminate it from other values must be a description of its nature"; and that "truth and error are values belonging to the experience of judging" (Moore, 1908, p. 430).[16]

These concerns about the relationship between the value judgments made by social researchers and what they describe as concrete facts in cultures often quite foreign to their own is very much a theoretical foundation of social anthropology. Value is therefore a fundamental aspect of the experience and formulation of social anthropology as a discipline, both theoretically and practically (Firth, 1953). In social anthropology, language, value, and action are acknowledged as being inextricably joined. The discipline is, "in general, concerned with social relations expressed in behaviour—verbal behaviour as well as non-verbal behaviour; words as well as acts" (Firth, 1953, p. 146). For Firth, value is the determining element in human social relations—it is what gives social action meaning. It is expressed in patterns of social "preference" or "decision-taking" (p. 146). And, as an analytical concept, value "gives reality to our structural concepts" (p. 147). Thus the "preferences in social relations, their worthwhileness, the standards of judgment applied, give a context and meaning to social action. This is the field for the study of values" (p. 146).

Firth's conception of value, and of social anthropology more generally, is social and dynamic. Value helps to clarify "the theory of stability and change in social action" (1953, p. 147). As such, it is a foundational category for social anthropology in its "getting an adequate theoretical basis for dynamic analysis" (p. 147). It is worth noting that more recent sensitivities to the conceptual tensions between social structure, function, form, agency, and processes are not something unique to the current age. Firth emphasizes that social anthropologists "must guard against reifying values, much as we should avoid reifying social structures" (p. 147). Therefore, "the anthropologist's notions of values may change in accordance with a changing climate of opinion," and the anthropological "definition of values in its widest meaning is an operational one" (p. 147). For these reasons, according to Firth, the anthropologist's conception and "treatment of value tends to be broader in cultural scope, more realistic in illustration, and still fitted to a general social theory" compared with other disciplines in the social sciences (p. 147).

The most broad semantic categories foregrounded by what Firth has to say about values are those of *Normativity* (meant as the accepted standards of behavior in a social system) and *Desirability*. For Firth, value-systems are expressed in *evaluative patterns* (p. 148). Anthropological research, like many other fields, sometimes makes the mistake of pushing values into "the realm of the irrational and the unconscious" giving "no basis for any change in value judgements" (p. 148). One way to avoid dismissing values in this way is to look at value in terms of "patterns" which "prescribe and delineate the *acceptable*" (p. 148). In this view, *Desirability* and *Normativity* are mutually conditioning aspects of value:

> A pattern is not merely a systematic regular chain or modal form of behavior. It also carries an invitation or command to reproduce the pattern as well as an exclusion and proscription of what is outside it and therefore unacceptable. By implication here is a most important aspect of value, namely its quality of being something wanted and felt to be proper to be wanted. (Firth, 1953, p. 148)

The classical distinction between use-values and exchange-values, a distinction that dates to Aristotle, becomes problematic from the perspective of functionalist social anthropology since preferences, or evaluative patterns, are seen to be firstly normative, social, and dynamic: exchange-value *can be* a use-value, and vice versa.

While social anthropology offers rich insights into the social symbolic relations of society, and a sophisticated perspective on the links between evaluation and social action, the scope of its early inquiries largely avoids the specific problems of mediation processes. This is in large part because of its concern with cultural forms that were construed as "primitive".[17] While the insights produced by social anthropology are relevant to this book in synthesis with other elements, they are derived from perspectives that have largely ignored new media or tended to see mediation processes as something else.[18]

Propaganda and public opinion: "The dictatorship of palaver"

In the development of social perceptions of value, very few identifiable groups, other than perhaps those associated with organized religion, have made such a deep impact on social perceptions of value than the propagandists of the early twentieth century. Propaganda emerged as an object of intellectual investigation following the First World War, just as the radio was coming into widespread use. While other figures, like George Creel (1941), George Gallup (1938), and Edward Bernays (1928, 1945), were co-pioneers in public opinion studies, Harold Lasswell (1927, 1941) remains, I think, the most sophisticated of the early propagandists in terms of theorizing the role of values in influencing mass action. In Lasswell's early studies of mass propaganda techniques, a systematic, theoretically sophisticated study of the relationship between new media, language, and value emerges for the first time. For Lasswell,

> Propaganda is the management of collective attitudes by the manipulation of sig-nificant symbols. The word attitude is taken to mean a tendency to act according to certain patterns of evaluation. The existence of an attitude is not a direct datum of experience, but an inference from signs which have a conventionalized signifi-cance. ... The valuational patterns upon which this inference is founded may be primitive gestures of the face and body, or more sophisticated gestures of the pen and voice. Taken together, these objects which have a standard meaning in a group are called significant symbols. The elevated eyebrow, the clenched fist, the sharp voice, the pungent phrase, have their references established within the web of a particular culture. Such significant symbols are paraphernalia employed in expressing the attitudes, and they are also capable of being employed to reaffirm or redefine attitudes. (Lasswell, 1927, p. 627)

Lasswell elaborates a clear picture of the tensions between the social and in-dividual, objective and subjective, and static and dynamic perspectives on value. In distinction to the early psychologists' approach, Lasswell sees that the "collective attitude" is not on a "plane apart from individual actions" (1927, p. 628). Rather, it is "the collective attitude," a "pattern" which desig-nates "standard uniformities of conduct at a given time and place" (p. 628). The "collective attitude" is a "distribution of individual acts and not an in-dwelling spirit which has achieved transitory realization in the rough, coarse facts of the world of sense" (p. 628). Lasswell differentiates between the techniques of attitude change by psychiatric means and those of propaganda. The former is based on having "access to the individual's private stock of meanings" whereas the latter is based on "the standard meanings of the *groups* of which the individual is a member" (p. 628)—propaganda is a proc-ess of manipulating collectively held meanings, something that can only be reliably identified through dialectical investigation. Once again, resonances with contemporary critical sociolinguistic perspectives on meaning are quite overt (Lemke, 1998; Weiss and Wodak, 2003).

Lasswell's is a context-based, culturally specific understanding of group behavior. He sees that the individual moves through what are known today as "multiple discourse communities," and that each of these groups has its own peculiar *attitudinal patterns* for making meaning (Lemke, 1995). Lasswell is not seduced by the idea that any of the categories successfully deployed in propaganda can be static. The categories of propaganda need to be regarded as ineffable and ephemeral: "No propaganda fits tightly into its category of major emphasis, and it must be remembered that pigeon-holes are invented to serve convenience and not to satisfy yearnings for the immortal and the immutable" (1941, p. 629). Propaganda may be positive or negative, but its object is always cultural values:

> Every cultural group has its vested values. ... An object toward which it is hoped to arouse hostility must be presented as a menace to as many of these values as possible. There are always ambitious hopes of increasing values, and the object must be made to appear as a stumbling block to their realization. There are patterns of right and wrong, and the object must be made to flout the good. There are standards of propriety, and the object must appear ridiculous and gauche. If the plan is to draw out positive attitudes toward an object, it must be presented, not as a menace and an obstruction, nor as despicable or absurd, but as a protector of our values, a champion of our dreams, and a model of virtue and propriety. (p. 630)

The means by which desirable or undesirable attitudes are organized towards the objects of propaganda are not "things," nor are they oriented towards "the acceptance of an idea without reflection," nor are they even concrete "suggestions"; they are, rather, the manipulation of "cultural material with a recognizable meaning" (1941, p. 631). Moreover, they are a "form of words" (p. 631), whether "spoken, written, pictorial, or musical, and the number of stimulus carriers is infinite" (p. 631).

When propaganda studies first emerged, the term *propaganda* did not have the typically negative connotation that it does presently. Propaganda is in fact necessary, according to Lasswell, because of "technological changes," especially the rise of literacy, the emergence of electronic communication technologies, and because most of what could "formerly be done by violence and coercion must now be done by argument and persuasion" (p. 631). The sum total of advanced technology, increased literacy, and the widespread "ventilation of opinions and the taking of votes" is that "[d]emocracy has proclaimed the dictatorship of palaver, and the technique of dictating to the dictator is named propaganda" (p. 631).

A singular and clear assumption—that mass propaganda has power over collective patterns of evaluation—is the single source of coherence linking the early propagandists. Bernays (1928) was more psychologically oriented in contrast to Lasswell. For him, public opinion "is the power of the group to sway the larger public in its attitude" (1928, p. 958). Its technique is "the psychology of public persuasion" (p. 959). But the techniques of "sociology" are just as important to Bernays' propaganda model (p. 961). The process of "manipulating public opinion" begins with "statistics" and "field-surveying" (p. 961)—the collection of existing values.

Bernays considers that "a circumstance or circumstances of dramatic moment" are the events that change and establish the "functioning of given attitudes toward given subjects, such as religion, sex, race, morality, nationalism, internationalism, and so forth" (p. 961). Whether the object is attitudes towards hats, sexuality, or politics, Bernays believed that in the "age of mass production" there must be a corresponding "technique for the mass distribution of ideas" and thus for the mass production of collective attitudes (p. 971).

Propaganda and the media environment: Lasswell's categories

By 1941, Lasswell had, through a longitudinal, worldwide study of mass media content, developed a system for categorizing the values attributed to particular symbols. Such a system, he argues, "supply us with data about many of the missing links in the process of political and social development" (Lasswell, 1941, p. 459). The term "symbols" here means construals of abstract entities with strong associations to cultural value systems, entities such as "Germany" or "The Prime Minister" or "Labor" (pp. 460-461). It is worth enumerating a "representative—certainly not an exhaustive—list of standards," or evaluative categories, developed by Lasswell (p. 460).

Lasswell's categories for understanding mediated evaluations are worth mentioning for their expansiveness, as well as to highlight the *hierarchical* nature of evaluative meanings (see Chapter 6). This is evidenced in how Lasswell arranges construals of values, showing *how* evaluations can themselves be evaluated. The broadest of Lasswell's categories are *Indulgence*, a positive presentation of a significant symbol when it is put "in a favorable light"; and *Deprivation*, a negative presentation of symbol "in an unfavorable setting." *Indulgence* may be "positive-realized" ("a gain is realized for the symbol"); "negative-realized" ("a loss may be avoided for the symbol"), "positive-promised" ("gains promised for the future"), or "negative-promised" ("future losses will be avoided"). *Deprivations* may be "positive-realized" ("actual losses sustained"), "negative-realized" ("gains are blocked in the past"), "positive-threatened" (losses "may be referred to the future"), or "negative-threatened" ("blocked gains may be referred to the future") (p. 460).

The following broad categories of evaluators may also appear in positive or negative polarities:

1. *Expediency* (*strength*): "describes the position of the object of reference in regard to such values as safety, goods, respect (*power and respect are sub-categories of deference*)";

    1a. *Safety*: the security "of persons, groups or things";

     1ab. *Efficiency*: the "level of performance of a function";

    1b. *Power*: "control over important decisions … measured according to the means of decision-making—fighting, diplomacy, voting …";

     1bb.   *Efficiency of Power*

1c.   *Goods*: "the volume and distribution of goods and services";

 1cb.   *Efficiency* of *Goods*

1d.   *Respect*: the degree of esteem attributed to a symbol;

 1db.   *Efficiency* of *Respect*

2. *Morality* (*obligation to adhere to moral standards*)

2a.   *Truth-Falsehood*: "the obligation to refrain from the deliberate dissemination of falsehood";

2b.   *Mercy-Atrocity*: "makes use of a moral standard to justify acts, the obligation to refrain from inflicting unnecessary cruelty";

2c.   *Heroism-Cowardice*: "the obligation to act courageously";

2d.   *Loyalty-Disloyalty*: "the obligation to serve a common purpose";

3. *Propriety*: "the obligation to learn a conventional code";

4. *Divinity*: "an obligation to abide by the Will of God";

5. *Legality*: "the standard is to abide by law";

6. *Beauty*: the "standard is aesthetic";

7. *Consistency*: the "standards are logical relationships among proposition [*sic*]";

8. *Probability*: "[p]robabability of a statement with no imputation of falsification";

9. *Euphoria-Dysphoria*: the "standard is agreeable or disagreeable subjective states";

10. *Omnibus*: "statements fusing many standards" (pp. 460-462)

Many of the categories that Lasswell identifies here are found in the more recent sociolinguistic approaches of Martin (1998, 2000), Halliday (1994), and Lemke (1998). Many are not, and the differences are analytically important. I outline these differences and their significance in Chapter 6.

Time, space, and opinion polls: The monkey bars of direct democracy

In the propagandists' work there is again an emphasis on the relationship between social influences and individual psychology, and between objective and subjective understandings of value. There is also an increasing emphasis on the role of language in value determination. Just as importantly, we see an acknowledgement of increased importance for *mass* media in propagating values, most notably the radio. For the propagandists, the objective social milieu tended to be seen as the extrinsic shaper of the subjective values that inhere in individual psychologies. We also see a strong emphasis on the relationship between perceptions of value, language, and media. Already, there is concern about the amounts of money being spent on US election campaigns (Poole, 1939, p. 371). But that is merely a quantitative aspect of a fundamentally qualitative change in the way value determinations are now being effected in the public sphere.

For Poole, elections and opinion polls are ways of arriving at "value judgments" (p. 371). Poole claims that "there is a choice between divine and human judgment" and, having given God short shrift, we must now rely solely on human judgment (p. 372). Poole reduces the "determination of values" by humans to two "principles" of judgment, one based in "the qualitative or heroic," the other, "quantitative and statistical" (p. 372). These are significant differences because they correspond to distinct dimensions of social life: *time and space*. Judgments

> by either the qualitative or quantitative principle may take place in two dimensions. These dimensions may be called conveniently *time and space*. The dimension of time is historical and its use opens up the store of human judgments found in the records of history and the enduring monuments of literature and art. The other dimension is simply that which we are more accustomed to think of in this ordinary connection, running at right angles to time. (p. 374)

Like Bernays (1945), Poole sees the possibility of what is now called "direct democracy" destroying representative government because of a tendency towards "laziness or moral cowardice" on the part of "legislators and executive leaders" (Poole, 1939, p. 374):

> They are honestly disposed to believe that the "voice of the people" (that is a majority) is the voice of God or Truth; or, to state the matter less theologically, that in a human world the best value judgment is the judgment of the greatest number of humans on any given problem at any given time. This is the quantitative or statistical, as opposed to the solely qualitative, idea. We have come to be so committed to it in our political philosophy that the cost and fuss and noise of the elections and polls are taken for granted—even welcomed, as adornments of our political life, which perhaps they are. (1939, p. 374)

The historical search for "judgments in the dimension of time" is firstly based on "the qualitative or heroic principle," a kind of "'Gallup poll' taken in the dimension of time" (1939, p. 375). With the introduction of Gallup's (1938) techniques, "value judgments in the domain of public affairs are come to, apparently, by an interesting, and rather reassuring, interaction and cross-control between the qualitative and quantitative principles *operating in the two dimensions of time and space*" (Poole, 1939, p. 375). Here we see introduction of an attempted synthesis between *static and dynamic* categories of value by assessing human action from points of view that correspond to specific types of space-bound (synchronic) and time-bound (diachronic) value-judgments. We begin to see the emergence of a form of consciousness that takes into account—or at the very least implies—the kinds of "bias" inherent in media that Harold Innis later specifies (Innis, 1950, 1951).

Gallup (1938) held no such conceptions of historical balance in terms of space and time where matters of judgment were concerned, preferring to think of democracy as a "hot," reactive relationship between political action and ongoing measurements of public opinion:

> James Bryce said that the next and final stage in our democracy would be reached if the will of the majority of citizens were to be ascertainable at all times.
>
> With the development of the science of measuring public opinion, it can be stated with but few qualifications, that this stage in our democracy is rapidly being reached. It is now possible to ascertain, with a high degree of accuracy, the views of the people on all national issues. (Gallup, 1938, p. 9)

The implications of manipulative activities in the public arena do not escape Gallup. The usefulness of polling is not to be confined to government or politics. It can be "equally useful in the field of social problems", as if the two were entirely separate (1938, p. 13).

Once sufficient is known about specific attitudes—opinions about welfare, religious prejudice, venereal disease, and any problem of attitude whatsoever—the issues can be addressed "with equal success" (1938, pp. 13–14). Consequently, Gallup believes "with many of our leading psychologists and social scientists" interested in the problem of measuring public opinion, "it will not be long before the final stage in the development of our democracy, as described by Bryce, has been reached—that the will of the majority of citizens can be ascertained at all times" (p. 14). Questions about the relationship between the "facts" of public opinion, centralized control of media, and the quality of government and its organs appear to elude Gallup in his enthusiasm for an early end to the History of Democracy. These questions, muted and smudged over by Gallup's methodological enthusiasms, were answered with a resounding blast from Western Europe, the shockwaves of which are still being felt today.

Total propaganda: The case of Nazi Germany

No mention of political economy, media, language, and values can exclude Nazi Germany. It is, if nothing else, an exemplar of the potential for concentrated use of mass mediated meanings to effect the most profound shifts of values in a technologically massified society. For the Nazi propagandists, as for Bernays and Lasswell, propaganda is qualitatively distinct from advertising; it is a matter of moral obligation to the public, a value and public good in itself:

> Political propaganda may not be confused with advertising. Advertising changes its target as needed. The Americans call it "ballyhoo." ... There is no thought of moral or national values. "Ballyhoo" is advertising at any price, with no moral content, no moral thought or responsibility ... . In a political sense, it is incite-

ment, distortion, and it is all immoral.

When we talk about the necessity of political propaganda, we seek powerful moral goals. We want to make our people a united nation that confidently and clearly understands National Socialism's policies, quickly and correctly. We cannot change our political principles as we would a consumer good, becoming random, irresponsible and immoral. We do not want to distort, confuse or incite, rather clarify, unify, and tell the truth. Political propaganda is the highest responsibility, it is a moral duty, a national duty. We may never think there is too much of it, or that it is superfluous. (Wells, 1936)

Moral and national values are conflated in the Nazi doctrine, and mapped directly onto an heroic human form. This following is characteristic: "For us, gold is not a measure of the value of money. Our foundation is German labor and confidence in the Führer" (NSDAP, 1939). Attitude and value are also synonymous for the Nazi propagandists. These are testable aspects of human experience which are open to manipulation. Again, *End of History* rhetoric resounds throughout:

The National Socialist worldview is an attitude, an attitude that must show a courageous face to the outside, but domestically be infused with camaraderie.

… world history today must be rewritten, and that we will do the rewriting. It would be a mistake to delegate the task to the teachers and professors who wrote previous histories, for they grew up under the old world and were educated in it. The 2000 year old Christian age is dying and a new national Socialist world under Adolf Hitler is being born. The youth are growing up in this new world. Our task is to serve these ideas and to lead the struggle. Then we will be able to look confidently into the future. (NSDAP, 1939)

The futuristic orientation of the Nazi regime is well-documented. Ideas and leaders were oriented to the emergence of a Thousand Year Reich. The paranoid values of "negative eugenics" (Herbert, 1913), social Darwinism, and the natural state of all-pervasive competition were propagated through film (Hippler, 1937), radio (Goebbels, 1933), printed materials, and by every means and medium available, including cultural gatherings, mass marches, even "stickers," and *especially* through the spoken and written word (Stark, 1930). Children were not to be excluded from the aggressive logic that inheres in seeing our world as a manifestation of the competition of every living thing against every other living thing. A fifth-grade textbook "for young girls" from the Nazi era is instructive here:

We have established that all creatures, plants as well as animals, are in a continual battle for survival. Plants crowd into the area they need to grow. Every plant that fails to secure enough room and light must necessarily die. Every animal that does not secure sufficient territory and guard it against other predators, or lacks the necessary strength and speed or caution and cleverness will fall prey to its enemies. The army of plant eaters threatens the plant kingdom. Plant eaters are prey for carnivores. The battle for existence is hard and unforgiving, but is the only way to maintain life. This struggle eliminates everything that is unfit for life, and selects everything that is able to survive. (Harm and Wiehle, 1942, p. 168)

No other species has more clearly benefited from cooperation than *homo sapiens*. Once this fact is overlooked, though, a clear set of imperatives for action flow from understanding life as a never ending competition of every living thing against every other living thing. Appeals to fear; to immutable laws of nature; to subjective psychology; to doctrines of scarce resources; to eugenic sociology; to work; to "the future of the nation"; to racial "hygiene" and "hygiene" in general; to science, technology, and truth—this combination of appeals forms the evaluative blueprint for National Socialist propaganda to expand *Lebensraum*.

The comprehensive range of the Nazis' appeals, combined with a centralized control of mass media, made its effects profound, widespread, and explosive. The objective was quite simple: *to change the nation's patterns of evaluation*. The task of propaganda

> is to free those who today still are rooted and anchored in the foreign ideas of liberalism and Marxism, to make them feel, think and act according to National Socialism, to bring them *to the point where they judge and evaluate everything according to National Socialist principles*. (Dietz, 1934, emphasis added)

The Nazis did successfully change the German nation's patterns of evaluation and the rest, as the saying goes, is history.

No more, no less ...

I leave my history of value here, recognizing that there have been many more recent developments: the visual values of television collage; the development of massive, global media monopolies in recent decades; the emergence of econometric theories of value based on particle physics, game theory, and complex systems theories; the development and implementation of the "Keynesian" system and the subsequent reinvigoration of allegedly "neoclassical" or "neoliberal" economics; the decline of Bretton-Woods and the emergence of new and powerful international legislatures and judiciaries; the gradual but thorough "entertainmentization" of news and current affairs; the worldwide, paranoid values of the nuclear Cold War and the subsequent withdrawal of Sovietism from the world stage; the latest "cold war" against "terror"—all of these are massive and complex histories in themselves, and all have had enormous impacts on the evaluative habits of whole blocs of humanity.

Yet the methods for analyzing, understanding, applying, and propagating perceptions of value on a mass scale had been fully developed by the 1930s and have changed little since, even though various departments of society have broken down value studies into ever more fragmented disciplinary silos, such as marketing, public relations, linguistics, rhetoric, advertising, professional and technical communication, design studies, social psychology, management studies, cultural studies, and the seemingly endless new branches of social and behavioral science that continue to emerge.

In retrospect, and especially in light of recent development post-September 11, 2001, World War II appears as a struggle not against totalitarianism, but over the types of totalitarianism that would come to dominate the early twenty-first century. The end of World War II might indeed be seen as the beginning of hypercapitalism's incubation period, during which global media infrastructures were built, international legislatures invested, and global financial systems implemented.

The vast shifts in the way official expressions of economic value have been produced, propagated, and enacted over the last three hundred years have shifted the centers of power from factory and foundry to mass media networks. By transferring official expressions of wealth from substances such as gold and land to paper to ephemeral bits of digital data, the trajectory I have called the linguistification of value has become increasingly overt, especially over the last century, and even more so during the last ten years. Economic value has been overtly linguistified over time. It has shifted in political economic discourse from being construed as a quality of an objective substance to being construed as the outcome of dynamic processes variously mediated in forms and modes of meaning-making. Even seen as a medium of exchange, money has moved from being a mass of precious metal moving slowly across perilous seas to being comprised entirely of data exchanged on high-security networks.

Marx's statement about the need for any political economic analysis to be underpinned by a theory of value is useful for understanding the kinds of changes that have happened in political economic systems in recent years. The brief history of value I have outlined here shows that social patterns of evaluation have changed significantly, especially in the realm of official expressions of economic value. It also shows an historical relationship between new and changed media environments, influential institutions, the values they propagate, culturally shared perceptions of value, and the imperatives for actions that flow from official theories of value. The interdependent nature and size of mass-mediated societies is now unparalleled in history. As societies become more thoroughly infused by mediation processes, the more official expressions of value become the products of valorized dialects. Where money-values are concerned, this has never been more apparent. The "appearance" and "disappearance" of hundred of billions of dollars in money now turns on the words of a central bank governor, the sexual proclivities of the US president, on an intern-concubine's intention to speak before a grand jury, or merely on "market sentiment."[19] Therefore political economy needs more than ever, not merely to acknowledge, but also to grasp the relationship between language, mediation, and perceptions of value, precisely because value is a far broader concept than price and has specific and recognizable social implications. Furthermore, "it" is unquestionably conditioned by mediation processes, as exemplified by the superlative efforts of the Nazi regime, the Creel Committee and, more recently, in the propaganda of the coalition of the willing in their rush to war against Iraq in 2003. The speed of mediation also greatly changes the character of the political economic system. Because values are produced by what people do, they are firstly time-based, even though values becomes manifest in more and less ephemeral substances which are then viewed as having a provenance that stands outside of all social processes. Money is just one of these substances. The historical description given here, though, does not explain value transformations. It merely situates the present system in an ongoing historical process. A theory of value is central to a critical theory of social change. Such a theory, I believe, cannot be situated solely in economics, psychology, sociology, anthropology, linguistics, or any other sub-discipline of social science. A dynamic theory of value *is* a theory of social change and social action, the basic assumption being that social patterns of evaluation and social patterns of action are inextricably related. With the historical linguistification of value, we can perhaps assume that definitions of value are expressed most obviously in language, albeit partially and implicitly. We can also assume that the means of inculcation—mediation processes—are a vital part of the process of production where perceptions of value are concerned. Perceptions are, by definition, the object of mediation processes— simultaneously the raw material and final products of media production processes.

CHAPTER THREE

Social life

☞nderstandings of social change proceed from particular assumptions about what "the social" actually is. A people's conception of its social character has both practical and logical implications. For example, if it is widely assumed that "there is no such thing as society" (Adey and Frisby, 1976 in Jarvis, 1998, p. 44), that society is nothing more than the collection of individuals at any specific period of time, certain imperatives follow from that assumption: the abrogation of social justice responsibilities by governments; the individualization of social needs; the "privatization" or private enclosure of public spaces and other goods; the promotion of unbridled competition; "user-pays" approaches to public services provision; the inability to define or identify public goods, and so on. Conceptions of the social situated at an even more abstract level have had significant long-term consequences. They are also, and always, products of historically specific circumstances.

Hobbes (1651) conceived of the State as a *Leviathan*, an enormous "artificial man"

> in which the sovereignty is an artificial soul, as giving life and motion to the whole body; the magistrates and other officers of judicature and execution, artificial joints; reward and punishment (by which fastened to the seat of the sovereignty, every joint and member is moved to perform his duty) are the nerves, that do the same in the body natural; the wealth and riches of all the particular members are the strength; salus populi (the people's safety) its business; counsellors, by whom all things needful for it to know are suggested unto it, are the memory; equity and laws, an artificial reason and will; concord, health; sedition, sickness; and civil war, death. Lastly, the pacts and covenants, by which the parts of this body politic were at first made, set together, and united, resemble that fiat, or the Let us make man, pronounced by God in the Creation. (Hobbes, 1651)

Hobbes's is a "natural order" view of the social, a perspective that sees the social order as eternal, given by God, but dynamic nonetheless. Hobbes's State has muscles, nerves, brains; it is a magnified version of a human being endowed with human organs and superhuman functions. In this view, the State is "on the move," driven by its soul which is embodied by the head of State. Hobbes's view stands at an historical juncture between the eternal and unchanging "divine order" described by the likes of John of Salisbury and Thomas Aquinas, and the massive automated "machine" view of society envisaged by twentieth-century corporate and military management elites (Noble, 1984, pp. 54-55).

When propagated with sufficient force and repetition, such metaphors of the social produce particular modes of relatedness and imperatives for political action. They also emerge from and reflect specific social and technological environments to provide a practical lens through which people make sense of their "place" in the world. Whether as a part of a divine plan, as a joint, muscle fiber, or nerve ending in an anthropomorphic State; as a cog in the machines of industrialized societies; as a competitor in the ultimate Darwinian struggle for survival; or as "bits" or network nodes in a cybernetic, "post-industrial" knowledge economy, dominant theories of the social have functioned to provide rationales, metaphors, and lenses for people to understand the character of their social order, and of their place in that order.

Like any intellectual products, theories of the social tend to provide grounds for their antitheses, alternative understandings of society that offer potential for radical change and emancipation rather than a rationalization of the existing order. What is called "critical theory" is typically oriented towards such ends. Put more explicitly, critical scholarship challenges existing systems of exploitation, though it does not necessarily propose a new system. Adam Smith is rarely thought of as a radical or a critical scholar. Yet his argument in *Wealth of Nations* is a thorough critique of a political economic system, that of late mercantilism, and an endorsement of a new system organized around private interests and a machine-based industrial division of labor. The political systems that emerged from Marx's critical scholarship are widely regarded as failures (regardless of whether they had anything to do with what Marx actually wrote). The same may be said of Smith. The economic and political "neoliberalisms" of the years between 1979 and 2001 relied heavily on a particular interpretation of Smith's "invisible hand," a passing metaphor used by Smith which, when inserted into Social Darwinist theories of the social and magnified by a global system of mediations, became the rationale for unbridled competition on a global scale. The consequences of global "competition policy" include enormous global corporate monopolies, the most powerful of which are now the global media, finance, and military corporations. I am reluctant to prescribe an alternative system, yet hope to provide understandings that can lead to a balance between the political economic extremisms that have become far too familiar throughout the twentieth century. In any case, perspectives upon what actually exists are of an entirely different type than those that deal with what might exist at some future time and how such a system might work.

The perspective on the social I am proposing here seeks to comprehend the implications of a globally mediated humanity. Human beings throughout the world have become connected as never before, and new technologies provide the potential for people throughout the world to interact in many unprecedented ways. Yet the results of global connectedness have, overall, been far from impressive. As I write, the formerly "globalized" world is fracturing into a volatile mix of violently competing interests. Religious and political fundamentalisms abound, most of them thoroughly hostile to all others. The counter-globalizing impetus to promote exclusive, localized cultural identities is evident in the often militant revival of cultural and political groups that had all but disappeared. Political engagement on the part of citizens appears to be futile because the political field is presented to "the public" as distant and untouchable. The global distribution of wealth is exercised within the realm of global currency markets. These markets constitute ninety-nine percent of all trade and are inaccessible to most people.

In a globalized system that depends mainly on the circulation of symbolic material for the bulk of its wealth production, and which emphasizes individualism and apolitical isolationism, the primary product seems to be systemic alienation—the illusion that our political, economic, and institutional environments are beyond our control, comprehension, and creative capacity in terms of our being able to influence them to any significant degree. That illusion is very powerful, and it is reinforced with the most extreme and extensive coercive powers in human history. At the same time, evidence of widespread dissent, often violently expressed, is almost everywhere to see. Still, it is difficult to comprehend the effects of, for example, the various "anti-globalization" movements that emerged during the late 1990s or, shortly afterwards, the globally coordinated anti-war protests that preceded the 2003 invasion of Iraq. In one sense, these movements indicate that resistance to the current system is strong and widespread (whether or not it is a majority of people). In another, the fact that the most massive public displays of protest in recent history made practically no difference to the policy decisions at which they were directed can be viewed as a reinforcement of the perceived distance between people and the political systems that govern them.

The social theory I put forward here is designed to reveal the modes of relatedness that characterize specific human social systems as such. It views social systems as *living* systems; not as Hobbes' giant anthropomorph, but as meta-organismic systems that reproduce themselves as recognizable entities over time. Issues of scale, scope, and complexity become immediately problematic in such a view (Lemke, 2000). In this definition, a family can be defined as a social system, as can a corporation, a township, a political party, a religious group, or a nation-state. The definition also accommodates international social systems, such as those through which scientific "disciplines" are constituted and maintained, or through which transnational political entities maintain, reproduce, and change themselves over time.

A mediation perspective can assist in defining the complexities of scale and scope in social systems. Social systems are maintained, characterized, delineated, and transformed by their systems of mediation. That is to say, the way participants in a social system typically move meanings through time and space, and the extent to which they do so, are definitive of the scale and scope of the system, and of its rate of change over time. Meanings that provide a system with identifiable coherence are those of most interest. Understanding the constitution of social systems entails an understanding of how meanings are made and moved, what meanings are made, who is allowed to make which kinds of meanings, and how specific classes of meaning are valued at different periods of time and in different contexts.

The perspective through which I define the social is based in Maturana and Varela's "autopoiesis," a perspective that sees self-producing and reproducing processes as definitive of life and evidence of systemic cognition (cf. Maturana and Varela, 1980, 1987; Luhmann, 1995; Graham and McKenna, 2000). It is the basis of a perspective that can foreground meaning, mediation, and modes of social systemic reproduction to comprehend the character and scale of social change. An autopoietic understanding of the social also emphasizes the centrality of language to the human social condition at a period in history in which thought and language are the raw materials of commodity forms produced for the "globalized" knowledge economy. Finally, it is a perspective that provides an understanding of the new kinds of labor—human activity—that are currently being brought under the logic of commodification.

From an autopoietic perspective, human knowledge is the natural product of relationships between persons operating on and within specific environments, social and otherwise. Once human knowledge becomes a primary commodity in political economy, language becomes the primary means of production, exchange, and evaluation. The basic commodity-form of the knowledge economy can be defined as a conscious distinction that can be exchanged between people in more or less valued forms of language.

The knowledge-value of any particular distinction, or any set of distinctions, is ultimately mediated by the language used to describe it, the context in which it is described, and the position of the person making the distinction in relation to that context. For example, in a global policy context, comments about the economy are far more likely to be recognized as official "wisdom" if they are made by an economist than if they are made by a shaman or a school child. What "counts" as knowledge in any given social system is at least as much a function of the person-system relationship as the accuracy of what is considered to be truth in any given context. The functional relations between social contexts and meanings made are therefore a key focus for any political economic analysis of a knowledge economy.

Autopoiesis and knowledge commodities

In human social systems, a sociocognitive metabolism emerges from the relationships between people and their environments. Marx (1970) describes a "social metabolism … which gives rise to definite social relations" (pp. 51-52). He specifically refers to the production, exchange, and consumption of relatively durable commodities, socially useful things that derive exchange-value from their usefulness; the socially necessary labor time to produce these; and the social relations that this arrangement entails at any given point in history (1970, pp. 50-51; 1976, p. 125). To focus on a knowledge economy, however, means disregarding the less ephemeral commodities of the social metabolism, those that retain a tangible, relatively fixed form over a period of time, such as cars, bricks, or bread. Rather, an analytical apparatus for a global knowledge economy foregrounds the social metabolism of intangible, ephemeral, and abstract sociocognitive commodities: ideas, attitudes, and meanings: "language" in its broadest definition. In language, as in image, music, and all other modes of human expression, people render their environments socially meaningful. This is the sociocognitive metabolism, the entire network of interactions and processes through which people produce and exchange meanings. While I acknowledge that humans make meaning with "every sort of object, event and action in so far as it is endowed with significance, with symbolic value" (Lemke, 1995, p. 9), I argue that language in the strictest sense—spoken or written words—is the ultimately coordinating element in which social perceptions of value are created, modified, and mediated (cf. Lemke, 1998; Martin, 1997, 1999).

An analysis of any knowledge economy foregrounds the immediacy of language and its evaluative dimension; the speed and geographical extent of mediation systems through which systematic patterns of evaluation are propagated; the relative power and ostensive social function of particular groups; and the collections of commodities that comprise the knowledge economy at any given time. In the current system, the most valuable knowledge commodities appear to act on their own volition, increasing their value as they circulate at the speed of light in a globally integrated system of self-valorizing commodities exchanged in more and less valued dialects of expertise.

Credit derivatives are exemplary of the knowledge economy's most exclusive and valuable commodity-forms. They are the invention of financial sector experts. Put simply, a credit derivative is an insurance note on future or "notional" debt which is raised against futures of one sort or another.[20] The basic idea of a credit derivative is that it is insurance on the difference between the face value of a futures trade (such as beef futures) and the notional capital raised against the goods claimed in the future. Credit derivatives realize value only in the occurrence of a verified "credit event," such as the bankruptcy of a large corporation or some other highly visible financial disaster. Financial commodities such as these are exchanged without any clear definition, agreement, or understanding about what they are (Edwardes, 1998a,b). As one financial commentator put it, they are hard for people "without a Nobel Prize in mathematics" to understand (Kohler, 1998). Yet trade in these pure abstractions generated $US 20 billion dollars in 1996, twice as much in 1997, $US 447 billion by 1999, and is estimated to exceed $US 2 trillion by the end of 2004 (Edwardes, 1998a; Kothari, 2004; *Business is booming*, 1999). Interestingly, these transactions are "notional" and therefore "off-balance sheet"—they are not included in a business's statement of assets and liabilities because they do not exist.

Credit derivatives exemplify the commodity-forms that sustain the digital knowledge economy and the exclusive character of the social contexts within which they are produced and exchanged. So do advertisements. Both credit derivatives and advertisements rely on the work of a specific buying audience to realize value (Smythe, 1981). They are both products of the imagination, made by relatively few people in order to produce a general attitude towards something that is realized as price at some later stage. Like credit derivatives, and all the proliferating forms of financial instruments, advertisements are products of language and thought—knowledge commodities for a knowledge economy. By viewing the products of thought and language as commodity-forms, my intention is not to endorse their economic appropriation, but rather to draw attention to the fact that they have become the central objects of commodification in hypercapitalism and are also at the foundation of social life in a very literal sense. In such a situation, social life itself becomes the primary commodity-form and the basis of human relatedness therefore becomes the raw material for the production of commodities. Such a view of social life has serious implications for how we see ourselves as life forms and for what it means to be human.

Autopoiesis, sociolinguistic processes, and living systems

Marx's metaphor of a "social metabolism" may be taken to suggest a Hobbesian view of society-as-organism. I make a very different assumption about the social. While I see social systems as living systems, I argue that they are necessarily meta-organismic collections of complex, dynamically related processes, structures, and participants with emergent properties and characteristics that are vastly distinct from those of the organisms that constitute them at any particular time. They are as different as cells are from organs, or organs from organisms. From an autopoietic perspective, human social systems are third-order, meta-organismic, living systems coordinated in the domain of language.[21] The presence of autopoietic organization—or self-producing and reproducing processes—within a system is both necessary and sufficient to classify a system as living and vice versa (Maturana and Varela, 1980, 1987; Varela, 1992). The historical character of human social systems, the most influential of which last many times longer than the people who constitute them, permits an explanatory apparatus that can describe the development of social systems without reducing those descriptions to mechanistic, evolutionary, anthropomorphic, technological, or entirely arbitrary terms.

The usefulness of an autopoietic perspective for understanding the significance of a knowledge economy is fourfold. First, it emphasizes social systemic continuities as well as changes, thereby allowing historical understandings. Second, it emphasizes that systemic cognitions and the way they emerge within living systems define the character of the system. Third, it foregrounds a relational perspective on social systems, situating them in relation to other systems and their environment in general. Finally, an autopoietic perspective sees that human beings' autopoiesis is made possible within an interrelated network of social environments that are created, coordinated, and maintained in the domain of language (Maturana and Varela, 1980, pp. 107-108; 1987, pp. 230-231; Maturana, 1995).

Systemic cognition is an emergent property of any living system because of the need for continual distinctions to be made by a system between itself and its environment (Maturana and Varela, 1980, p. 9). Because human social and cognitive systems are constituted, coordinated, and maintained in the domain of language, and because language is a fundamentally social phenomenon, a socially grounded approach to language provides the most appropriate analytic for understanding the systemic and creative role of language in a global knowledge economy (Graham and McKenna, 2000). Such an approach is necessary in the study of a knowledge economy because, to study the way knowledge is created in living systems, we "are forced to discover 'regions' that interweave in complex manners, and, in the case of humans, that extend beyond the strict confines of the body into the sociolinguistic register" (Varela, 1992, p. 14).

In such a view, the commodification of language and thought appears as far more than a mere extension of capitalism into more intrusive and intimate domains. It calls attention to the fact the system called capitalism is on the verge of consuming, or at the very least expropriating, the very foundations of human social life. That is because a knowledge economy assumes the appropriation of cognition, recognition, and language as resources to build its staple commodity-forms. Cognition is the distinguishing criterion for any living system. Language is the ultimately coordinating, fundamentally creative social phenomenon that most marks the human species as unique. Language—the means of abstraction—is the definitive feature of human social systems.

The human tendency to alienate and reify our own abstractions often leads us to see ourselves as being separate from, or alien to, the language that we live in and through. Consequently,

> we live existing in our language as if language were a symbolic system for refer-
> ring to entities of different kinds that exist independently from what we do, and
> we treat even ourselves as if we existed outside language as independent entities
> that use language. ... The main consequence of our existing in language is that we
> cannot speak about what is outside it. (Maturana, 1995)

In other words, language first appears as an alien system that defines the boundaries of human understanding and relatedness. Capital is recognized in critical terms as a system of exploitation that operates through the alienation of human life forces. The move to commodify the creations of language—understandings, relationships, values—is therefore the most thorough expression of capital.

By developing technologies to appropriate and commodify thought and language, a knowledge economy encourages the sociolinguistic creations of expert dialects to operate as reified abstractions that can be produced, appropriated, bought, deployed, and sold within the proprietary domains of the knowledge economy's infrastructure. By providing the technical means to produce a global system of self-valorizing abstractions, whether credit derivatives; advertisements; call warrants, options, or shares; roubles and baht and money in all its forms—the global technological infrastructure of the knowledge economy facilitates the global propagation of thought, value, and power, all of which are ultimately packaged and sold in language in the current context. More than ever in a global knowledge economy, "language *is* practical consciousness" (Marx and Engels, 1846/1972, p. 122).

The knowledge economy can also be seen as the form of political economy in which individual identity becomes a commodity because the environment of language also provides the resources with which persons constitute their self-descriptions. Human social systems also maintain their identity in language. It is the means by which communities "build solidarity, patrol and extend their boundaries, and perpetuate themselves in the life of a general culture" (Killingsworth and Gilbertson, in McKenna, 1997, p. 191).

A self-conscious knowledge economy has emerged at a time when language, value, power, and the resources of social and individual identity have become exposed to processes of commodification. A critical sociolinguistic analysis of human social systems as living systems is, I argue, essential for understanding the implications of the knowledge economy. The knowledge economy has as its object the means of human relatedness—language and thought. In analyzing how valued meanings are made requires an understanding of how various modes of meaning are made in language, and of how meanings are differentiated in a social systematic way. For instance, a school child, a university professor, and a politician may all speak about "the economy." Only certain of these people will be listened to when it comes to making the rules that define how the economy works, and that will have a lot to do with their social position, how they talk about the economy, including the words they use and the attitudes they express. These are the key aspects for analyzing meaning: the "aboutness" of what is said, the attitudes expressed in doing so, and the way these are textured.

Social autopoiesis, technology, and social change

> Machines have developed out of a complex of non-organic agents for converting energy, for performing work, for enlarging the mechanical or sensory capabilities of the human body, or for reducing to a mensurable order and regularity the processes of life. (Mumford, 1934/1963, pp. 10–11)

The approach to understanding the social I have thus far outlined entails knowledge of a social system's history. It proceeds on the assumption that, within a given social system, intertextually constituted *"thematic patterns …* recur from text to text in slightly different wordings" but are "recognisably the same, and can be mapped onto a generic semantic pattern that is the same for all" texts about a particular aspect of the world (Lemke, 1995, p. 42). This is consistent with dialectics and there is an implicit theory of technology and mediation embedded in such a view. For a social system to retain, change, and propagate the systems of meaning through which it defines itself, there needs to be an understanding of precisely *how* this happens at any given time in the history of the system.

To see how meanings are moved through times, spaces, and social contexts is to see mediation processes (Silverstone, 1999). When we focus on a social entity, we are delineating boundary conditions for that entity, defining who and what is "in" the system, who and what is not, and *how* the constituents of a social system are related internally and externally. The work of delineating one social system from another includes defining the size, age, and type of social organization, as well as the relationships of one social system to many others. There are at least two ways to do this. One is by taking a synchronic view that sees a specific point in time. Like a family photograph, a synchronic perspective will take an audit of social systemic goings on at a given moment. Another is to take a diachronic view that sees changes in systemic composition over time. An analogy for this view is a "family tree." Both views are useful, but to see and describe social systems as living entities, we need to focus on changes in the system over time.

One entry point into social change more generally is technological change. Technology, as Lynne White Jr. puts it, "is the way we do things" (1940, p. 161): technologies are the many "hows" of social happenings. The mediation processes that provide coherence for social systems are in some significant way a function of technological change. McLuhan's "global village" is an impossibility without a global communications network (McLuhan, 1964). So is the phenomenon described as "globalization." Further, as Mumford (1934/1963) and McLuhan (1964) point out, technologies typically extend, amplify, or conserve the potentialities, faculties, and actualities of human energies. Even though in our current environment the most overt technological changes are essentially non-organic in composition, they are nonetheless human and social in origin, and they can affect social relatedness in significant and often unexpected ways.

Integrating the technological into an autopoietic perspective means merely to acknowledge that *how* people in a social system enact the relationships which define the system—how a social system produces and reproduces itself as a recognizable entity—is a significant part of the character of that system. Changes in a system's character imply changes in its technological character, and can often be seen as such. For example, the bureaucracy of the Roman Catholic Church has a very different character today than it did in, say, the tenth century, even though the stated aims and claims of that particular bureaucracy have not changed vastly over the last millennium. The difference in the Church bureaucracy's character can be seen through the changing technologies it has deployed in achieving autopoiesis throughout the last millennium. It has moved from a scribal and oral organization concentrated in Western Europe to being a global institution that uses every medium available to provide its constituency with the means to constitute itself as a coherent social system.[22]

The extent and duration of a social system's autopoiesis relies upon the kinds of technologies it deploys in the maintenance of its identity. Social systems that use only oral and aural technologies to provide coherence are far more limited in their ability to extend themselves across large geographical spaces than are literate societies (Innis, 1951). The kinds of technologies a social system has at its disposal also have effects on the temporal extent of a social system (Innis, 1951). Social autopoiesis in human societies are dependent on numerous technologies, and the "global society" promised by techno-utopianists is no different. But technological capacity alone is not enough to bring such a system into existence. The mere fact of technologies that are capable of bringing formerly disparate social systems into relatively sudden contact with each other does not mean that those systems will necessarily "merge" into a relatively cohesive, new and larger system, although that can happen. But the opposite seems more generally to be the case: faced with changes to their identity-forming traditions and practices, social systems seem to become more resistant to change to the point of becoming overtly hostile to outside influences (Carey, 1989, pp. 132-133). Twentieth century history is a monument to increased capacities for social systemic interconnectedness on a massive scale paralleled by unparalleled levels of violence between social systems, regardless of whether their organizing principles are based in ethnicity, religion, politics, or whatever.

As with other features of a social system, its technological aspect can also be understood in terms of "Presentational," "Orientational," and "Organizational" meaning, just as language can (Lemke, 1995, 1998).[23] As numerous studies of technologies have shown, technologies have social meanings in and of themselves and are therefore susceptible to comprehension through an analysis of their meaning.[24] *How* people do what they do is as much a product of their socialization as it is of the technologies they deploy, whether consciously or unconsciously. It is also a marker of social "belonging" or, in the context of studies of political economy, their social standing—their value as socially situated persons. Technologies are as much means of reproduction and production for social systemic identities as they are for the production and reproduction of commodity-forms. Implicit in the industrialization and mechanization of human life forces in "mass society" is the potential, if not the inevitability, of the industrialization and mechanization of human relatedness. Since social autopoiesis is a function of relatedness, a view of how we relate must today include the technologies of relatedness.

The deeper biological implications of technologizing or industrializing social autopoietic processes can be seen when the clock emerges as a general way of understanding and regulating the social meaning of time:

> Abstract time became the new medium of existence. Organic functions themselves were regulated by it: one ate, not upon feeling hungry, but when prompted by the clock: one slept, not when one was tired, but when the clock sanctioned it. A generalized time consciousness accompanied the wider use of clocks .... (Mumford, 1934/1963, p. 17)

The effects of the clock and its regulatory functions are now so thoroughly infused throughout industrialized nations that the inorganic and synthetic qualities of clock-time go practically unnoticed. Indeed it is impossible for industrialism to have emerged without the coordinating facilities that clockwork technologies provided.

By including technology in the analysis of meaning, we have a concrete basis on which to develop an understanding of social systemic change. I will continue with the clock as an example. At a concrete functional level, the Presentational aspects of clocks include displays of hours, minutes, seconds, and many subdivisions of seconds. They also include size, shape, constituent materials, layout, setting, and the many other visual and audio features that clocks can have. The Orientational (or Attitudinal) aspects of clocks include Mumford's "time consciousness." The very concepts of "busyness" or "lateness" imply attitudes towards time and its social meaning. The Attitudinal character of a living human system that lives by clock-time is very different to that of one that lives according to the movements of the sun and the seasons (Mumford, 1934/1963). The Organizational functions of the clock include the myriad punctuations and coordinations in industrialized social systems that are entirely dependent on clocks keeping time—transport schedules, school lessons, working hours, meetings—the list of activities organized according to clock-time is seemingly endless.

Historical changes in the meaning of a day are useful to see how social systemic modes of cognition emerge from social systems in respect of technology. But a technological perspective sees only changes in *how* we relate in social, historical, and material ways, and how specific ways of knowing and saying are propagated. It does not see the "what" of these aspects. That is a function of language because in human societies, social life is maintained and coordinated in language (Maturana and Varela, 1981). The meaning of a piece of music or a painting can only be shared in language. The meaning of any event, practice, thing, person, or circumstance can only be shared in language. Despite the proliferation of different modes of meaning, such as still or moving images, language remains the domain in which these modes attain socially shared meaning.

Implications for analysis

To understand a social system, the perspective I have outlined so far entails an analytical method that focuses on regularities in social systemically produced themes of description, propositions, and proposals about itself or aspects of the world that concern it. The statements (propositions) produced by a discourse community about a particular subject are firstly analyzed thematically and historically in order to assess the way the community traditionally construes its world, its attitudes to its own and others' discourses, the way it relates the elements of its discourse to each other, and how these change over time. Once recurring propositions about a given subject are distilled into thematic patterns, attitudinal coherence between systemically and individually produced propositions within a given social system about a given subject can be assessed. These can then be analyzed at the semantic level to determine the lexico-grammatical features of a particular social entity, including those concerning value. The theoretical and analytical perspectives I have outlined here highlight the inseparable relatedness of language, thought, identity, history, and society. Each of these factors interdependently creates the circumstances of instantiation for each of the others. Language is the processual, socially interactive means by which we coordinate, contest, describe, create, and exchange understandings that emerge from each instance of humanity, and which mediate the production and reproduction of the social systems within which these instances occur. Social systems are, in turn, the environment in which humans flourish, albeit to widely varying degrees of satisfaction and success. Language is an empirical and constitutive process. It facilitates the socially shared distinctions by which we come to know and describe our world, our societies, and ourselves. At a time in history when little, if anything, in Western society remains outside the technological apparatus that expedites increasing concentrations of communicative and economic power, a critical approach to "the social" must attempt to understand and challenge the meaning of various mediations, and the extent to which they influence social consciousness. Language by its very nature is the only analytical entry point we have through which to address these critical issues. Given this, I will now situate language, technology, and social relatedness in the political economic system that currently prevails.

Hypercapitalism

The emergent political economic system facilitated by new media first appears as a collection of new *things*: computers, satellites, and various other parts of the global communication infrastructure. But, as Marx points out, "capital is not a thing, it is a definite social relation of production pertaining to a particular historical social formation, which simply takes the form of a thing and gives this thing a specific social character" (1981, p. 953). Nevertheless mainstream economic thought has treated capital, since well before Marx's time, as various sorts of "things": plant and equipment, linen and cotton, money, cars, and so on (Marx, 1976, p. 169). To avoid confusing these two distinctly different conceptions of capital, I distinguish between capital as a specific form of social organization, hereafter *systemic capital*, and capital as a collection of "self-valorizing things" that are deployed in pursuit of surplus value (1976, p. 255), which I will call *phenomenological capital*.

The development and diffusion of technology within systemic capital has tended towards an emphasis on its ability to firstly appropriate, and commodify, and later to replace, more intricate aspects of human energy. Systemic capital firstly concerns itself with raw, "physical" labor power. Then the division of labor engendered by the application of technology to production "gradually transforms the worker's operations into more mechanical ones, so that at a certain point a mechanism can step in to take their place" (Marx, 1973, p. 703). Consequently, the art of invention "becomes a business, and the application of science to direct production itself becomes a prospect which determines and solicits it" (p. 704). This trend has continued since the early twentieth century, and there has been an increasingly sharper focus on applying science to the attitudinal and intellectual aspects of labor (Noble, 1989).

At the earliest stages of systemic capital, the labor process was oriented towards the production of durable commodities: cotton, steel, and linen for instance. At that time, the emphasis was upon muscular aspects of labor. But industrialists quickly realized that advantages conferred by the use of industrial machinery were offset by the large amounts of labor required to operate it (Marx, 1976, pp. 922-923). Systemic capital therefore tends to increase the ratio of machinery to people in the workplace (1976, p. 1051). Spurred by economic incentives, technological innovation has accelerated as production and management processes have incorporated scientific methods (Mandel, 1975, p. 248).

According to Ernest Mandel, the years between 1919 and 1939 is the period during which "intellectual labor" is finally subsumed under systemic capital (1975, pp. 249-250). During that time, management became self-consciously "scientific" (Noble, 1989). Ford began mass-producing cars. Electronic mass media became a world-shaping influence. The hype surrounding the early radio and film industries has a recognizably utopian tone:

> We want a radio that reaches the people, a radio that works for the people, a radio
> that is an intermediary between the government and the nation, a radio that also
> reaches across our borders to give the world a picture of our life and our work. ...
> The purpose of radio is to teach, entertain and support people, not to gradually
> harm the intellectual and cultural life of the nation. (Goebbels, 1933)

And so, under the guise of what is now described as "universal access," "the intellectual and cultural life of the nation" found itself within systemic capital's immediate processes of production. By the time Horkheimer and Adorno (1947/1998) had completed their bleak appraisal of "the culture industry," electronic mass media had been deployed to incite and coordinate opinion in the most massive, rapid, and destructive exercise in propaganda the world had seen: World War II. Hitler, Roosevelt, and Churchill used the radio to transform national patterns of evaluation with equal success. At the same time, research into public opinion had turned knowledge about public attitudes into the most valuable of all commodities (Creel, 1941). The historical point at which opinion became commodifiable was the point at which thought became a commodity "and language the means of promoting that commodity" (Horkheimer and Adorno, 1947/1998, pp. xi-xii).

Systemic capital has continued to extend its reach into every sphere of life. "Leisure" itself has become an established field of university instruction and research, and an enormous complex of industrial activities. As a result, "free time" has steadily become a "shadowy continuation" of labor (Adorno, 1991, p. 168). In hypercapitalism, economically "productive" activities can consume the entire waking life of people. One example of how this is achieved can be seen in the efforts of advertisers to occupy "space" in the consciousness of whole populations. Advertising not only generates economic value in the process of its production, it ideally creates value in its "consumption" by producing a predisposition in people to purchase a specific brand, product, or service at inflated prices, or to hold specific attitudes towards someone or something (Samarajiva, 1996, p. 137). Advertising is perhaps an obvious example of how "intellectual labor" is appropriated, objectified, and manipulated to produce value outside what are most usually called production processes. However, the long standing distinction between intellectual and manual labor has performed a specific social function.

The most cursory inspection of class distinctions throughout history reveals that the differentiation between "intellectual" and "manual" work has largely served to sustain "a spurious means of social distinction" (Schiller, 1996, pp. 20-21). Apart from anything else, it is a mistake to think that labor of any kind can be conducted without some degree of intellectual engagement (Schiller, 1996, p. 20; Weber, 1930/1992, p. 63).[25] At the same time, intellectual processes are material processes, and the "labour of representation," whether by writing, speaking, painting, or whichever means, is a material process of production that results in the materialization of meaning (Bourdieu, 1991, p. 164). Reading and writing, for example, both entail labor in the most general and abstract sense—the expenditure of human energies on the transformation of some aspect of the world or other. Reading and writing are, again, obvious examples in this respect, but the same principle extends to the whole enterprise of meaning making, from a child's acquisition of language, to the consumer's acquisition of knowledge about the virtues of various products, to the scientist's acquisition and dissemination of knowledge.

That is why, in hypercapitalism's knowledge economy, the term "labor" must be understood in the broadest possible sense, and why Marx's more restricted definition of labor requires expansion to include the labors of abstraction and representation. While Marx focuses largely on labor of human muscle, he sees that from one perspective labor is "the entire productive activity of man, through which his metabolic interchange with nature is mediated" (Marx, 1981, p. 954). That necessarily includes cognitive production—the production of language and social consciousness. Understanding a knowledge economy also entails understanding *production* in the broadest possible terms. From the autopoietic perspective I described in the previous chapter, the term "production" refers to the entire network of activities by which societies produce and reproduce themselves. The social process in a knowledge economy, because of its focus on commodifying the products of language and thought, includes the entire network of activities and artifacts through which individuals and societies reproduce themselves at every level: materially, spiritually, socially, relationally, intellectually, and technologically. Such expansive, all-embracing conceptions of "labor" and "production" may seem far too broad to be of any use. Nevertheless they reflect the trajectory of systemic capital as it extends its processes of commodification to include every aspect of existence from "goods of the mind" to DNA, allegedly the "essence of life" (Barlow, 1998, pp. 5-9).

The appearance of the term "knowledge economy" in political discourse is symptomatic of these tendencies in systemic capital. Because a knowledge economy is concerned with the production, distribution, and exchange of knowledge commodities, there emerges an imperative to produce new—or at least seemingly new—knowledge that can be turned into money values. Many principles of industrial era commodities apply to the hypercapitalist knowledge commodities: built-in obsolescence becomes a necessity for the knowledge commodity, which is ephemeral by nature; and the expansion of knowledge markets to a global scale, combined with the mass and immediacy facilitated by new media networks creates an imperative for increased production of new knowledge in place of old. Combined with this is an increased imperative for new knowledge *about* knowledge. The result is a proliferation of ostensibly new ideas, stories, beliefs, sciences, and technologies. All of this has an effect on the character of labor in hypercapitalism. Since the production of valuable knowledge entails specific ways of discovering, knowing, and representing aspects of the world, it requires some degree of shared capacity on the part of knowledge "consumers." For people to recognize the value of a knowledge commodity (whether a scientific journal article, a television program, or an advertisement) they must *work* in the process of "consuming" new knowledge commodities. Merely believing, or suspending belief, to accommodate new ideas requires significant effort. A generalized "knowledge economy" entails a systemic assault on social memory—one that requires huge amounts of effort on the part of "consumers."

As I have previously noted, the largest sector of the current knowledge economy is the financial sector. It derives its appearance as a system of wealth creation through the efforts of experts who labor to concoct the abstractions upon which the system thrives, and from the propagation of these forms through a global system of mediations. But financial "commodities" have no intrinsic use-value except as exchange-values. They generate "value" only as long as they are continuously exchanged. This system quite overtly mediates perceptions social and personal worth to the point at which nation states are often compared with particular individuals or corporations, based entirely on their comparative levels of "paper" wealth:[26]

> The world's richest man is currently worth some $64bn, according to the Bill Gates personal wealth clock. That means that there are only 63 countries in the world whose GDP is bigger than his personal fortune. Among those that don't quite make the mark are Syria, Bulgaria and the United Arab Emirates. Looked at another way, Bill Gates is worth more than the world's 70 smallest countries in terms of GDP combined. (Lennard, 2004)

Believing that Bill Gates, or anybody else, is "worth more" than Syria or Hungary or any other nation requires significant effort—it literally defies all logic, except that of the abstract global financial system. In successfully propagating illusions that a person can be worth more than an entire nation, people's

processes of perception rather than more tangible aspects of labor have become the primary objects of production in developed countries today and,
therefore, the most common form of labor in hypercapitalism. This is made
possible by an advancing technological ability to commodify increasingly
intimate aspects of life, the intrinsically social character and functions of language and thought, and the necessity of the knowledge "consumer" to work
in the process of consuming the products of these. This has led to the total
subsumption of human energies under systemic capital.

Conflating production, consumption, and exchange

In a technologically mediated global economy, the largest sector of which
produces abstract financial instruments designed to be continually exchanged
but never "consumed," questions about precisely *what* is being produced and
consumed, and by whom, become quite difficult to answer. Unlike shoes or
cabbages, knowledge need not be destroyed in the process of its "consumption"—it merely ceases to be "new." Further, a knowledge economy implies
that particular cognitive predispositions have become a central focus for productive processes. In a system with such an abstract focus, production,
consumption, and exchange become an inseparable whole, and "value creation" becomes an immediate, continuous process that unites these formerly
distinct spheres of activity.

Consequently there is little analytical usefulness in separating these moments within hypercapitalist political economy. That is because the
conceptual, physical, and temporal boundaries between them are dissolved by
new media's ubiquity and speed; by the work habits engendered by new media; and by the mass, and more importantly, the speed of exchange in
hypercapitalist social systems. Marx treats these spheres as analytically separate and differentiates between "productive" and "unproductive" labor, but
sees that from one perspective it is possible that "the entire time of the
worker is taken up by capital" (1976, pp. 1002-1045). But he gives little cre-
dence to such a view, perhaps because of the pre-eminence of "material"
commodities which were the main objects of the labor process at the time he
wrote.

Marx defines the sphere of consumption as the sphere in which the "means
of subsistence" are consumed (1976, p. 1004). Since they disappear from circulation after being consumed, the means of subsistence "form no part of the
physical elements in which capital manifests itself in the *immediate process
of production*" (1976, p. 1004). But today, trade in means of subsistence, and
in tangible goods more generally, constitutes a miniscule percentage of the
global economy (Saul, 1997). Marx views the relationship between the
spheres of production and consumption as being mediated by exchange be-

cause this is where labor is purchased—i.e., where human energy is reduced to the status of a commodity (1976, p. 302). However, this leads him to see that once exchange-value had "acquired a definite, independent *form*, distinct, albeit ideally, from its use value," and that when "all produce necessarily assumes the form of the commodity and hence all producers are necessarily commodity producers," then "use-value is universally mediated by exchange-value" (1976, pp. 951-955). And that is what has happened: hypercapitalist production processes have commodified almost every conceivable aspect of human social life, including life, birth, death, sexuality, opinion, and thought. Every aspect of life is measured, at least for policy purposes, in money values, whether in health, education, justice, defense, or whichever ends policy directs itself towards.

Knowledge commodities are not necessarily removed from circulation after they are produced, exchanged, and "consumed." In the process of consuming knowledge commodities, the consumer's reproductive process is oriented, not towards physical reconstitution or subsistence, as is often the case with "material" consumption, but towards reproducing themselves in the "descriptive domain" of human cognition, the domain in which social and individual identities are constituted (Graham and McKenna, 2000; Maturana and Varela, 1980, 1987, p. 231). The commodities of the information economy can be a source of self-identity "when and if social actors internalize them, and construct their meaning around this internalization" (Castells, 1997, p. 7). But this is not a two-step process in hypercapitalism. The exchange and consumption of knowledge is immediate—knowledge is produced and consumed at the same time it circulates and is exchanged. Further, knowledge exchanges immediately produce new knowledge, as well as forming the foundations for the production of even more knowledge. In a knowledge economy, production, circulation, and consumption become analytically inseparable because they happen in the same moment: the moment of exchange.

Knowledge and language as exchange systems

The novel aspect of hypercapitalism, and what makes it different from past forms of social organization, is that today's new media facilitate the production, consumption, distribution, and exchange of thought and language—knowledge commodities—on a planet-wide scale with a mass and speed that is historically unprecedented. Thought and language have themselves become the primary objects of production, distribution, and exchange within this emergent system. But that is merely to say that a knowledge economy must, self-evidently, be communicative in nature; its commodities must be the products of conscious distinctions between various aspects of the human environment; and these distinctions, to be exchanged with any political economic efficacy, must be exchanged in more and less valued forms of language, which are necessarily the products of more or less valued social contexts (Bourdieu, 1991; Gal, 1989, pp. 349-352; Schiller, 1996, p. 21).

At the most fundamental level, knowledge production is a continuous sociocognitive exchange between people and their environments. New knowledge is new meaning, and any instance of meaning-making is "a sociological event ... through which the meanings that constitute the social system are *exchanged*" (Halliday, 1978, p. 139). The process of sociocognitive exchange—meaningful interaction—is a process of production that is at the very heart of social organization. Because the hypercapitalist labor process operates by appropriating language and thought as its raw materials, in a knowledge economy it becomes very apparent that "production is simultaneously consumption" and vice versa, and both production and consumption are necessarily material processes of exchange (Marx, 1970, pp. 195-196).

Consumption and production of knowledge commodities are, at one level, necessarily processes of destruction and reproduction. But unlike the more durable commodity-forms that dominated previous eras, the ephemeral commodities of the knowledge economy are not destroyed in the process of consumption, even if they are materially produced and consumed. One cannot destroy information merely by "consuming" it—fire, eternal monopoly, and digital disasters notwithstanding. Once "consumed," though, a particular knowledge commodity ceases to be immediately informing for an individual: its functional utility *as* knowledge is exhausted, except for the purposes of future exchange. However, once informed, people can then reproduce, reconfigure, and redistribute their knowledge in an infinitely complex cycle of social interactions and exchanges. "Consumers" of knowledge are simultaneously its producers. Language is the primary means of exchange. This holds for all kinds of valuable knowledge, from currency trades, to advertising and political propaganda, to secrets sold by inside traders on the stock market, to the inventors of new techniques for manipulating DNA.

A corollary to all of this, considering the "division of intellectual labor" that knowledges of varying value entails, is that certain dialects are more amenable to commodification than others: valuable knowledge is necessarily the product of valorized dialects and, therefore, of privileged social contexts (Jarvis, 1998, pp. 87-88). At any given time in history, dominant interests give their "ideas the form of universality, and represent them as the only rational, universally valid ones" (Marx and Engels, 1847/1972, p. 138). Knowledge of the world is identical to one's understanding of the world, and, consequently, to understanding one's self in relation to the epistemological universe of dominant ideas, regardless of where a person is situated in this field. In a system dominated by the idea of exchange-values, the social worth of a person becomes a function of their monetary worth.

Capital, labor, language, new media, and social consciousness

Phenomenological capital embodies labor which has finished its work, or as Marx puts it, "dead" labor (1976, p. 342). The purpose of systemic capital is to extract surplus value from the living labor it appropriates (1976, p. 302). Systemic capital is therefore "a perpetual pumping machine for surplus labour" (Marx, 1981, p. 961). Phenomenological capital is "dead labour which, vampire-like, lives only by sucking living labour, and lives the more, the more labour it sucks" (Marx, 1976, p. 342). In a knowledge economy, products of human cognition simultaneously become the primary source of surplus-value, the primary means of production, and the primary *object* of production.

Because the ratio of machines to living labor increases as systemic capital advances, systemic capital becomes increasingly technologized:

> The more thoroughly developed the means of production and its associated division of labour, the less living labour can set its own goals: the less, indeed, living labour is living. The shift in the proportion of constant and variable capital is extended into the proportion of living and dead elements in individuals. (Jarvis, 1998, p. 71)

I do not mean this in any facile sense as the inevitable "mechanization" of people, as if they were "something static which, through an 'influence' from outside ... suffer certain deformations" (Adorno, 1951/1974, p. 229). It is, rather, the result of existing in social relations in which people appear in language as "things," as, for instance, in the ultimately objectifying terms "human capital," "human resources," and "labor market" (e.g., Latham, 1998, pp. 46-47). It is only when the process by which labor "is first transformed into a commodity" has thoroughly infused the consciousness of individuals, thus objectifying "each of their impulses as formally commensurable variations of the exchange relationship," that persons themselves are perceived as phenomenological capital: they become categorically objectified in language—they become categorically "dead" (Adorno, 1951/1974, p. 229).

The tendency towards objectification is an intrinsic function of language in technologized society (Halliday, 1993, p. 10). By accretion, like mechanical clock-time, technologized language slowly infuses social consciousness to the point at which people think of their life force firstly in respect of the exchange system and act in accordance with that system—*unconsciously*. But "labor," whether living or dead, is not a matter of content or form. Rather, the definition of "labor" is a matter of its place within systemic capital's categorical universe. To exemplify this assertion, it is worth considering the way Marx distinguishes between unproductive labor (that which people do by

their very nature, and which falls outside systemic capital's sphere of appropriation) and productive labor—labor that can be appropriated by systemic
capital in pursuit of surplus value (1976, pp. 1043-1045). In contrast to
Marx's time, hypercapitalism has extended its reach into education, knowledge, art, leisure, and what has generally become known as the "service
sector":

> A schoolmaster who instructs others is not a productive worker. But a schoolmas-
> ter who works for wages in an institution along with others, using his own labour
> to increase the money of the entrepreneur who owns the knowledge-mongering in-
> stitution, is a productive worker. But for the most part, work of this sort of work
> has scarcely reached the stage of being subsumed even formally under capital, and
> belongs essentially to a transitional stage. (Marx, 1976, p. 1044)

Here we see the implications of what a knowledge economy entails under
hypercapitalism: the formal commodification of education, art, sexuality, spiri-
tuality, psychology, personal intimacy, privacy, just to name a few aspects of
life that have become "industrialized." Even personal humiliation has become
systematically commodified with the proliferation of so-called "reality TV"
programming.

The objects of systemic capital's technology have changed. They have
moved from being primarily an instrument for the "domination of nature," or
that which is seen as external to human societies, to being more concerned
with manipulating human nature itself, in particular, human relatedness and
social consciousness (Adorno, 1991, p. 61). This begins and ends with the
commodification of human interaction, with the *products* of language. These
are products of a particular kind. Language is a material and social product. It
is

> not a superstructure on a base; it is a product of the *conscious* and the *material*
> impacting on each other—of the contradiction between our material being and our
> conscious being, as antithetic realms of experience. Hence language has the power
> to shape our consciousness; and it does so for each human child, by providing the
> theory that he or she uses to interpret and to manipulate their environment. (Halli-
> day, 1993, p. 8)

That is why, quite literally, perception, language, meaning, consciousness, and
consequently, knowledge and identity, have been progressively dragged into
systemic capital and subsumed under its mechanisms of appropriation. If we
are to understand the effects of new technologies of mediation, we must understand their relationship to, and impact upon language.

The functional convergence of language and new media

After millennia of technologization, objective technologies and technologized
language have converged to the point at which

> Language is no longer just a mode of social control; it is also the [direct] mode of
> control over physical systems and processes. The immediate impact here is the

> technologising of language itself. Here we have a direct line of evolution from the
> printing press to the computer, via the telephone, typewriter and tape recorder.
> (Halliday, 1993, pp. 68)

Language, knowledge, power, and new media are historically inseparable.
They emerge together as the very beginnings of recorded history itself:

> When language enters history its masters are priests and sorcerers. Whoever harms
> the symbols is, in the name of the supernatural powers, subject to their earthly
> counterparts, whose representatives are the chosen organs of society. (Horkheimer
> and Adorno, 1947/1998, p. 20)

In hypercapitalism, the most sacred of all symbolic systems is money. In its
many forms, it has also become the most valued commodity. Like the commodities that formed the basis of previous forms of systemic capital,
knowledge commodities are "self-valorizing" (Marx, 1976, p. 255): the more
widely and rapidly they are circulated, the more they appear to accrue value
independently of the people who produce them. The difficulty in "seeing"
knowledge commodities as such is that they become manifest only as ephemeral "things," as specific instances of "technologized" meaning making
(Fairclough, 1992); or, as instantiations of "the *labour of enunciation* which
is necessary to externalize the inwardness, to name the unnamed and to give
the beginnings of objectification to pre-verbal and pre-reflexive dispositions"
(Bourdieu, 1991, p. 129). Because they exist primarily in the realm of exchange, knowledge commodities cannot really exist as discreet "things."
They are the continuous products of social interaction, the public expressions
of thought, knowledge, power, and attitudes. As socially situated "things,"
each utterance, text, and work of art has different values for different people
(Bourdieu, 1991, 1998).

The "labor of representation" is like any other form of labor. It is a materially, socially, and historically conditioned process, the value of which is
established through and within socially and historically conditioned contexts,
through the institutionally contextualized processes by which "symbolic
power" is enacted, realized, and (mis)recognized as such (Bourdieu, 1991, p.
164). The producers of "authorized" or "legitimate" knowledge become fet-
ishized, valorized, and self-valorizing the more widely their knowledge gains
socially validated authority. This is the point at which economic, political,
and institutional aspects of value are expressed in specific political forms as
recognizable systems for the exercise of power.

Assuming that the right to produce officially sanctioned knowledge is a
source of power, the value system of a knowledge economy can be viewed as
an expression of the power system specific to the society in which particular
knowledge commodities are produced and exchanged. That is to say, in any
given social situation, particular persons are endowed with the social significance of legitimate "expertise"—the US President, the World Bank

economist, the foreign policy bureaucrat, the record company executive, the journalist, the financial pundit, the art critic—each of whom exercises a form of authority over specific symbolic realms, each of which must be transformed through mediations of one sort or another into money-values. They are recognized as "expert" producers and purveyors of knowledge (Bourdieu, 1991, chap. 4).

Throughout history, new media have had quite specific "implications for the character of knowledge" (Innis, 1951, pp. 3-4). The result has been that "a monopoly or an oligopoly of knowledge," and therefore power, has formed around the institutions that regulate access to new media, and to the most valued, sacrosanct forms of knowledge specific to these (1951, pp. 3-4):

> The imposition of a sharp divide between sacred and profane knowledge, which underlies the claims of all groups of specialists seeking to secure a monopoly of knowledge or sacred practice by constituting others as profane, thus takes on an original form: it is omnipresent, dividing each word against itself, as it were, by making it signify that it does not signify what it appears to signify, by inscribing within it … the distance which separates the 'authentic' from the 'vulgar' or 'naïve' sense. (Bourdieu, 1991, p. 145)

At the very moment knowledge commodities become "visible," their alien character, their status within the hierarchy of "authentic" knowledge, and their immediacy as forms of technologized language, renders their social origins invisible. They may not even appear as artifacts of knowledge, but as reified artifacts of socially sanctioned power—as specific persons. At the same time, the value system associated with particular forms of knowledge becomes more alienated from its source because the value attributed to knowledge of particular kinds appears to be "attached" to particular people and social groupings. As Bourdieu puts it, "the profit of distinction, procured by any use of the legitimate language, derives from the totality of the social universe and the relations of domination that give structure to it" (1991, p. 73). But the fact that socially significant power is embodied by particular groups of "legitimate" people gives rise to the illusion that symbolic profit "appears to be based on the qualities of the person alone" (1991, p. 73). This hides the social nature and generative logic of symbolic power.

The fetishisms that cleave to persons who have a recognizable and institutionally legitimate mastery of valorized dialects, along with the social sanction of the "sacred" institutions within which such knowledges are produced, is also a cumulative function of technologized language. Historically, language has tended towards "thinginess," towards objectification (Halliday, 1993). In the first instance, the historical "shift into the written medium" transformed embodied discourses into static "things," "and the abstractions— the written symbols and their arrangements—are transformations of processes into things" (Halliday, 1993, p. 10).

Written language, the first materially enduring communication technology, transforms "processes into *things* [which are then] construed as commodities; they take on value, and can be drawn up and itemized into lists" (Halliday, 1993, p. 10). In writing, meanings are technologized and value is alienated from its source. By separating thought from its embodied thinker, writing forms the generative and organizing principle of the physical alienation—the literal objectification—of language, thought, and value.

Writing is the historical source of the seamless trajectory that propagates objectified meanings across space and through time. Similarly, exchange values—money in the current context—now appears as something external to us. It appears as an objective system that expands its power independently of what we do as individuals. That is because, like language, "money is an ideal measure, which has no limits other than those of the imagination" (Marx, 1973, p. 190). The money system, like language, arises

> from the mutual influence of conscious individuals on one another, but [it is] neither located in their consciousness, nor subsumed under them as a whole. Their own collisions with one another produce an *alien* social power standing above them, [and] produce their mutual interaction as a process and power independent of them. (1973, pp. 196-197)

These historically entrenched contradictions, which inhere in all technologized forms of language, have never been so exposed as in the self-conscious presence of a knowledge economy. It is a system in which technologized forms of thought and language, value and money, appear as forces of nature, as forces beyond the control of human intervention.

The functional convergence of technology, language, and specialized thought as mechanisms of social control, mechanical control, and commodity production has quite definite and concrete implications. According to Coates (1998), within the next twenty-five years in "World 1," "[n]o aspect of the human being, whether physical, mental, intellectual, social, psychological or physiological, will be beyond practical manipulation and change, all of which will be made possible and practical through technology" (1998, p. 41).[27] Coates assumes that, by this time, knowledge *about* people will converge with the technological means to apply that knowledge. As a result, he argues,

> [b]rain technologies will go well beyond disease, offering relief for the person who is short-tempered the person who has no sense of humour, the person who is overly emotional. And relief from these conditions will find a substantial market. Beyond that will be the possibility and later the practice of enhancing people's cognitive processes, enabling them to think more clearly, to have a better command of arithmetic, to have a better memory for faces, to be more generous and loving, or to be less prideful or slothful. (1998, p. 42)

An historical heteroglot of privileged social voices is evident in this statement: we hear the fluent voice of the economically-minded technocrat (technological *relief from these conditions will find a market*); priestly pronouncements and predictions upon at least five of the "seven deadly sins" (by my estimation Coates has covered pride, sloth, envy, anger, greed, and implicitly, lust); the condescending and banal platitudes of patriarchy prescribing what are, and will be, considered as "valuable" qualities for a person to have (*a better command of arithmetic*; *a better memory for faces*, etc.). In short, Coates's statement collapses millennia of technologized thought, and the power and value systems which inhere in these. The mixed modes that new communication technologies facilitate combine almost the entire range of resources developed throughout human history.

Such is the legacy of a literate industrial society: meaning is "made manifest and progressively 'technologised'" (Iedema, 1999). In being technologized, meaning moves from "temporal kinds of meaning making, such as talk and gesture, towards increasingly durable kinds of meaning making such as printed reports, designs, and buildings" (1999, p. 1). Each step away from embodied meaning-making that technologizing processes take are made manifest in less negotiable, more "technologized" forms: a report is less negotiable than a meeting; an architectural design is more negotiable than a building, and so on. Similarly, casual conjecture is far more negotiable than the "facts" of technologized orthodoxy. By the same systemic logic, not all ways of knowing are perceived as having similar value. The logic of a system historically based on more and less valuable knowledges presupposes an assumption of inequality between social contexts of knowledge production, and so between individual persons and social groups; it presupposes *scarcity of access to privileged knowledge*. A challenge for critical research into new media is creating egalitarian access, not merely to knowledge and technology, but more importantly to privilege. Of course egalitarian access to privilege immediately abolishes privilege as a category.

The systemic contradictions of hypercapitalism are exemplified in Castell's post-Fordist maxim: "I think therefore I produce" (Castells, 1998, p. 359). Here, in the knowledge worker's ontological slogan, Castells highlights the paradox of hypercapitalism's knowledge economy: according to the utopian rhetoric of technology policy and technology industries it would seem that anyone with the capacity for thought and language, and with access to the technological means of production, would instantly qualify as a producer of "valuable" knowledge. That is patently not the case. Hypercapitalism therefore offers an opportunity to view some of the most fundamental contradictions inherent in the logic of systemic capital's social relations—the basic, seemingly objective and immutable inequality of people. In addressing this issue from an historical materialist perspective, I must reassert that, although they appear to be ephemeral, thought and language, and more importantly, *the perceived value of their social context of production*, are as much a material product and a producer of specific material social relationships as are mass-produced motor cars (Adorno, 1991, p. 99; Bourdieu, 1991; Gal, 1989, p. 352).

Value-alienation, knowledge, and valorized language

By definition, knowledge commodities are fundamental to the operation of a capitalist knowledge economy. Knowledge commodities are necessarily produced and exchanged in one sort of language or another. To be of value, knowledge commodities need to be technologically stored, harnessed, exchanged, and circulated. Moreover, they need to be *recognized* as valuable and significant "things." New communication technologies have played consistent roles throughout human history because they are the means by which specific groups of people have produced, maintained, manipulated, and eventually destroyed historically specific forms of "knowledge economies" and their associated "knowledge monopolies" (Innis, 1951, chap. 1).

Neither knowledge commodities, knowledge monopolies, nor the specialized groups of people who produce them, are new features of human society. Specialized language and thought have, to the best of historical knowledge, always been at the center of social, political, economic, and technological developments in human societies.[28] Historically, knowledge specialists have included priests, philosophers, technocrats, bureaucrats, military officers, scientists, scribes, poets, artists, musicians, and so on.[29] What is often ignored in accounts of systemic capital's development of commodities is the first mechanically mass-produced products: books and pamphlets (Innis, 1951, p. 139). In other words, the industrial revolution and the emergence of systemic capital as a recognizable form of social relations followed the "information revolution" that the printing press sparked almost 350 years before the industrial revolution was fully realized (Weber, 1930/1992, pp. 44-45).

Innis's (1950, 1951) insights show the current environment as a stratified historical complex of communication technologies—from oral traditions and the earliest writing, to the mixing of these in ancient Greece, to the first electronic media, to the proliferating technologies of the digital age. Of course, we must include boats, trains, the telegraph, radio, and television—anything that has affected modes of social communication, organization, and control, especially the means and modes of *distribution* for meanings (Innis, 1950, 1951; Marx, 1973, p. 524). Today's new media conflate the processes of production, exchange, and distribution of self-valorizing language and thought within a domain of globally interconnected "things." Alongside this self valorizing system of knowledge commodities is its arbiter, partner, and facilitator—the system of symbolic values that constitute the globalized system of monetary exchange.

The history of communication technologies is also a history of knowledge monopolies being built and destroyed. Corresponding to this is a history of social control systems and subsequent revolutions against them. In short, the history of communication technologies is a history of the most fundamental and violent changes in social relations (Innis, 1951, pp. 31-32). It is also a history of how people preserve and exchange language, knowledge, and power at temporal and spatial distances. Each major historical advance in communication technologies has corresponded to identifiable social ruptures as new ways of "technologizing," exchanging, and propagating knowledge— whether sacred or profane—become available to specific groups of people (Innis, 1950, 1951).

Languages, technologies, and societies, and the people who inhabit, these, each mediate changes in the others' circumstances of production and repro-duction. This necessarily includes the production and reproduction of conscious experience, an inalienably material process. Conscious experience in turn shapes and is shaped by other environmentally embedded actions (Halliday, 1993; Marx, 1846/1972, pp. 123-124). Historical changes in the interdependent factors that comprise society bear the marks of the historical conditions within which they become manifest. Language is no exception:

> [T]he particular mix that characterizes the elaborated tertiary styles of the Eura-sian world languages, from Japanese and Chinese at one end of the continent to English, French and Spanish at the other, is the result of layering, one on top of another, of all these various "moments" in their history through which experience has been ongoingly reconstrued in successively more abstract and objectified terms. (Halliday, 1993, p. 11)

Technological advances, of all kinds, can also be seen to be "layered" upon preceding innovations. For instance,

> [e]lectricity was the central force of the second [industrial] revolution, in spite of other extraordinary developments in chemicals, steel, the internal combustion en-gine, telegraphy and telephony. This is because only through electrical generation and distribution were all the other fields able to develop their applications and be connected to each other. (Castells, 1996, pp. 38-39)

This historical overlaying of techniques or modes of expression, and their integration with new technologies, forms a retrospectively perceptible pat-tern. But this implies neither a linear nor deterministic view of technological development: 'the pattern is a helical one … . Mixed modes engender mixed genres" (Halliday, 1993, p. 68). In the "field of power," these "mixed genres" are historical manifestations of technologically reconciled power struggles that have been acted out within and between specific social domains throughout history. Mixed genres are the result of historical power struggles involving technologized meanings (Bourdieu, 1998, p. 34).[30]

History, language, new media, and society

Language defines social realities and propagates the value systems that shape the way we live. New media have specific and profound effects that are never quite recognizable, before, during, or perhaps even after their general diffusion and deployment. Relations and modes of production are delineated and defined in people's language, and that is why language provides an important, if not a vital focus for research into the social impacts of any new media. But that is no simple matter. Language practices

> cannot be understood *outside of* their historical contexts; but neither can they be *derived* from these contexts by any simple relation ... language is at the same time a part of reality, a shaper of reality, and a metaphor for reality. (Halliday, 1993, p. 8)

Technologized language is like any other historically significant human achievement. It contains, shapes, and represents the context of its production. It contains traces of its past within its present which, in turn, contains the seeds of all its possible futures within each utterance. It contains the sediments of history within its formal and informal instantiations. It delineates myriad aspects of the world from each other, and gives social life to thought across generations and continents. The material artifacts of language—for example, recorded speech, the written word, video recordings—appear as technologized, objectified, and alienated forms of social interaction which, once alienated from people and their social contexts, appear as objective historical resources of varying value for making *more* socially significant meanings.[31] In this respect, technologized meanings can be viewed as vital to both systemic *and* phenomenological capital: as means of production and reproduction; as arbiters of distribution and exchange; and as products and producers of social relations—all at the same time. When viewed as such, technologized language becomes technologized symbolic capital—valorized artifacts of privileged social interactions.

The point at which language, thought, and technology converge in their mass and immediacy, while being collectively deployed in controlling technological *and* social systems, is also the point at which knowledge *about* these systems becomes the most valuable knowledge of all. In such conditions, an individual's *mind* takes on the qualities of the commodity-fetish. It simultaneously appears as an in-itself value and as an artifact which can be construed as if it were external to the person who "uses" it:

> If some nerdy kid can go from zero to being worth 45 billion dollars in 25 years on nothing but the power of his mind—defeating the most powerful corporation of his time and now actually competing with whole nation states for control of the future—it is obvious that scale and economic momentum have lost a lot of their formerly fearsome credibility. (Barlow, 1998, p. 12)

Here, the propaganda of an apparently "neoliberal" logic becomes manifest. Rather than being liberal in any way, though, it much more resembles the logic of nineteenth-century eugenic thought—Bill Gates as the exemplar of Galton's "class X" man (see Chapter 2). Again, we see the nation-state and individual rendered as commensurable "things" that are conceptually fungible with each other based entirely on the logic of a synthetic value system—money. The reified, apparently autonomous system of money takes on a distorting and ostensibly determining role. The nation-state and moneyed individual are qualitatively identical based solely on accumulated amounts of symbolic wealth.

Such displays of anti-social logic are a recognizable feature of techno-utopian language. Barlow refers to economic power on an historically unequaled scale wielded by a single individual, Bill Gates, to show that where nation-states are concerned, "scale and economic momentum" have lost their ability to "control" the future. But if anyone were naïve enough to believe that Gates rose to "power" single-handedly by deploying "nothing but the power of his mind," some commentary from Friedman (1999) might help to illuminate an important aspect of the social context within which Gates has achieved his success:

> The hidden hand of the market will never work without a hidden fist—McDonald's cannot flourish without McDonnel Douglas, the builder of the F-15. And the hidden fist that keeps the world safe for Silicon Valley's technologies is called the United States Army, Air Force, Navy and Marine Corps. "Good ideas and technologies need a strong power that promotes those ideas by example and protects those ideas by winning on the battlefield," says the foreign policy historian Robert Kagan. (Friedman, 1999, p. 84)

Knowledge, power, value, and language are, as ever, interdependent, mutually conditioning "things" in the knowledge economy in a very literal sense. Dialects of power provide "access to material resources" and are, unquestionably, materially produced, socially embedded practices (Gal, 1989, p. 352). In being produced and exchanged, the products of valorized dialects—like the other products of industrialized societies—produce and reproduce specific, though not immutable, social relationships (Fairclough, 1992; Lemke, 1995). In short, knowledge commodities, because of the symbolic values attributed to their contexts of production, have a fully fungible relationship with the languages in which they are exchanged. More visibly, they have a fungible relationship with money, the mysterious system that can render relationships between all "things"—even the nation state and the individual—rational and equivalent. In a knowledge economy, "language makes power; power gets valued" (Martin, 1998, p. 429).

A prelude to time and space

Systemic capital "by its nature drives beyond every spatial barrier. Thus the creation of the physical conditions of exchange—the annihilation of space by time—becomes an extraordinary necessity for it" (Marx, 1973, p. 524). In short, systemic capital is considered to have become more "productive" when circulation time—the transformation of money into commodities and back again—decreases (Marx, 1973, pp. 524-549). Today, the dominant ideal is exchange itself. The emergence of hypercapitalism and its knowledge economy emphasizes that language is a material social practice with very real effects. Language is the source of money-values and is now globally mediated through new ICTs. Systemic hypercapitalism privileges money-values at the expense of perceptions about what human societies are and what they mean. Language is also a commodity and a technology, or at least has become increasingly commodified and technologized within new media environments. A focus on language practices once again appears to be the only way to assess changing perceptions and social relations in newly mediated political economic systems. Our perceptions are conditioned by the way we talk about and deploy new media, and by the way language, new media, the labors of abstraction, and the social technologies of money are converging in their social function.

By foregrounding some of the contradictions and tendencies inherent in hypercapitalism, it becomes clear that systemic capital's valorization process operates within and upon human relationships. The ultimate expansion of systemic capital constitutes nothing less that the *total* colonization and commodification of human life: "labor" in the current context. Hypercapitalist processes are aimed at the most ephemeral, intimate, and intangible aspects of human energies and social relatedness. Historical materialism is analytically based in the specifics of existing material conditions. Such a method, in the face of hypercapitalism and its knowledge economy, needs to eschew, reinvent, or further refine theoretical distinctions within political economy. Terms such as "material" and "non-material" production; "productive" and "unproductive" labor; production and consumption; forces and relations of production; base and superstructure; and distinctions between politics, society, and economy, have all been convenient distinctions in earlier historical materialist studies of political economy. But now these distinctions need to be redefined or dispensed with altogether in favor of a new conception of the social, and of what social goods are.

Because of hypercapitalism's immediacy, which is a function of its expansive scope, its circulation speed, and its ephemeral commodity-forms, such distinctions appear to be more obfuscatory than explanatory. Under conditions of hypercapitalism, forces and relations of production; base and superstructure; the valorization process; material and non-material production; and production and consumption are analytically inseparable because of the immediacy and pervasiveness of the social and technical domains within which they operate, and because of their intimate involvement with language and thought. While Marx noted that means of communication limit the speed of circulation time, and therefore of the valorization process, he largely ignores communication technologies in his apparent assumption that more tangible commodities would remain of primary importance in creating values. This may yet prove to be the case. But under systemic hypercapitalism, the illusion of value takes on a grossly distorting role, especially where utility and social worth are concerned. The role of value has become inverted, and social utility is now relegated by a mute, blunt, and fictitious value system that is all but entirely alienated from its source. Value is mediated, legitimized, and defined in language. Rather than being seen as a useful fiction, it has been used to appropriate and commodify the most intimate aspects of human experience. Therefore to engage hypercapitalism as the object of effective critique requires constant consideration of the fact that human perceptions have become systemic capital's primary objects of production. Having commodified, consumed, and inhabited much of the useful space on earth, the emphasis for dominant commercial institutions in developed countries today is upon commodifying temporal abstractions, most specifically those pertaining to some imagined future. These imaginary future commodities exist only in the minds of specific people. Nevertheless they are traded in enormous quantities and make up the largest part of "the global economy." Such a path raises insuperable paradoxes in conceptions of materiality, social and economic stability, and social equality. It forces us back upon the most general and basic concepts in political economic and social organization: time and space. The various ways we have organized these aspects of existence are functions of language and mediation systems, and they define the historical character of political economies. Alternating emphases upon these aspects of organization seem to operate in antithetical cycles throughout history. The current state of their interaction underpins hypercapitalist political economy. These trajectories involve intricate, and to a large extent unpredictable, interplays between time and space on the one hand, and mythology and rationality on the other.

CHAPTER FIVE

Time, space, and new media

> In the past five years Jules Vernian impressions of radio and radio broadcasting
> have been driven into people's minds by the active publicity man with his circus
> ballyhooing about the romance of radio and the wonders of the wireless. The press
> agent has convinced many of us that there is practically nothing the radio cannot
> do, all the way from communicating with Mars and transmitting millions of kilo-
> watts of electrical energy thousands of miles without wires to giving a college
> education to the nation and keeping wayward husbands at home. (Beuick, 1927, p.
> 615)

Innovations in communication technologies throughout history have invariably coincided with ruptures in social relations. That is neither a
contentious nor surprising statement. That communication technologies
and social relations have mutually determining, constraining, and disruptive
effects on each other is also self-evident. What *is* surprising about the period we
live in is the apparent amazement with which researchers from many disciplines view the effects that current advances in communication technologies are
having within our societies.

Communication technologies have performed fairly consistent functions
throughout human history. They have been central in the preservation of
knowledge, the creation of new knowledge monopolies and the destruction of
old, the maintenance and expansion of centralized powers, and the eventual
erosion of these (Innis, 1950, 1951). The social effects of today's new ICTs
are no different. We are merely seeing the continuation of historically recurrent effects rebadged in the most up-to-date technical jargon. While each new
communication technology, like each dominant faith system, has its historically unique form and content, their intended purpose at the time of
deployment remains consistent throughout history: social control in the maintenance of a political economic elite. But that is clearly not their sole effect.
The social consequences of new communication technologies are an entirely
different matter from the intentions of their designers. And my comparison of
communication technologies with historically dominant faiths is more than
just a rhetorical device. The two are inseparable throughout history. Each
successive faith has relied on a unique suite of communication technologies,
and each new communication technology can be identified with the emer-

gence of new forms of faith (Innis, 1951; Noble, 1997).

Working the myth of circulation time

> This is the nature of capital, of production founded on capital, that circulation time becomes a determinant moment for labour time, for the creation of value. The independence of labour time is thereby negated, and the production process is itself posited as determined by exchange, so that immediate production is socially linked to it and dependent on this link—not only as a material moment, but also as an economic moment, a determinant characteristic form. (Marx, 1973, p. 628).

My central focus in this chapter is circulation time and its implications for a global knowledge economy. Circulation is the economic sphere most apparently relevant to new communication technologies and their effects. Circulation is a matter of time *and* space. Today's communication technologies circulate information at close to light speed. They are very recent and significant historical developments. Prior to electricity and the telegraph, the circulation time of communication was limited and equal to the fastest means of transport (Marx, 1973, p. 628). Goods, news, people, and ideas have traveled together throughout most of history. The invention of the telegraph changed this, and for the first time, select people in select places could communicate over vast distances in the time it took for electrical impulses to be encoded, decoded, written down on paper, and delivered. With the telegraph, communication and transport were separated in time and space—they became separate spheres of circulation. Conceptually, though, space and time had taken a step towards each other.

In the separation of communication and transport, we see historical indications about the functional trajectory of communication technologies. Writing meant that a person's thoughts could be turned into static "things" with an existence separate from their thinker. As societies and technologies changed over time, more sophisticated means of production, reproduction, and transport facilitated communication across greater expanses of space, enabling empires and organizations to exert their influence over shorter and shorter periods of time (Innis, 1951, pp. 64-65). With each historical breakthrough in transport, media durability, and media transportability, high levels of financial speculation become manifest. This is most evident in recent history with the emergence of the bullionist and mercantilist economies of the seventeenth century. Stories brought home by Dutch traders about the riches of the orient, combined with the emergence of a new credit system in Holland, gave way to "tulipmania." At the peak of the tulip craze, between 1634 and 1637, one tulip bulb could buy three houses in Amsterdam (Thurow, 1996, pp. 220-221; Hyma, 1938).[32] The unsustainable levels of speculation in the Netherlands resulted in a form of bankruptcy from which it has never fully recovered.[33]

As physical space continued to give way to improvements in navigation and chronology—accurate measurements of space and time (the perfection of which are in large part attributable to Isaac Newton)—South America offered its El Dorado to the British mercantile imagination in the form of maritime narratives, literally, rumors. But war between Britain and Spain, which at that time controlled the South Pacific, prevented the British from capitalizing on the promise of South American gold. The war with Spain, mercantile economics, and colonial expansionism had taken its toll on the British public purse. Following the French lead, the British government decided to relieve itself of the national debt by "privatizing" it and allowing a franchise to sell shares in the debt to members of the public. In doing so, they initiated the first of the many massive joint-stock swindles which continue to this day. People had begun speculating *en masse* by trading paper promises of shares in future wealth. In 1720, the "South Sea Bubble" burst.

With the South Sea bubble, a recognizable phenomenon emerges. The directors of the South Sea company had secured a monopoly on trade in South America and throughout "all the south seas." They made a proposal, sweetened with bribes for the appropriate officials, to assume the entire national debt of Britain in return for the right to sell shares in it to the public (Mackay, 1841; McNeil et al., 1996). This is the historical point at which hype and public perception first enter as significant commodities in capitalism, as valuable "products" of the labors of representation. By deploying hype and manipulating opinion in the stock trading communities,

> [t]he Company immediately starts to drive up the price through artificial means; these largely take the form of new subscriptions combined with the circulation of pro-trade-with-Spain stories designed to give the impression that the stock could only go higher. (McNeil et al., 1996)

Public gullibility, fuelled by the prospects of fast money, rose to hysterical levels. The frenzied pitch that speculation reached became evident upon the issue of an enterprise with an especially vague purpose statement. It was announced, namelessly, as "A company for carrying on an undertaking of great advantage, but nobody to know what it is' (McNeil et al., 1996). The prospectus for the company stated that

> the required capital was half a million, in five thousand shares of 100 pounds each, deposit 2 pounds per share. Each subscriber, paying his [or her] deposit, was entitled to 100 pounds per annum per share. How this immense profit was to be obtained, [the proposer] did not condescend to inform [the buyers] at that time, but promised that in a month full particulars should be duly announced, and a call made for the remaining 98 pounds of the subscription. Next morning, at nine o'clock, this great man opened an office in Cornhill. Crowds of people beset his door, and when he shut up at three o'clock, he found that no less than one thousand shares had been subscribed for, and the deposits paid. He was thus, in five hours, the winner of 2000 pounds. He was philosophical enough to be contented

with his venture, and set off the same evening for the Continent. He was never heard of again. (Mackay, 1841)

It is an historical commonplace that breakthroughs in ICT are followed by periods of irrational speculation.

The hype, scepticism and bewilderment associated with the Internet—concerns about new forms of crime, adjustment in social mores, and redefinition of business practices—mirror precisely the hopes, fears and misunderstandings inspired by the telegraph. Indeed they are to be expected. They are the direct consequences of human nature, rather than technology. (Standage, 1999, p. 199)

The speculative impulses associated with the telegraph can be seen throughout history in similar phenomena that appear to be contingent upon advances in communication technology, including transport:

In the 1850s, the railroad was widely expected to greatly increase the efficiency of communications and commerce. It did, but not enough to justify the prices of railroad stocks which grew to enormous speculative heights before collapsing on 24 August 1857. Radio in the 1920s also promised to create a revolution in the economics of communications and commerce. Indeed, an entirely new industry grew out of the invention. Euphoria over the promising new technology came to an abrupt end in October 1929. Even stock in RCA, the only company that had successfully built a profitable business from radio, lost 97% of its value between 1929 and 1933 (iTulip, 1999).

Any technological improvement that increases the speed of circulation seemingly results in speculative activity, whether financial, military, or political. Speculation, communication, electricity, and news joined forces in the person of Julius Reuter (1816–1890). Reuter thought that telegraphy would transform the *meaning* of news (Hobsbawm, 1975, p. 77). It did. It also prompted some adventurous bankers to try sending money electronically, small amounts at first—$100 at the very most (Standage, 1999, pp. 112-114). Standage notes an instructive historical aside here: as soon as it became widely known that money was being sent by telegraph, mothers whose sons were in the American civil war began taking food to the telegraph office to send to the battlefield to provide the comforts and worldly goods of home. If money could be sent by electricity, they apparently thought that food surely could. That historical nugget does not reflect a general misunderstanding of the telegraph's technical capacities. Rather, it is an expression of a general misrecognition of money: the objective social character of money (as coins, gold, etc.) at the time permitted no understanding of money as a form of information and communication (i.e., as "pure" price information). Today, the problem of understanding money is that trillions swirl around the globe on a daily basis, not as a mere aid or adjunct to business, as were the first electronic funds transfers, but as a freestanding business in itself—the massive global currency trade. Significantly, a large part of the infrastructure for global currency trade and general financial speculation is today owned, and naturally promoted, by the Reuters news organization. It is no historical accident that the most prolific, publicized, and valorized sector of hypercapitalist economy is the trade in financial abstractions.

The ongoing, serial collapses of whole national and corporate economies, from the late eighties through to the present day, are the direct result of financial speculation and manufactured illusions of wealth, mostly in the form of debt in its manifold, abstract forms, and of artificial and deceptive practices designed to inflate prices (cf. Hellyer, 1999; Saul, 1997). The most serious financial collapses in East Asia, South America, and Eastern Europe throughout the last decade have all been the result of speculative excesses compounded by hyperinflated currency and stock markets, and the tendency of the financial sector to conjure financial abstraction upon financial abstraction, dub these "new products," and send them into circulation around the globe at the speed of light. Exacerbating these phenomena is the simple and age-old problem of greed, in combination with new global regimes of corporate "self-regulation." These emerged from the allegedly "neoliberal" economic policies that began with the Reagan-Thatcher regimes of the late 1970s. The serial collapses of Worldcom, Enron, HIH, Kmart, Adelphia, Global Crossing, and the many others during the early twenty-first century, are directly attributable to rampant speculation, the distance of corporations from national regulatory systems, sheer greed, and an unflinching belief that the circulation of exchange-values is a productive economic end in itself (CBS, 2004)

The contradictions of space, time, and number

Circulation speed is a relation between space and time. For the duration of this chapter, I use the term "space" to refer only to geological space. In distinction to social and symbolic spaces, geological space has an existence independent of what humans think and do. Geometry is the mode of measurement most usually used to define its expanse. Time, as measured by clocks, is a purely human contrivance expressed in numerical form. Number systems, like all aspects of language, are also uniquely human inventions (Innis, 1951). The conceptual difference between time and space emerge from very different aspects of experience. Space, while always being fluid at some level, is a bounded expanse delineated by specific and substantial elements: rivers, mountains, seas, oceans, borders, fences, and so on. In its most technical sense, time is a system of numbers that marks off recurring cycles of more or less regular duration: minutes, seconds, weeks, years, and so forth. Space is expanse; time is duration. But once translated into the realm of number, space and time become commensurable to the human intellect. Ancient Greek geometry, perfected by Euclid in about 300 B.C., emerged from a concern with the relationship between space, time, and number (Innis, 1951, p. 110). From that point onwards, the abstract system of numbers pushed the concept of space ever closer to that of time, to the point at which Einstein theoretically fused the two. At this point in human thought, number emerges from analytical history alone and triumphant, as a separate and independent system capable of simultaneously grasping and fusing human concretions of space and time.

The triumph of number is a significant moment in human history. It is the triumph of quantity over quality. Only in this realm of human expression do time and space become commensurable, able to be thought of in a single system of expressions. Throughout history, whenever the relation of time to space time challenged the number system, that is, when equations describing space were challenged by new mathematical descriptions of time, the reality of space was numerically manipulated to compensate. Such was the innovation of Newton's concept of eternal and uniform space, for example. And when the reverse happened, when space became a numerical problem in relation to new mathematical expressions of time, concepts of eternal, constant time became necessary inclusions. But the fundamental laws of number have remained constant throughout. In the abstract realm of numbers, anything that "cannot be counted and measured, ceases to exist" (Adorno, 1951/1974, p. 47).

So it is no surprise that in political economy, problems are reduced to ones of space, time, and number—respectively, land, labor, and capital. Historical triumphs notwithstanding, the relationship between capital, land, and labor, the "holy trinity" of classical political economy, "is like that of lawyer's fees, beetroot, and music" (Marx, 1981, p. 953). They are qualitatively antithetical phenomena that gain little in the way of explanatory power from being reduced to numerical expression, just as the tedium of commuting in heavy traffic gains scant edification by being explained in terms of Einstein's theory of relativity. Number cannot explain its source—human imagination—nor can it describe the nature of the qualities it expresses.

Where new media are concerned, meanings of time and space become problematic. Apart from the problems associated with new media that Innis identifies—specifically, those of religion, empire, and knowledge monopolies—there remain other more challenging paradoxes that the emerging crop of new communication technologies foreground. Again, advertising provides a simple example of the paradoxical relationship between the meaning of time and space as it pertains to new media.

Advertising became an influential force in newspapers, both in the United States and Britain beginning in the late eighteenth century (Innis, 1942; Williams, 1976, chap. 2). Newspaper advertising is purchased in quantities of unambiguous space, by the page or column inch for example. Measures of a print advertisement's "reach" are based on the number of papers sold on any given day and the best estimate of how many people read each publication. Newspapers therefore provide a clear means of working out precise measurements of how much physical space a given advertisement occupies, of how many acres of advertising a "full page" constitutes on any given day in any given paper. Not that that is any indication of the success or otherwise of a given advertisement, because the space an advertisement really occupies, in terms of its meaning, effectiveness, recall, and so on, is an abstract sociocognitive space within the social consciousness that can only be measured indirectly, and even then very imperfectly.

When radio enters as an influential medium, advertising begins to be sold in quantities of time. During the first seven years of radio broadcasting in the United States, listenership grew from "a mere handful to over six and a half million people" (Hettinger, 1934, p. 284). By 1934, the number of broadcasters had grown to 598, including foreign language stations, and regional and national networks. By 1931, "time sales to advertisers totalled slightly in excess of seventy million dollars" (Hettinger, 1934, p. 285). Space appears not to be a problematic issue in radio advertising. Time is what is sold. Nevertheless, the *spatial* dimensions of radio emerged as a conceptual problem even prior to its becoming an influential broadcast medium:

> Writing on "Air as Raw Material" in the *Annals of the American Academy* for March, 1924, Walter S. Rogers, American adviser to the Peace conference in Paris, said that one of the serious problems in dealing with the subject of international electrical communications was the question of who owns the right to use space for communication purposes …
>
> Of course air has nothing to do with the matter, whether as raw material or otherwise. Nothing is property unless it can be reduced to possession and exclusively occupied and held. The newspapers of Washington, D.C., called attention, some few years ago, to the purchase of space overlying a lot of ground by the owner of a tall building adjoining, in order to secure the right to the perpetual use of whatever light and air might fill that space. Air drifts in and out with every zephyr, and light passes through at the rate of 186,000 miles per second.
>
> The purchaser can only own so much of them as he can use. What he here bought was something more imponderable than light. In economics it is known as land, or natural resources; in everyday English it is space. (Childs, 1924, pp. 520-523) [34]

In a very real sense, wireless transmissions occupy space: a specific amount of electromagnetic bandwidth, or "electrospace" (Hinchman, 1969 in Smythe, 1981, pp. 300-318). Like all communication technologies, radio also creates quantitatively and qualitatively new social spaces, whether seen as "communication between the announcer and each individual listener" or "between one person and massed millions" (Hettinger, 1934, p. 290).[35] Selling radio time is the selling of several amounts of qualitatively different kinds of abstract space all at once, the most important of which is direct and centralized access to the "sociocognitive metabolism" (Graham and McKenna, 2000).

Television poses similar problems in terms of defining what aspects of time and space it occupies. While television advertisements are sold by the second, receivers vary in price according to screen size and quality. But in the internet, advertising becomes another matter altogether. Space and time again dissolve into number. Numbers, in the form of "namespaces," and hits thereon, become the contested space in the knowledge economy: advertisers currently compete for marketshare, for numbers of numbers, which of course can only be expressed as other numbers. When interested enthusiasts of internet advertising attempt to deviate from quantity to describe the internet environment, the effects range from banal to outright vicious. For example, Mr. Burns, the CEO of Xerox Australia in 1998, tells us that "Australians spent 130 million hours browsing the internet in 1997, double the number of the previous year ... at the same time, the number of hours watching television fell by 470 million hours to 15.5 billion hours" (Burns, 1998 in Witts, 1998, p. 32). Burns's understanding of people and their interests requires that he abstract according to the laws of number to describe people's intellectual activities as qualitatively cattle-like. He then deploys a strong behaviorism to reshape the consumer's habits: "The behaviour is typically like foraging for food. The consumer clicks on a site, but if they don't find what they want quickly, they move on to the next site or paddock. We are developing a formula of predictability and then we can change their behaviour, modify it" (Burns, 1998 in Witts, 1998, p. 32).

This is a qualitative step away from concerns with returns on investment in abstract space and time—it is direct psychological aggression. The importance of the new psychosocial space is evidenced by the US Department of Defense's (DOD) first *Information Operations Doctrine* which classified "cyberspace," along with "air, land, and sea," as "battlespace":

> The Information Operations doctrine "moves information operations from an ad hoc process and institutionalizes it." The individual services already had taken steps to formalize their information operations, Kuehl said, and the new doctrine brings these operations into the joint realm. ... The doctrine published by the chiefs takes warfare to a new dimension with the "ultimate target human decision-making." (Brewin, 1998)

Here, in a numerically defined space-time, the US military identifies a system, the ultimate aim of which is to manipulate the human decision making process. It is a space that is now defended by the US military, the most expensive and technologically intense organization on earth. Having officially identified and defined the space in which "information operations" take place, the military has effectively objectified and institutionalized the spatial ontology of digitally mediated exchanges by committing to patrol and defend the "territory" in which they are produced and effectively take place. In this respect, it may be said that communication between people, the basis of societies, has been raised to the status and significance formerly enjoyed only by nation-states. The number system developed to describe space and time has itself become a form of space-time.

A uniquely human folly

The measurement of space and time—and for that matter space *in* time—is description by numerical ratios, description by the exercise of quantitative rationality. Human emotion cannot be understood by the same means, nor can emotions be measured in the same way. Nor can number typically rouse people's passions in the same way as can music, personal intimacy, poetry, and religion.[36] Number is a technology of commensurability, a means of rendering qualitatively different aspects of experience comparable. Translating equations into everyday language necessarily results in a much longer expressions because mathematics is a form of linguistic compression. In mathematics, logical expressions are compressed into a system of expertly derived symbols. Further, valid equations are typically tautological. Numerical formulae demand and assume balance and perfection, whatever their solution. Consequently, particular forms of quantitative rationality, distinct as they are from what we understand as religion, paradoxically appear to develop what can only be described as religious dimensions in so far as they tend to inspire disproportionate levels of faith in human systems of abstraction. In respect of the scientific revolution based on experimental scientific method, Horkheimer and Adorno (1947/1998) called this phenomenon "the dialectic of enlightenment," emphasizing that "the enlightenment" itself has its basis in methods developed within religious institutions.

Innis also recognized a similar trajectory, although he viewed it somewhat differently as having more to do with the bias of a medium towards control over the meaning of space and time, and therefore over the lives of people occupying particular spaces and times:

> A medium of communication has an important influence on the dissemination of knowledge over space and time and it becomes necessary to study its characteristics in order to appraise its influence in its cultural setting. According to its characteristics it may be better suited to the dissemination of knowledge over time than over space, particularly if the medium is heavy and durable and not suited to transportation, or to the dissemination of knowledge over space than over time, particularly if the medium is light and easily transported. The relative emphasis on time or space will imply a bias of significance to the culture in which it is imbedded. (Innis, 1951, p. 33)

But Innis did not merely focus on the medium as a collection of physical things. He also put forward a more important and subtle understanding of the various forms of signification as technologies in themselves, like money and other numbers systems:

> The price system with its sterilizing power has destroyed ideologies and broken up
> irreconcilable minorities by compelling them to name their price. Unrestrained, it
> has destroyed its own ideology since it too has its price. In a sense religion is an
> effort to organize irrationality and as such appears in all large-scale organizations
> of knowledge. (Innis, 1944, p. 97)

A global knowledge economy is the apotheosis of a "large-scale organization of knowledge," and to exist it requires the most massive organization of irrationality in history. The rationalizing myth of this essentially religious system is the supposed productivity of circulating exchange values. Since recorded history, mythology and rationality—together in antagonistic tension, always appealing to different aspects of human nature—have been deployed to organize the meaning of time and space in human societies. This is especially evident in times of cultural decline. For example, at the very height of Roman technical achievements there arose an "abrupt flight from reason to faith," a movement that was evident "in every quarter of society" and which both signified and hastened the fall of the Roman empire (Mumford, 1944/1973, p. 79).

In any age, the predominance of symbol and myth indicates an emphasis on the meaning of time by groups in power, whereas the predominance of number and rationality indicates an emphasis on the domination of space (Carey, 1989, p. 155). Horkheimer and Adorno recognized the same recurring phenomena: an antithetical oscillation between rationality and mythology, the one with an emphasis on space, the other on time:

> Before, the fetishes [of religion] were subject to the law of equivalence. Now
> equivalence itself has become a fetish.

> The doctrine of the priests was symbolic in the sense that in it sign and image
> were one. Just as hieroglyphs bear witness, so the word too originally had a picto-
> rial function, which was transferred to myths. Like magical rites, myths signify
> self-repetitive nature, which is the core of the symbolic: a state of being or a proc-
> ess that is presented as eternal, because it incessantly becomes actual once more
> by being realized in symbolic form. (Horkheimer and Adorno, 1947/1998, p. 77)

Today, the system of monetary exchange, which gives substance to the sphere of circulation, has become an object of mythological proportions. It incessantly appears as eternal and omnipresent in nature, precisely because of its circulatory operation. As such, it creates two illusions: first, one of universal equivalence, by which money represents the measure of all things, including various symbolic species of itself (e.g., Pounds Sterling, Dollars, and Yen, as well as the myriad forms of exchangeable debt, insurance notes, and so on); and, second, the equivalence of time and space as numerical expressions. Marx comprehends the transitory and transitionary character of periods during which the mass and speed of circulation can stand in for real production:

The frequency with which capital can repeat the production process, self-realization, in a given amount of time, evidently depends on the speed with which this space of time is run through, or on its duration. … The velocity of turnover therefore—the remaining conditions of production being held constant—substitutes for the *volume* of capital. (Marx, 1973, p. 518) [37]

In such a system, human activity also becomes merely an element in the space-time continuum: "the magnitude of labour appears as an amount of space; but expressed in motion, it is measurable only in time" (Marx, 1973, p. 321). The economic measurement of time is money. Thus the

tendency to find mental satisfaction in measuring everything by a fixed rational standard, and the way it takes for granted that everything can be related to everything else, certainly receives from the apparently objective value of money, and the universal possibility of exchange which this involves, a strong psychological impulse to become a fixed habit of thought. (Innis, 1944, p. 82) [38]

The speed of monetary circulation in hypercapitalism is close to the speed of light, and the system spans the space of our planet. In Einstein's system, it would, indeed, by definition must, have close to zero mass: almost no substance whatsoever. But new communication technologies and the spatiotemporal biases of our symbolic history have combined to give the appearance of a *universal*, concrete substance to the money system, which nonetheless remains a product of imagination. While it is still "possible to believe that God is not a mathematician as some philosophers would have us believe," this is becoming harder as the cacophony of speculative, money rationalism rises to a deafening pitch (Innis, 1944, p. 84). The monetary exchange system encompasses the entirety of social space. It appears everywhere, as if from nowhere. It lays claim to the future because of its link with our past and its claim on massive amounts of past and future life. In this sense, the money system has become truly God-like, at least in the eyes of its most fervent acolytes.

Mass producing the money myth

Today the monetary system of exchange has become as powerful a force for social organization as language itself, perhaps more so. Its organizing logic is hypnotic, numbing, and ultimately impenetrable.[39] With a minimum of slippage, one might easily be fooled into thinking that money *is* a language—a system of abstract descriptions and promises that define the social value of everything from ideas to nations to DNA. But such a seemingly massive system of qualitatively homogenous promises—however expedient—can only be analyzed on its own terms, that is to say quantitatively. The exchange system easily insinuates itself everywhere because of its impenetrable, self-referential logic. Simultaneously, it hides itself from its source: human imagination. Now that the imaginary source of money is sufficiently obscured, money appears to take on an objective form, independent of people, history, and circumstance. Money has reached its mythological apotheosis when, as with religions, "products of the human brain appear as autonomous figures endowed with a life of their own, which enter into relations both with each other and with the human race" (Marx, 1976, p. 165).

The sheer velocity of hypercapitalist circulation facilitates the most extraordinary phenomena, not the least of which is the mass propagation of speculative excesses. Speculation is merely a way of trading in non-existent phenomena which will potentially exist in some imagined future, whether it be the possibility of a certain number of cows in the future, the possibility of victory in war, and the possibility of particular forms of disaster (insurance are exemplars of these forms). In itself, speculation about the future has been part of the human condition since debt became a decisive force in Draconian Greece. Speculation in Greece began with free people risking their own freedom—their own lives—for money in the hope that things would get better for them in the future. A great majority of them lost the gamble (Mumford, 1944/1973, pp. 19-20). We might call this first-order speculation, a personal claim against one's own future welfare expressed in the form of indebtedness to another person or group. In such expressions, we see the human capacity for imagination and statistical probability at work: the debtor imagines a future in which she or he will be better off. On the other hand, sheer desperation or imagined future fortunes can drive a person to mortgage their entire life. In either case, though, it is what I will call first-order debt: an agreement (or bet) between two parties about some future happening and its value in the present.

Second-order speculation abstracts from the first and adds a layer of conceptual complexity to it. This happens when a debt is sold or exchanged for some similar conceptual abstraction, like money. This has two immediate effects. First, it gives a more alienated and objective character to the debt, insofar as such an exchange, which is originally an agreement between two parties, is viewed and treated as if it existed independently of the parties who made that original agreement. Second, it adds another level of probabilistic calculation to the debt, which is already an expression of two individuals' probabilistic views of the future. While it is not necessarily the case, the sale and purchase of debt will usually entail further expectations about some future state of affairs, and more importantly, of the monetary *value* of that state or event. Put plainly, someone who buys debt usually expects to profit in some way. Such profits are therefore doubly derived from beliefs and expectations about the future.

Either at or above this level of abstraction, the conceptual aspects of speculation become daunting, if not entirely irrational. For instance, when speculation becomes socialized, as it is in the concept of "the national debt," and when it becomes further distanced from the individual in space and time, debt, and the money it purportedly represents, becomes conceptually incomprehensible. Even though its probabilistic nature may be grasped by the shorthand mathematics of econometrics, its conceptual characteristics are ultimately incomprehensible.

For example, when governments set policy based on such high levels of future oriented abstraction, policy cannot help but ignore actually existing states of affairs. Instead, policy becomes the servant of institutionalized probabilities: not for the first time in history, whole nations have become enslaved to the *idea* of debt, socially propagated beliefs about the future calculated in number (Saul, 1992).[40] Here number becomes the authoritative agent that dominates massive amounts of space and enormous numbers of people (time) over decades, and in some cases, centuries. As an intergenerational expression of debt, the authority of number encloses space *and* time. Time after time, all over the world, government surpluses are directed away from public goods, such as education, communications, health, clean water, and housing, to "pay down the debt" (see, e.g., Freeman, 2004).

The most insidious forms of debt emerge with the modern notion of "futures" in the mid-nineteenth century. These forms first become most ubiquitous with the widespread use of the telegraph by speculators (Stevens, 1883). The remarkable aspect of futures is that their basis is a promise by a commodity producer to provide a certain quantity of goods at a certain price, months or even years in advance of the produce existing. But the future bill of sale, or "option," is never binding on either party. In fact the buyer never takes delivery of the commodities and no goods ever change hands. It is only the prospective possibility of goods at a certain price some time in the future that is traded (Stevens, 1883, p. 38). Stevens quotes an 1887 edition of the *Mark Lane Express* to exemplify contemporary grievances about futures trading: "these contracts (futures) are framed to allow of differences in value at a certain date or within a certain time being paid or received, the commodity itself never being intended to pass from one party to the other. The seller does not possess it. The buyer does not expect to receive it" (1883, p. 38). With the proliferation of futures as a form of tradable commodities, the exchange system once again begins to dominate the fate of persons. Time—the future— becomes the probabilistic commodity, and the speed of circulation is once again foregrounded.

The public debate over the worth of futures continued into the twentieth century. But by 1917, intense political lobbying by banks, merchant groups, and traders on Wall Street had all but silenced debate. As early as 1895, policy makers were asking how the world of commodity production could ever have survived without the beneficial acts of futures speculators, specifically in respect of price fixing:

> The establishment of this future price for the delivery of a commodity is the great
> service of speculation. We are wont to think of speculation as beneficial chiefly
> through holding back supplies in times of plenty for use in less prosperous times.
> This is indeed an important service, but it is no longer performed directly by the
> speculators. Since the production and distribution of commodities, as to both time
> and place follow their probable values according to the most enlightened opinion
> of the most competent men, we may, then, sum up the function of speculation in
> produce as follows: It directs the production and distribution of commodities into
> the most advantageous channels, by establishing, at any particular moment, rela-
> tive prices for different commodities deliverable at different times and places.
> (Emery, 1895)

The same rhetoric is familiar in "globalization" discourse: let "the market" de-
cide the future of persons. But in this context, "market" means price, and price is
actively manipulated by the speculative class: financial experts whose political
control has been established over centuries. Their expertise is in numerical, probabilistic models of the future based on debts held against future action. The
collateral for this kind of debt is the future life of billions of people, as expressed
in the term "national debt." Since Emery praised the "beneficial" activities of
futures speculators, abstraction has been piled upon abstraction in the futures
markets. Futures were supplemented by notional capital: money lent against the
potential future referents of futures: "pretend" money loaned against the future
likelihood of cattle, cotton, and grain prices rising or falling. To ensure the validity of these tradable debts in imaginary money, insurance notes were invented,
issued, and immediately traded. Future time, space, and life were further enclosed within the boundaries of the exchange system. The practical effect of
developing intergenerationally transmissible claims against future life is to limit
possibilities for substantial social systemic change any time in the future. The
result is that, today, the most widely propagated myths are manipulated to control the meaning of the future rather than the past, and this is achieved on a
global basis.

Enclosing social time and space through applied idealism

The logic of technologically mediated exchange is the logic of alienation: it is
the logic of thought alienated from its thinker, and of value alienated from human activity. Today, that logic has become the dominant logic of consumption
and production; creation and destruction. It is manifested in the notion of a
"knowledge economy," something that has always existed. Exchange-values—
forms of money—have become the most important use-values; the very definition of success and social worth. Money appears as the means of self-production
and reproduction—physical, psychological, and social—for each and every human subject to the logic of production for the sake of exchange. This provides
some clues to the political economic trajectory of global society: capitalism
has advanced by extending its processes of appropriation, alienation, and

production from raw nature and gross human energies to the most intimate aspects of social life. It reaches into the future at the expense of the present. It appropriates social space by occupying it, and colonizes and appropriates social time by placing double and triple mortgages on the future. And it does so just as Innis suggests: by the calculated creation and manipulation of knowledge monopolies, and by the mass propagation of myth as rationality. The term "public opinion" is insufficient to describe the deep effects of the present money economy upon people's consciousness.

The quasi-spatial domains created by the technologized domains of mediated communication is the arena in which the knowledge economy's social relations of production are constituted, and its knowledge commodities are wholly social in their source, significance, and impact. This is a fact largely obscured by the massive, monolithic, and impersonal system of exchange that confronts individuals as if it were a force independent of human agency, origin, or control. The state of hypercapitalism is the point in the development of the money economy that alienated forms of thought become the predominant commodity-forms, and at which the products of human imagination dominate perceptions of the social and the individual alike.

This is the perfection of capital's paradoxes: an idealist system that operates by attributing independent and supernatural forces to an illusory system of exchange-values; the product of imagination burdened with nothing substantive reduced to the sole source of social utility and inclusion. Under hypercapitalism, pure exchange-values become the object of the production process. Marx had extrapolated this logic to its illogical conclusion:

> the rule of person over person now becomes the universal rule of the *thing* over the *person*, the product of the producer. Just as the *equivalent*, value, contained the determination of the alienation of private property, so now we see that *money* is the sensuous, corporeal existence of that *alienation*. (Marx, 1844/1975b, p. 270)

The most intimate aspects of human relatedness are hypercapitalism's primary source, means, and object of production. Communication, emotion, sexual and emotional intimacy, public displays of humiliation—practically every process and product of social relatedness has become a productive "thing" in the global knowledge economy. As a result, societies continue to disintegrate under the social pressures "engendered and amplified by the logic of competition of everyone against everyone" (Bourdieu, 1998, p. 27). Desire for, and identification with increasingly abstract commodities underpins this logic: "… the felt need for a thing is the most obvious, irrefutable proof that the thing is part of *my* essence, that its being is for me and that its *property* is the property, the peculiar quality peculiar to my essence" (Marx, 1844/1975b, p. 267). And so exchange-value, the number system that has become the basis of universal fungiblity in all human interaction, has thus become the ultimate force in forging new social spaces.

The double dialectics of mythology and rationality

Since recorded history, various mythologies and rationalities have redounded against each other in violent, cyclical social upheavals, each reaching in turn for dominion over its specific terrain: respectively, time and space. Mythologies, mostly in the form of organized religions, have historically sought control over the meaning of time, and thus over time itself. Rationalities, from Pythagoras to Poincaré and onwards, have sought control over the meaning of space. Yet even the most astute thinkers remain confounded by the current rise in fundamentalisms and nationalisms (Castells, 1997). But these ought not present us with any surprise whatsoever.

Since mechanization, and even more so since electrification, societies, mythologies, and rationalities have degenerated into increasingly violent struggles over the meaning of space and time. Whether manifest in the constant redrawing of national boundaries, or in the innumerable struggles over working hours and conditions, the major struggles of classes, cultures, and political systems are all closely tied to struggles over the meaning of time and space. This has never been more clear than in the monstrous and violent upheavals of the twentieth century. Just as in ancient Greece, the seventeenth-century literate minds of Europe found a sense of freedom from the constraints of time by rationally conquering problems of space. In the twentieth century, the literate mind gave birth to the thought that would abolish theoretical distinctions between these two conceptually and violently contested terrains of social control. At a single stroke, Einstein fused space and time. Then, with the introduction of Heisenberg's quantum uncertainty, God eventually re-emerged from between the cracks of a mathematical rationality pushed to its limits. Religion, ever the adaptive force in human affairs, embraced the new rationality from the very beginning, precisely because of its religious implications and origins (Noble, 1997).

In the first quarter of the twentieth century, the electronic culture industries emerge on a mass scale, taking center stage in the shaping of public consciousness. As space and time were fused in the new physics generally attributed to Einstein, the culture industry showed the populations of the developed world that a linear experience of reality in the form of myth could be alienated from its social origins, mechanically duplicated, and circulated *en masse*. The spatial contours of the Church and Town Hall became anachronistic. "Community" became alienated from the people who comprise it, a fact highlighted on the auspicious or tragic occasions when the terminology of "the international community" is invoked. The democratic process gradually became pure entertainment, and vice versa (Postman, 1985). From the early

1980s onwards, the tension between mass mediated mythologies, mass programs of rationality, and massified themes of social belonging collapsed under the burden of relativized space and time. Today, this trajectory is manifested in "globalization," the "knowledge economy," and "the market"—the "holy trinity" of technophilic mythology (Saul, 1997). It has become manifest in fundamentalisms of every type: religious, linguistic, ethno-nationalist, economic, and political. The emerging social realities are unerringly repressive and profoundly violent. That is because the commodities of a global knowledge economy—alienated thought and value—and the conceptual dominions over which they rule—time and space—are conflated in a global network of circulating exchange values that propagates opposing value systems, bringing them into close proximity and assigning them relative values. Previous struggles are exacerbated by the claustrophobia of a system that has no "outside." Tensions between different social spaces and times, and between opposing mythologies and rationalities, now redound against each other at logarithmically faster speeds, in ever greater numbers, producing strange and ancient antagonisms, new forms of collaboration, and new forms of organization. Knowledge commodities hold these intense contradictions in tension: knowledge commodities conflate alienated thought and alienated value. To attain and retain value, they must be produced in valorized contexts and situated in narrative spaces where they can be given the appearance of concrete "things," attributed relative values, and circulated in distinction to other such "objects."

Circulating myths through new mediation systems

Since thought and language were separated in the written word, ostensibly independent, "objective" thought has spread through space and time, largely at the direction of those who have controlled the most valued mediation spaces of the day. Different groups throughout history have manipulated and patrolled these spaces to produce, reproduce, control, and destroy particular social configurations. Such groups have been variously organized along religious, partisan, royal, scientific, ethnic, commercial, military, bureaucratic, and academic lines. Today, the most influential systems of thought and language are those specifically designed to regulate the character of social systems: law, legislation, policy, and corporate mediations of all kinds. The groups currently involved in the production of laws include people from all these spheres of expertise: priests, bureaucrats, soldiers, academics, politicians, company directors, and experts of almost every kind. Consequently, contemporary policy environments conflate the historically disparate value systems that have developed within these fields, often over the course of centuries. The tensions inherent in this arrangement are made manifest in political discourse of all kinds. Here is an excellent example:

See, I understand the limitations of government. Governments can hand out money. But governments cannot put love in a person's heart, or a sense of purpose in a person's life. The truth of the matter is that comes when a loving citizen puts their arm around a brother and sister in need and says, I love you, and God loves you, and together we can perform miracles. (Applause.)

And miracles happen—all the time—in America. They happen because loving souls take time out of their lives to spread compassion and love. And lives are changing. Listen, our society is going to change one heart and one soul at a time. (Applause.) It changes from the bottom up, not the top down. It changes when the soldiers in the armies of compassion feel wanted, encouraged, and empowered. And that's what the faith-based and community initiative is all about. How do we gather up the strength of the country, the vibrancy of faith-based programs? The social entrepreneurs—how do we encourage them? (Bush, 2004a)

The full text of this speech uttered by George W. Bush expresses centuries of the most influential and often antagonistic value systems. He conflates and collapses these systems in the production and unilateral ratification of a Presidential *Executive Order* that specifies the *Responsibilities of the Department of Commerce and Veterans Affairs and the Small Business Administration with Respect to Faith-Based and Community Initiatives* (Bush, 2004a). Bush blends and bends the often conflicting value systems of religious faith, secular law, commerce, politics, militarism, economics, and science in a demonstration of his power to rule unilaterally on behalf of the faithful:

... I wanted to make sure that the faith-based groups simply got equal access and equal treatment when it came to the billions of dollars we spend at the federal level. That was the first step toward making sure the faith-based initiative was strong and vibrant. And of course, it got stuck in the Congress. (Laughter.) [...] So I got frustrated and signed an Executive Order. (Laughter.) (Bush, 2004b)

The laughter noted in the transcript is a quite ominous response to an announcement of totalitarian solutions. The enlightenment supposedly separated church and state once and for all, ending the executive privilege of "divine right" royalty and allegedly enthroning Truth and Reason as the principle guiding values of governance. Yet today the President of the most technologically advanced nation in the world appeals simultaneously to miracles, money, and science, wielding unilateral executive privilege to reassert the relationship between god and government, as if it represented some sort of progress.

Such manifest upheavals in the political climate of the age are epiphenomenal of new forms of relatedness, which are made possible by new communication technologies, enabling (if not demanding) the formation of supranational bodies designed to exercise global political influence. These organizations are clearly not exempt from the religious provenance of economic doctrine and the various confusions that a religiously grounded economic fundamentalism entails. Here is the head of the WTO speaking in

2000 to the *International Military Chiefs of Chaplains Conference*:

> I believe that we are all brothers and sisters, born in the image of God, thus created equal. We are equal, but not the same. Trade and business is only one aspect of the interchanges and the civilising effect of cooperation. Moreover, trade and increasing interdependence among nations is nothing new. Neither is the exchange of ideas and the movement of peoples across borders.

> Indeed, one of the first multinational institutions was the Church. Faith knows no boundaries. Faith has withstood nationalism, persecution, empires and ideologies. It is eternal. (Moore, 2000)

Moore's desiderata are insightful: religions are oriented towards control over the meaning of eternal time; rationalities are oriented to control over the meaning of finite space. The religious impulse knows no temporal or national boundaries and is based on myths of universality. Rationality, on the other hand, serves to divide time and space into discrete segments that can be separated, delineated, counted, and accounted for. In the presence of a global system of instantaneous circulation, exchange-values have come to dominate and mediate the religious impulse—faith in "the market" and "the economy," so amply demonstrated by governments these past few centuries, especially so over the last three decades, is merely religion: faith in the products of human imagination. In the present case, it is money in all its forms and tenses (Noble, 2004; Saul, 1997).

The central paradox of circulation in hypercapitalism's knowledge economy lies in the contradictions of a quantitative system (money) being used to rank qualitative aspects of knowledge, the effect of which is to make certain ways of knowing more valuable than others. Money has thereby taken on an objective appearance as a social force, even while its form has been ephemeralized into the digital realms of cyberspace and the linguistic domains of financial expertise. The more rapid and massive the circulation of "virtual" money becomes, the more powerful a social force it appears to be. But in the sphere of circulation, the value of money also becomes fragile and unstable to the point at which the worth of whole nations can suddenly be "talked up" or "talked down" by persons of mythological proportion:

> For several months, as a way of justifying his mammoth $1.6 trillion tax cut, George Bush has been talking down the economy. [...] Now he's finally succeeded. The market's taken a nosedive. In one day alone, American investors lost over $3 trillion in personal wealth. And Bush finally acknowledged the damage he had done: "I'm sorry people are losing value in their portfolios." [...] Maybe Dick Cheney should tell him: (1) He's president of the United States. (2) When a president speaks about the economy, people listen. (3) It's immoral to bad-mouth the economy and destroy people's personal savings in order to score cheap political points or sell a tax cut. (Press, 2001)

The rational, which is to say quantitative, aspect of money provides very specific ways of knowing and ordering the world. It also emphasizes the importance of social situatedness in the determination of values. In the "knowledge economy," according to Press, the words of a single person can make three trillion dollars simply disappear. We see in Press's statement explicit connections between moral worth (it is *immoral to bad-mouth the economy*); economic worth (slandering the economy can *destroy people's personal savings*); and social worth (if a *president speaks about the economy, people listen*). Not just anyone can "talk down" an economy to the tune of $3 trillion per day. In all of these "domains" of value—the economic, the moral, and the institutional—it is the same talk that simultaneously determines and instantiates these dimensions of value. Of course, these ostensibly disparate "types" of value are reducible to money, the socially sanctioned measure of *personal* worth. In a "globalized," digitized sphere of circulation, money comes into contact with the circulation of all others sorts of meaning-making materials, including the resources of television, radio, and print media. These come with their own axiological traditions, mythologies, and rationalities—literally, more and less valued ways of meaning.

The historical weight of millennia dominated by sacred texts of one sort or another has helped much of humanity view language and thought as separate "things," making the conception of a knowledge economy seem new. The extended capabilities of digital communication technologies emphasizes control over space at the expense of time. It is a system that is global in its spatial reach, yet unpredictably ephemeral in time, especially where social stability is concerned. The temporal instabilities of such a system can only be tamed by deploying myth on a mass scale, and even then only temporarily. Myths have their cultural provenances and people tend to resist myths that overtly threaten the narrative structures that provide coherence for their cultural lives.

As members of literate societies, we continue to alienate ideas about ourselves from ourselves. We continue to believe that the products of our intellect are "things" with an existence and value independent of our activity. Mythology is the result. Illusions of this type have typically led to speculation based on an intrinsic belief in the power of ideas. Speculation has plagued societies throughout history, whether in war, trade, or any sphere of human relatedness. Since the mass "democratization" of literacy made possible by the printing press, enlightened Western elites have typically viewed technology as the highest expression of human achievement (Mumford, 1934/1963; Noble, 1997). We are yet to recognize to any significant degree the profound violence of our technological complex and its attendant mythologies. Consequently, we continue to be hypnotized whenever we are exposed to the latest technological developments, precisely because they reflect aspects of ourselves (McLuhan, 1964/1997).

Adorno sees in organized consumption "the primitively narcissistic aspect of identification as an act of *devouring*, of making the beloved object part of oneself" (Adorno, 1991, p. 120). So it is with our technologies: we identify with them, consume and devour them; in turn, they devour our time, our lives. In the absence of shared social time, in any event a physical impossibility in "global society," the propagation of mythology on a global scale becomes an absolute necessity for any global order. That cannot be achieved by isolated individuals. It requires the cooperation of education systems, governments, religious groups, media industries, and the rest of the "organized" world. To propagate myth on the scale required to "organize the irrationality" of a globally connected humanity requires technical infrastructure that can harness the creative energies of many millions of people, whether as "producers" or "consumers" of mythology. A globalized cultural fabric, as unstable as it must be, requires flexible and diverse means of symbolic production that can accommodate "different cultural roles for different groups of people to play, and different sets of myths or different cultural pleasures to go along with them" (Tetzlaff, 1991, p. 17). That implies a technical ability to produce flexible understandings and attitudes, in itself a massive project of organization and centralization. Throughout the twentieth century, "media producers have continued to maintain or expand the diversity of their products while control of production has become ever more centralized" (Tetzlaff, 1991, p. 17). One significant consequence of this system is that what is a socially accepted fact or attitude one day can easily be replaced by an entirely contradictory fact or attitude the next (Postman, 1985, chap. 5). Finally, and most importantly, political structures that both permit and depend upon such conditions are necessary. It is in policy that standards for communication infrastructure and content are set. It is in policy that education and training objectives are defined. It is in policy that particular axiologies are given the stamp of legitimacy. We turn now to the language of policy to see how its authors attempt to produce, express, and propagate the axiological preconditions for a global knowledge economy.

CHAPTER SIX

Making value with policy

apitalist social relations have led to a purely monetary understanding of the term "value" in contemporary mainstream political economy. Classical political economy, regardless of its flaws, sought to achieve an understanding of human interaction that embraced the whole human experience. As a field of study, political economy emerged from the more general field of moral philosophy. Since the mid-nineteenth century, political economy has withered in its scope while enjoying an ever broader sphere of influence. Because it is a collection of quantitative terms, the price system has thrived under post-enlightenment science, becoming the single most important public expression of value. Mainstream econometrics, with its emphasis on abstract formulae for predicting price and worth, provides the primary tools for measuring and predicting the efficiency of public policy. The withering of political economy into a mathematics of pure price has had far-reaching implications for the production and analysis of policy. The monetary reductionism of economics has been further exacerbated by the so-called "neoliberal" policy agenda that has been in play throughout developed countries since the late 1970s.

Ignoring the various meanings of what might be understood by the "liberal" part of neoliberalism, the basic tenets of neoliberal economic theory are as follows. First, competition for resources, market share, more skilled or cheaper labor, and so on is assumed to be beneficial regardless of its consequences. Second, such competition is assumed to be global, natural, and inherently efficient, producing the best outcomes for individuals and societies. Third, any interference to competition is tantamount to a crime against society, as evidenced in the many legal challenges launched by one government against another in extrajudicial contexts such as the WTO. Fourth, government is expected to promote and enforce competition, even between its own departments. Finally, it is assumed that the benefits and effects of competition can be understood solely in terms of price. Put as simply as possible, neoliberal economic theory is based on tenuous interpretations of Adam Smith's "invisible hand" and Charles Darwin's theory of natural selection.[41] Neoliberalism's most valuable analytical framework is comprised of econometric tools, a highly abstract, mathematically rigorous discipline that has an often tenuous relationship with reality (Saul, 1997). In the econometric framework, the whole of reality is reduced to models of the price system, past, present, and future.

Any contemporary study of the knowledge economy must take the influence of neoliberal discourse into account. It must also consider the social function of policy as well as *how* it is made. Policy, and political science more generally, are most expressly concerned with how we ought to live. In other words, the "political" part of political economy has been charged with legitimate authority over social mores. Yet the framework within which political science operates, whether at the level of bureaucratic process or political discourse, is influenced and shaped by the tenets of modernist science, as is the "economic" part of political economy. In other words, policy must be based on "good science," or at least be seen as such.

The scientific impetus of modernity raises problems for contemporary policy makers. "Good science" is objective, replicable, universal and, most important of all, "value free." Therefore policy makers who are charged under the tenets of their discipline with legitimate moral authority must, according to the tenets of "good science," divest themselves of their moral values in order to make "good" policy. This presents problems and paradoxes for policy makers. To produce objective, value-free policy, the social world must be reduced to a set of universal, objective, value-free, quantitatively derived "laws." Econometrics and quantitative sociology supply such laws.

The paradox of contemporary policy goes to the heart of arguments about the differences between "hard" and "soft" science. Good "hard," rational science is based on experimental methods that produce predictable and replicable results across multiple and often unrelated contexts: Newton's laws, for example, are assumed to be as valid on earth as they are on Mars, or as they are in yet-undiscovered galaxies and solar systems. Further, such laws are assumed to be valid throughout eternity: the presumption of "hard" science is that the laws are eternal. Yet any social science that produces identical results across all contexts, cultures, and times can probably be described as either fallacious, trivial, uninformative, or all of these. That is because societies and cultures of all kinds change over time, at least to some extent. That is the most interesting and difficult aspect of social science. Social science that can only show that which does not change, or that which is not different across different places and times, is of limited use. But the various forms of social science that focus on change, difference, and unquantifiable aspects of human experience are generally held to be "soft science" and therefore unsuitable for making policy.

So contemporary policy makers are subject to a number of conflicting forces, the most apparent of which are: the unruly characteristics of social life and the unpredictability of social change; imperatives to do replicable, quantitative science that is most amenable to the system of monetary values; and the tenets of neoliberalism I have outlined above. Policy makers are required to formulate policies that are evidence-based, scientifically rigorous, and economically sound. Policy must also be presented in appropriate forms of language. The language of science is the language of *fact*. It is the language of objective, expert descriptions based on verifiable, quantifiable, predictable, and replicable aspects of experience. Policy documents therefore appear as a collection of scientifically derived *propositions* (statements and descriptions). However, to be effective, policies must also function as a collection of *proposals* (specifically, commands or exhortations) that result in people acting and interacting in specific ways.

The language of fact and description is very different from the language of command and exhortation, even though the two can spill over into each other in functional terms (Halliday, 1994). That functional spillage can be demonstrated with a simple example. Almost every parent has been confronted with a child who says "I'm hungry"—a clear truth claim. Now, the nature of propositions, and what defines them as such in distinction to proposals, is that they are open to argument, whereas proposals are not (Halliday and Martin, 1993). The child who says "I'm hungry" is putting forward a proposition that a parent can argue with. Usual arguments would include "But you just had lunch …" or "You can't possibly be hungry, I just fed you" and so on. However, as most parents understand, when a child says "I'm hungry" what the child means is "Feed me!" What happens here is that the child draws upon social and cultural relationships to turn a statement of fact ("I am hungry") into an exhortation ("Feed me!"): it is, in most cultures, the obligation of a parent to provide food for his or her children, a social fact understood by both the child and the parent, however implicitly. The obligation that a parent feels is an expression of long-standing axiological formations in a culture. It is from the axiological pool of cultural and social situatedness that the utterance "I'm hungry" derives its social force as a command. It is in the realm of cultural values that the functional transformation between statements of fact and demands for action is operationalized.

The same functional transformation is constantly operationalized within the realm of policy. That is a matter of necessity. Because contemporary policy makers must present their products as the result of a scientific process, contemporary policy relies upon operationalizing what can only be described as an ongoing naturalistic fallacy: a continual movement from "is" to "ought," from fact to exhortation. As in the example of the parent-child interaction above, policy makers rely on a multitude of social and cultural patterns to produce a functional transformation from statements of fact to mass exhortations (Graham, 2002).

My emphasis on analyzing policy language is of threefold significance for my purposes here. First, it is axiomatic that what we call knowledge is inherently bound up in language: how we know is shaped to a large extent by what we say to each other, and by how we say it. Therefore language assumes the utmost significance in any knowledge economy. Second, the "commodities" of the knowledge economy are necessarily products of more or less valued types of language. Finally, language (whether mathematical, spoken, or written) is at the same time a key means of production and distribution for knowledge commodities. To further complicate the matter, policy is almost completely an achievement of language and exists to propagate new cultural patterns of evaluation—it is simultaneously an expression and legitimation of particular axiologies that are oriented towards producing specific actions and outcomes by drawing on and reshaping cultural patterns of evaluation. Further, in a knowledge economy, policy is a most valuable commodity and it is no secret that it can be bought and sold. Billions are spent each year on its production, purchase, and dissemination, and much of it has global implications. In the US presidential campaign of 2004, more than $600 million had been donated to candidates by October for an election set to run in November (Center for Responsive Politics, 2004). That figure does not include "soft money," nor does it include the billions spent each year on political lobbying, the closest thing to "direct democracy" people have yet to see in mass society.

Two further problems face evaluative analyses of contemporary knowledge economy policy. The first is the institutional imperatives for policy authors to rely on extremely abstract nouns to convey meaning.[42] The second is in the essentially future oriented nature of policy: it is essentially hortatory; its primary function is "to get people to do things" (Muntigl, 2000, p. 147). However, in operationalizing the hortatory function of policy, contemporary authors are driven by technocratic imperatives to "rationalize" exhortations with "facts," and then to turn these facts into the basis of exhortation. The hortatory content of knowledge economy policy is therefore usually implicit, disguised as ostensibly "value-free," "objective," statements of fact (Lemke, 1995, pp. 60-61).

These aspects of policy introduce the need to make some very basic distinctions. Because the objective of policy is always future oriented, time and tense, especially in the interplay between proposal and proposition, become problematic. There is little point in trying "to get people to do things" in the past; the explicit and implicit proposals in technology policy is only ever a future oriented, *irrealis* (roughly meaning potential or imagined) function of language (Lemke, 1998, p. 36). For the same reasons, the propositions of policy are similarly oriented, often concerning themselves with describing future circumstances to produce normative outcomes.

There is a distinct division between aspects of language that can describe the world in terms of *Substance* and those that can describe the world in terms of *space-time*; or, between language used "to specify a set of properties" or attributes for, or predicates of, a particular "thing" (*Substance* language), and the language used to locate a particular thing at a particular time and place (space-time language) (Harvey, 1973, pp. 38-40). An uncomfortable fact of language is that "space itself can enter into either language but in different ways" (p. 39). So can time. Spatial and temporal positioning are necessary properties of particular substances (Harvey, 1973, p. 41). Consequently, the second main distinction between "types" of language I emphasize here is that between the kinds of evaluations that typically indicate *Substances* and those that typically indicate movement through space-time (*Process* language).

Substances (which can include particular people or groups of people) are expressed in language, explicitly or intertextually, as having attributes that define them in relationship to *other* substances within particular conceptual or ideational spaces (geographical, social, aesthetic, scientific, cultural, etc.). Scientific taxonomies are an example. In Process-relationships, the time element—movement and action—gets foregrounded. Substances (and substantial spaces), as well as other processes, are set in various relationships to one another over more and less specific periods of time with causative and functional effects implied or expressed. These two aspects of language are marked by grammatically and conceptually different types of evaluative possibilities but are nevertheless deeply interdependent. That is because the "things" of policy are often complex nominalized processes that function to compress meaning, an exemplar being "globalization." It is not only useful and informative to see which "things" get to act in policy, but also which processes get turned into "things," and which of these "things" are construed as being able to act upon the world.

The approach to analyzing policy that I am advocating here recognizes that both Substance and Process languages inevitably play into evaluative meanings of any kind, even while containing irreconcilable linguistic resources. In a more "concrete," or everyday, context than that of policy, we might expect to see Substances described and delineated by the deployment of "relational processes" that assign attributes to things and situate them in various relations to others (Halliday, 1994, pp. 124-129). Similarly, Process language is most recognizable in the deployment of material, transitive processes: "Your son threw a stone through my window." But because of the heavy reliance on nominalization in policy discourse, and because the purpose of policy is to translate scientifically produced language into the future actions of whole populations, analysis cannot easily delimit realizations along these lines.

The analytical framework for understanding how values are formalized in policy that I briefly outline here synthesizes the methods of Jay L. Lemke (1998) and James R. Martin (2000), both of whom take systemic-functionalist and sociolinguistic approaches to their analysis of meaning. I developed this approach while analyzing a large corpus of "knowledge economy" policies from throughout the world (Graham, 2002, 2003). The method is designed to foreground how axiologies are propagated in policy over very long stretches of text, and how these axiologies draw upon cultural resources to translate fact into imperatives for action. Existing realities typically have little to do with the kinds of assertions made in technologically oriented policy texts, largely because they are concerned with anticipating, describing, and shaping future states of political economic being. Because of the social function of policy, all else is subjugated to its future orientation. The axiologies that provide cohesion for these texts can only be grasped through fairly close textual analysis. That is because policy documents typically propagate axiologies at high levels of abstraction. Contemporary producers of policy have developed elaborate lexical mechanisms that work tense, modality (likelihood or probability), metaphor, and myriad other cultural resources that enable them to avoid explicit statement of the axiologies that nevertheless underpin the texts produced. The function of policy language is to orient the axiological compass of a society.

The inclusion of a method for understanding the axiological dimension of language is at the core of understanding political economic change, especially where policy and its effects in mass society are concerned. Policy is the means through which specific forms of power are legitimated and made manifest in most developed societies. The apparent identity between power and money, which can now be seen almost everywhere, is the consequence of policies that take the predominance of money values as their basis. It is also the result of many years of legal and technical developments, and the consequence of axiological influences and assumptions in the formulation of policy.

As Ralph Barton Perry (1916) notes, money is only one expression of value; it is a particular manifestation of the way people evaluate the world. The extent to which money is permitted to influence the operation of a political economic system, and the forms that money is permitted to take, is directly tied to the political administration system of any age. Whether as salt, cows, pepper, corn, glass, gold, certified paper, or digital bits, the form and distribution of money relies for its social force on "agreements" or "understandings" which must be made explicit in the realms of policy to realize official and legitimate status. To understand how money has come to be generally misrecognized as the basis of value in human societies requires an understanding of policy assumptions and how these are transformed into cultural presuppositions.

A unique historical marker of the current age is the extent to which almost identical axiological presuppositions are echoed throughout the world in legislatures at every level, often in direct opposition to the unique and variegated cultures that these legislatures supposedly represent. This fact points to key elements in the argument I have presented so far. The relative global homogeneity of "knowledge economy policy" is direct evidence of the *spatial* bias of new technologies as identified by Harold Innis and elaborated by James Carey: "structures of consciousness parallel structures of communication" (Carey, 1989, p. 161). With the emergence of a global network of institutionally and technologically integrated policy production systems, there emerges an "isomorphism" of both structure and content in the production and distribution of policy (Kim, Jang, and Hwang, 2002). In this view, not only is policy a technology and a technologized process, it is a medium of social and cultural control. Its seemingly homogeneous content reflects the spatial orientation of "post-enlightenment" systems of mediation. James Carey's explanation of Innis is most helpful in seeing how and why the global policy community has developed in such an isomorphic way:

> Innis argued that changes in communication technology affected culture by altering the structure of interests (the things thought about) by changing the character of symbols (the things thought with), and by changing the nature of community (the arena in which thought developed). By a space-binding culture he meant literally that: a culture whose predominant interest was in space—land as real estate, voyage, discovery, movement, expansion, empire. In the realm of symbols he meant the growth of symbols and conceptions that supported these interests: the physics of space, the arts of navigation and civil engineering, the price system, the mathematics of tax collectors and bureaucracies, the entire realm of physical science, and *the system of affectless, rational symbols that facilitated those interests.* In the realm of communities, he meant communities of space, mobile, connected over vast distances by appropriate symbols, forms, and interests. (1989, p. 160, emphasis added)

The global policy community expresses all these aspects in its language about knowledge, value, and new media. It is a globally connected community concerned with the coordination of national and international regulatory regimes. To see the contemporary bases of official axiologies, including and especially those that define economic worth and the official forms it can take, international policy language provides an essential focus. The language of global knowledge policy has been quite literally spatialized according to the principles elaborated by Carey above. It typically turns processes into things—quite literally turning time into space—in order to conceptually appropriate the world and propagate an axiology that promotes and represents the interests of the "growthism" Halliday (1993) has identified in languages throughout the world.

A brief tour of axiological analysis

I have attempted in the following paragraphs to provide an accessible overview of a grueling, detailed, and sometimes tedious method of analysis without boring the reader who has little interest in the finer-grained aspects of linguistic analysis. For those who are interested, much more detail can be found in Graham (2002), Halliday (1994), Lemke (1998), and Martin and Rose (2003). The most important thing to keep in mind as you read the following analysis is the difference between the semantic labels I use (marked in *italics*) and the words as they are commonly used. The semantic label refers to a domain of evaluation: each label is an abstraction for organizing specific realms of axiological resources that pertain to different realms of experience. In what follows, I briefly outline and synthesize the approaches of Jay Lemke (1998) and James Martin (2000) to show how such a synthesis can be used to understand the role of policy in the propagation of "knowledge economy" values.

To put it as briefly as possible, Lemke's approach is organized around the broad semantic "evaluative dimensions" that seem to be the only ones deployed to evaluate propositions and proposals in English: *Desirability*, *Warrantability*, *Appropriateness*, *Usuality*, *Significance*, *Comprehensibility*, and *Humorousness/Seriousness* (1998). After working with the policy corpus, I added the categories of *Ability* and *Utility* (which can typically be used only to evaluate proposals) because they are a feature of policy axiologies, fusing *Desirability* and *Significance* while being reducible to neither. Martin's approach is organized with a more overtly grammatical and lexical orientation around the concept of "Appraisal" (2000). One of the basic assumptions I make is that the perceived *Desirability* of a process, person, circumstance, or thing is identical to its "value," however conceived. However, I understand the *Desirability* of anything is a socially, historically, and biologically conditioned attribute that requires significant amounts of work, and the propagation of other "types" of value—*Appropriateness*, *beauty*, *power*, *efficiency*, and so on. In the language of policy, we see that the *Desirability* of certain orientations "scaffolded" by other types of evaluations. I have called the approach predication and propagation.

Synthesis

Analyzing evaluative patterns from a predication and propagation perspective means approaching a text from both directions, and at two distinct levels.

Predication directly inscribes or attributes a *Substance* in a text with particular characteristics and sets it in taxonomic relationships to other *Substances*. To focus at this level is to begin from the text and move "outwards" towards context. From the perspective of "evaluative *propagation*," we are interested in seeing axiological patterns that emerge over the whole course of a text and, just as importantly, how these patterns provide coherence for the text (Lemke, 1998, pp. 49-53). So Lemke's approach is to begin from "outside" the text, from the context of a culture's axiological traditions, and move inwards.

Substances are defined by their *predicates*. In less abstract types of texts than policy we would expect to see *Substances* described within propositions though the deployment of what Michael Halliday calls relational *processes* (roughly, *verbs* in Latinate grammar) (1994, pp. 124-129). Similarly, what I am calling *Processes* here are typically expressed in everyday terms through the deployment of "material" verbs, such as "hit," "kick," "throw," and so forth. (1994, pp. 109-112). In the following, relatively concrete example of policy, the dynamic process of knowing is presented as a *Substance*:

Knowledge is a strategic resource in the digital society (Sweden1: 385).

Apart from throwing *knowledge* into the realm of corporate logistics, it is worth noting that following the use of the relational process "is," the authors present an enormous "thing"—a single nominal group—as a definition: *a strategic resource in the digital society*. *Knowledge* is attributed with valuable characteristics at a particular place in history by being assigned a type of use-value within "the digital society." At the same time it is placed in new taxonomic relations as an industrial "resource." In systemic functional terms, these are called Token^Value [Tok^Val] and Carrier^Attribute constructions (Halliday, 1994, pp. 124-129). An explicit evaluation is made for the Token or Carrier (in the above case, *knowledge*): it has a particular (*strategic*) value in a particular context (*the digital society*).[43] One clear reason that this text can be identified as foregrounding the *Substance* (or spatial) aspect of language is that there is no action happening here—"knowledge" is presented as a thing occupying a position in a particular field. To see how much this kind of language depends on objectifying *Processes*, all one need do is try the sentence using a *Process*-oriented expression of knowledge as Token: "*to know* is a strategic resource ...*" Such a construction of knowing precludes it being understood as an industrial resource. Knowing must be turned into a "thing"—*knowledge*—to fit comfortably into the "industrial resource" taxonomy.

Process language foregrounds change over time as a result of interaction. Action happens and something changes, as in the following example which is, again, a relatively concrete example:

> The government has adopted a whole of government approach to the application
> of information technology and telecommunications, to ensure consistency, cost ef-
> fectiveness, interoperability and transparency within government. (noie1: 7391)

In this example we can begin to see the difference between *Substance-* and
Process-based evaluations. Entirely different "types" of evaluation become evident. These are operationalized in different ways and at different levels of
abstraction. In the first example, a direct evaluation is being made for *knowledge* in a particular historical circumstance. As an epithet of *resource*, the
predicate *strategic* makes a relatively explicit evaluation of knowledge as a *Desirable* thing to have *in the digital society*. In the second example, an abstract
Agent (*The government*) has done something that will lead to all sorts of supposedly *Desirable* outcomes (*consistency, cost effectiveness, interoperability,*
and *transparency*). In the first example, the authors explicitly evaluate a particular *Substance* (knowledge). In the second example, neoliberal axiology is
simultaneously drawn upon and propagated when *Desirable* outcomes are designated as the necessary result of a particular *Process* (*adopting a whole of
government approach*).

But in the second example, the value of the outcomes must be inferred intertextually. That is to say, the authors rely on the assumption that *consistency,
cost-effectiveness, interoperability,* and *transparency within government* are *Desirable* and that others will share this assumption. The second example is an
example of how, in *Process* language, evaluations happen at a different level
than in *Substance* language. They are propagated. There is a more overt tendency in propagation towards dependence on cultural attitudes towards globally
dominant axiologies, and a tendency for the range of evaluations to narrow or
"focus" as a text gets longer and more complex. Unlike the predicates that define *Substances*, evaluations made in *Process* language must often be inferred
unless the action itself is explicitly evaluated ("it is good that the government
has adopted a whole of government approach"). In the second example, for
instance, the *Government* has done something with particular outcomes in
mind. The authors rely on assumptions that whatever produces those particular outcomes will be perceived as *Desirable, Important,* and indeed
Necessary outcomes for any action warranting policy attention from the government. At the same time, by their very appearance as the focus of policy,
these terms and concepts take on a social importance.

In other words, evaluations for *Desirability* and *Importance* are propagated
for, and from within, the value system upon which the policy authors draw
when they describe action and its outcomes. Also, the axiology that is being
deployed in the second text is not an explicit "part" of the text, even though it
provides much of the sentence's coherence: *efficiency is good*. Another aspect

worth noting is the mixture of proposal and proposition operationalized in the second example, especially in terms of time and tense. First there is a description of something the government did at some time in the past (it *has adopted* a particular approach to information technology already). Then we are told why the government did it. Those reasons are future oriented (they are done *to ensure* outcomes). But the future orientation is hidden where the outcomes are concerned. That gives the impression that the stated outcomes are inevitable or have already happened. That in turn elides the need for an explicit claim for the *Warrantability* (or, roughly, truthfulness) of the outcomes.

As I noted above, the two texts I have shown so far are relatively concrete examples of policy language. But even in those comparatively simple examples, it becomes evident that reliance on nominalization combined with policy's function of translating words into mass action, we cannot strictly or neatly delimit *Substance* or *Process* realizations along lines of proposals or propositions. In policy, *Substance* and *Process* aspects of language are often functionally "collapsed" into each other. For instance, the following from Norway is a good example. It demonstrates how *Substance* and *Process* aspects can get blurred in mixtures of descriptive and hortatory functions:

> It is important to see the administration as a whole, with interaction between levels and across sector boundaries. (Norway1: 3038)

In this example, *the administration* is being presented by the authors as a *Substance* and assigned attributes by the authors: it is a coherent *whole*. But the propositional (truth) claim made in the text is for the *Importance* of *seeing* the administration *as* such. Whether or not the administration is actually an integrated whole is not up for argument here. Only the importance of it being seen as such can be argued with, which is really an argument about obligation rather than truth. This is an exhortation that stresses the need to *see* (or "understand" or "treat" or "conceptualize") the administration as a whole, regardless of whether it is or not.

Speakers and writers of technical languages have developed many resources for presenting *Processes* as *Substances*, a metaphorical substitution that has developed as a technology over centuries, and which has become a necessity for science as we know it (Halliday, 1993, p. 10). Experts of all kinds have also developed ways to use verbs metaphorically. In the above example, the "phrasal verb" *to see ... as* appears to function primarily as a "mental process"—a process typically pertaining to the world of human perception (Halliday, 1994, pp. 207-210). But it is also made to perform a relational function by taking part in an implicit proposition that defines "the administration as a whole." It also performs an abstract-material function by suggesting that people "treat" the *administration as a whole*. So although distinctions between *Substance* and *Process* languages are possible, the metaphorical resources that facilitate contemporary policy functions often make such distinctions difficult.

In synthesis, predication and propagation views on evaluations made in policy can be used to see these and can provide coherence for a text over long passages, often relating logically unrelated aspects of the world. Consider the following predications, marked in *italics*, made in a policy text from Hong Kong:

> As economic activity has globalized, particularly in the financial and services sectors, a few *major* cities—*world* cities—have become *vital* centres for managing and co-ordinating economic activity on a *global* basis. Furthermore, *successful* world cities appear to share a number of common characteristics. First, *world* cities have a *distinctive* economic structure and exert a level of *influence* which is *far greater* than their size might suggest. This is because they have developed *tremendous strengths* in *internationally oriented* service industries and other *high-level* corporate service functions, which generate *significant* levels of added value as well as good employment opportunities. (hongkvis: 5,235)

The predications italicized in the above text all fall along the broad, semantic seam of *Importance* or *Significance*. They are the attributes of *world* cities and their institutions. They are *major, vital, successful, distinctive, high-level, internationally oriented, influential* centers that operate on a *global* basis because of their *tremendous strength* in *significant* areas. In other words, they are presented as *Important* because they perform *Necessary* and *Powerful* functions that affect the whole of humanity. This "secondary" set of attributions do not appear explicitly in the Hong Kong text, and here is where we see the effects of evaluative propagation. The predicates of particular elements in the text propagate evaluations of a more abstract and broad semantic categories. They do so within, across, and beyond the propositional content of the text.

To see the interaction between *Substance* and *Process* aspects of language in the propagation of evaluative meaning, let us take a look at the Hong Kong text from a different "angle." This time I am focusing on the text's propositional content—that which claims to be telling truth (or claiming *Warrantability*) about elements in the world and the relationships between them. Propositions, or truth claims, are [enclosed in square brackets] and the processes at the center of the propositions are *italicized*:

> As [economic activity *has globalized*], particularly in the financial and services sectors, [a few major cities—world cities—*have become* vital centres for managing and co-ordinating economic activity on a global basis]. Furthermore, [successful world cities *appear to share* a number of common characteristics]. First, [world cities *have* a distinctive economic structure *and exert* a level of influence which is far greater than their size might suggest]. This is because [they *have developed* tremendous strengths in internationally oriented service industries and

other high-level corporate service functions, which *generate* significant levels of added value as well as good employment opportunities]. (hongkvis: 5,235)

The major propositional claim put forward here is that *world cities* control and organize [*manage and coordinate*] global economic activities because of their *distinctive economic structures*. For this reason they are *Powerful*, *Important*, and *Necessary*. Or, to rephrase the evaluative propagation here in the broadest possible terms: world cities are *Important* because they *control* global economic activity. Although they clearly participate in *Important Processes*, their aspect as *Substance* is foregrounded at the expense of their existence as a network of dynamic, time- and place-bound relationships, that is, as the expression of multiple *Processes* done by people in historical and cultural contexts.

Compressing Reality

By nominalizing complex processes, policy authors engage in what Lemke calls thematic condensation:

> what is a proposition at one point in a text readily becomes "condensed" … as a participant at another, and participants (especially abstract nominals) are often meant to be correspondingly "expanded" by the reader into implied propositions through reference to some known intertext, as well as through reference to the immediate co-text. (Lemke, 1998, p. 43)

What holds for thematic condensation also seems to hold for evaluative condensation, an important device in policy texts that provides a means by which attitudes are expressed and propagated.

Let us return again to the policy example from Hong Kong to display a preliminary synthesis of the two approaches. Propositional content is (surrounded by parentheses), evaluative condensations are IN SMALL CAPITALS, predications are *marked in italics*, and the processes concerned with Warrants are **marked in bold**:

> As (economic activity **has globalized**), particularly in the FINANCIAL AND SERVICES SECTORS, (a few *major* cities—*world* cities—**have become** *vital* centres for MANAGING AND CO-ORDINATING ECONOMIC ACTIVITY on a GLOBAL basis). Furthermore, (*successful world* cities **appear to share** a number of *common* characteristics). First, (world cities **have** a *distinctive* economic structure **and exert** a level of INFLUENCE which is *far greater* than their size might suggest). This is because (they **have developed** TREMENDOUS STRENGTHS in INTERNATIONALLY ORIENTED SERVICE INDUSTRIES and other HIGH-LEVEL CORPORATE SERVICE FUNCTIONS, **which generate** *significant* levels of ADDED VALUE (as well as GOOD EMPLOYMENT OPPORTUNITIES). (hongkvis: 5,235)

We could go on ad infinitum highlighting nuances in the axiologies propagated in this text were we to be so inclined. But even this fairly rough mark-up demonstrates an example of what Lemke calls "evaluative cohesion" along the same semantic dimension. It creates cohesion, or "links between separated elements," that are not otherwise easily identified (Lemke, 1998, p. 50). Positive degrees of *Importance* are propagated throughout the Hong Kong text, supported by intertextual evaluations for *Desirability*. At the predication level, "appraisal" resources of "appreciation" are deployed in the terms *successful, major, vital, distinctive, significant,* and *tremendous.* The "things" being appraised—*world cities*—are essential to a functioning *global* economy, and they are central to, or "do," *Important* processes, namely managing and coordinating *economic activity on a global basis.* This confers an enormous degree of *Power* upon world cities.

The evaluative resources located on the level of abstraction at which *Power* is propagated here (which is more abstract, in higher polarity, and broader scope than the explicit realization of *Power* in *tremendous strengths*) is of an order between the direct lexical resources available at the predication level of *appraisal,* and those at the most broad propagational level of *Importance.* These "middle-range" values occupy quite a different and distinct level in the axiology of policy language. For instance, they are not typically (or cannot typically be) used to evaluate propositions and proposals, but may appear as direct lexical appraisals of elements in the text, as may the semantic labels of the most abstract and broad dimensions of evaluation.

This somewhat confusing aspect is to be expected because of the intrinsically relational nature of language, as well as circularity that arises from the need to describe evaluations in language that uses the semantics of evaluation. The semantic labels from any "level" of evaluative meaning can appear as predicates of an element in the text: a *desirable* circumstance; a *necessary* evil; a *beautiful* place; a *fearful* child. But only evaluations of a certain order of abstraction and ineffability can propagate. For example, we cannot sensibly say, using Lemke's (1998) probe, "*It is* very Powerful *that* John is coming." But we might say "John is very *powerful,*" just as we might say "Beethoven's fifth is a *powerful* piece of music." But the order of abstraction at which an evaluation for *Power* is propagated in the Hong Kong policy text, as well as the degree of its polarity, clearly lies "above" inscribed predications and "below" the most abstract and forceful propagation of *Importance. Power* does not appear in the text as a predicate of the cities. Yet the reader can hardly avoid "seeing" *Power* propagated in the semantic interplay of explicit and implicit evaluations. The process of evaluative propagation therefore appears to be relational, intertextual, multi-dimensional, hierarchical, and "syllogistic."

I cannot place enough stress on the importance of distinguishing between the use of semantic labels for evaluative categories and their direct deployment as words in a text. For instance, what becomes clear is that the degree of evaluative propagation changes the evaluative orientation of the attribution, *Powerful.* The statement, John is *powerful,* might construe an evaluation bordering on "appreciation" of John's social (or perhaps physical) makeup, or a "judgment" about his social *standing*. We would need to know more about context to say which it might be, and more importantly, how the predication of John as a *powerful* person might be evaluated within certain groups who are talking about the "sort" of *Power* that John might have. A statement that "Beethoven's fifth is a *Powerful* piece of music" deploys an appreciative (or perhaps metaphorically affective) appraisal of some music. But in the text from Hong Kong about *world cities*, *Power* appears as a sort of *judgmental* evaluation: the world cities' global economic functions are endowed with "social esteem" and "social sanction" (Martin, 2000, p. 156). The propagation of *Power* here happens at a level "below" the propagated value of *Importance*. That can be demonstrated by observing that we can sensibly say "it is *Important* that world cities are *Powerful*," but not "it is *Powerful* that world cities are *Important*." Here, *Power* is propagated by the *Process* aspects of evaluations in the Hong Kong text and is metaphorically "transferred" to the *Substance* called *world cities*. The *Process* aspects that propagate *Power* are buried in a nominal group (*managing and coordinating*) and in the "range" of the nominalized processes (*economic activity on a global basis*). World cities are quite necessarily *Powerful* in this view because they *control* the world economy. They are therefore *Important*. Here we begin to see the syllogistic aspect of evaluative propagation, or how evaluative propagation has its own "logic."

Understanding the "logic" of values

> If we consider evaluators as semantic operators, and ask what is their *scope*, i.e., to what precisely does their evaluation extend—we find that quite often evaluations propagate or ramify through a text, following the grammatical and logical links that organize it as structured and cohesive text as opposed to a mere sequence of unrelated words and clauses. (Lemke, 1998, p. 49)

At the most abstract level, evaluations seem to have a "logic," a term that typically refers only to the evaluative domain of *Truth* (or *Warrantability*) (cf. Hunston and Sinclair, 2000; Lemke, 1998, pp. 50–51). This is most obvious when texts are seen from the perspective of "syntactic propagation" (Lemke, 1998, pp. 50–51). Syntactic propagation occurs when an evaluative stance towards an element in a clause transfers its evaluation to another element elsewhere in the text. In this mode of analysis we can exclude "explicit evaluators," appraisal resources such as epithets and auxiliary modalizers, and "there are still a host of other phenomena" that can propagate evaluations (1998, p. 50). Even though evaluative propagation can be analyzed without recourse to analyzing appraisal resources, we need not ignore them because they do, as I have demonstrated above, provide a rich grounding for seeing the lexical resources that provide linguistic scaffolding for evaluative propagation.

In the following passage from a Greek policy statement, an overall evaluation of the *Necessity* (a manifestation of *Importance* when directed at irrealis proposals) for institutional change propagates across positive and negative evaluations for *Desirability* where the effects of new technology are concerned:

> The **initial** tendency for a **decline** in the demand for labour as a result of the intro-
> duction of **labour-saving** technology is counteracted by the **increased** demand for
> products and services that follows the **higher** productivity, **lower** prices, and the
> creation of **new** markets for the **new** products and services. In order for **sufficient**
> jobs to be created, it is **necessary** to establish a policy framework for the labour,
> product and service markets which facilitates such **dynamic** adjustment, encour-
> ages the **necessary new** investments, and prepares the labour force for the **new**
> skills that **will prevail** in the job market. **New** technologies are a source of ***new***
> ***employment opportunities*** but at the same time create the need for **difficult** ad-
> justments. Experience shows that policies which focus on safeguarding **existing**
> jobs in **declining** sectors and professions at all costs cause **significant** delay in the
> renewal of the industrial fabric with **adverse** consequences for **healthy** compa-
> nies. It is therefore **necessary** to establish an institutional framework for the
> labour market where the restructuring of jobs and skills can take place **faster** and
> **easier**. Employment policy in the Information Society aims at creating a **flexible**
> institutional framework for the labour market and is accompanied by **initiatives**
> for training and the **upgrading** of skills. (Greece1: 20,857)

In this text, the syntactic propagation of *Necessity* for wholesale structural reform of labor and its institutions in Greece depends "on a single variable which must be assigned intertextually" (Lemke, 1998, p. 51). In this case, it is the high degree of *Desirability* for *new employment opportunities* that are assumed to automatically flow from the use of new technologies. These will allegedly offset the negative effects of *labor-saving* technology.

To establish the organizational weight of *new employment opportunities* as an evaluation for the *Desirability* and *Importance* of new technology, it is helpful to trace out the elements that are most explicitly inscribed with evaluations in the above example. Overall, new technology is presented as having both positive and negative effects upon society. We are told that *la-bor-saving technology* tends to reduce *the demand for labor* when it is first "introduced." But this *un-Desirable* effect is indirectly offset by *increased demand for products and services*, the result of *higher productivity*, *lower prices*, and *new markets for new products and services*. All these outcomes are presented as unqualified effects of new technologies, despite all evidence to the contrary. Once given, the positive "facts" of technological development are transformed into imperatives for action: *it is necessary to establish a policy framework* that *facilitates dynamic adjustment*, *encourages necessary new investments*, and *prepares the labor force* for *new skills that will prevail in the job market*. In other words, the technologies that reduce the demand for labor, and which are the cause of all the change that people have suddenly had to deal with, also create *new employment opportunities*. The authors resolve the consequent logical tensions by operationalizing an alternative evaluative "logic."

First, *increased demand*; *higher productivity*; *lower prices*; and *new markets*, *products*, and *services* are attributed to technological advances. The benefits appear from nowhere and we can only assume that they are causally related to the introduction of new technologies. The prospect of protecting *existing jobs in declining sectors* is dismissed based on the facts of *experience*. The decrepit state of the Greek economy is acknowledged in the implied need for *a renewal of the industrial fabric*, thus doubly reinforcing the futility of maintaining the status quo. Next, the image of *healthy companies* is set against itself to imply "sick" ones thus situating *declining sectors and professions* and *sick* companies in a burdensome relationship with *healthy* ones. The outcome of all these positive and negative effects is *Necessity—for difficult adjustments*; *for training and the upgrading of skills*; for *an institutional framework*; and for *a policy framework*, all oriented towards *creating a flexible institutional framework for the labor market*. All the difficulties implied here are offset by a single lexical item *new employment opportunities*. Without this item there would be no solution to the problems of technology identified by the authors. Technology would otherwise be the primary cause of economic decline and social disruption without offering any mitigation. The *Desirability* of *new employment opportunities* dominates the evaluation that propagates syntactically throughout the Greek text.

This is achieved by a kind of evaluative "syllogizing." The evaluations of particular elements in the text do not merely or obviously "add up to" an overall evaluation of *Desirability* for the benefits of technological change, even though the "pluses" and "minuses" of introducing technology are laid out according to neoliberal axiology. The evaluations are not merely stacked up, but are set in opposition to one another and, at times, to themselves. In brief, using the form of the deductive syllogism, we can express the axiology of the Greek text in three related syllogisms:

> A
>
> | | |
> |---|---|
> | *Major premise*: | All new employment opportunities are Desirable |
> | *Minor premise*: | New technologies are a source of new employment opportunities |
> | *Deduction*: | New technologies are *Desirable*. |

B

Major premise: New markets, services, and products are Desir-
                         able

Minor premise: New technologies create new markets, services,
                         and products.

Deduction: New technologies are *Desirable*.

C

Major premise: The overall effects of new technologies are
                         Desirable.

Qualifying premise: New technologies require people to gain new
                         skills.

Deduction: It is *Necessary* that people gain new skills.

If the major premises are taken for granted it becomes a matter of mere
"common sense" that education gets oriented towards employment, and that
employment policy is oriented towards re-education of the Greek population
so that the economy can reap the inevitable benefits of new technologies.
Neoliberal axiology provides the organizing, supporting "logic" for the text,
so there is no need to justify or elaborate the *Desirability* of *restructuring
jobs and skills*; the *un-Desirability* of *safeguarding existing jobs in declining
sectors and professions*; or *Warrantability* for the claim that new technologies
will result in *higher productivity, lower prices, and the creation of new markets for the new products and services*. Once these are presupposed as facts
by the authors, it becomes a necessity that all the organs of Greek labor production, including and especially the entire education system, can be turned
towards training people to use new technologies. In this way, new media are
embedded in the daily lives of people through their education systems, their
employment opportunities, their industrial structures, and their policy directions. These are achievements of policy.

Modeling multiple dimensions in evaluative meaning

While the evaluative dimensions of *Necessity* and *Desirability* are foregrounded in the Greek text, we might just as fruitfully model the dimension
of *Probability* to find impetus for structural change. More and less subtle jux-
tapositions of *Probability* for various elements in the text "support" the
overall evaluations for the *Necessary* re-education of Greek people in a

knowledge economy. For example, while the introduction of technology is attributed with an *un-Desirable* "initial tendency" to reduce jobs, the assumed benefits of technology that offset these come with an evaluation for unmitigated *Truth*. *Necessity* for change is juxtaposed to the *Desirable* outcomes of new technology to propagate an overall degree of *Probability* in respect of policy outcomes: *In order for sufficient jobs to be created, it is necessary to establish a policy framework for the labor, product and service markets … .* When we model for *Probability*, a threat becomes apparent: if an *Appropriate policy framework* is not put in place, then the benefits of technology *will Probably not* be realized in Greece.

Similarly, we might model the text for *Warrantability*. The following claims are just a few of the key truth claims made in the Greek text:

the new skills that **will prevail** in the job market;

new technologies **are** a source of new employment opportunities; and

experience **shows** that policies which focus on safeguarding existing jobs in declining sectors … **cause** significant delay… .

All these statements deploy high positive degrees of *Warrantability*. They are statements of "fact," past, present, *and* future (note that the past is condensed in the nominal, *experience*). While time and space do not permit anything like a complete axiological analysis here, it will suffice to say that various degrees and polarities of *Normativity*, *Comprehensibility*, and *Usuality* are brought to bear on elements of the text, although these are more opaque, especially because of their reliance on the tense system (e.g., that specific skills *will prevail* is a contentious claim untestable by anything other than definite evidence of what happens in the future). For instance, under neoliberal axiology, it would be considered *incomprehensible* for the government of an economically struggling country to take up protectionist policies, even though these may be *prima facie* quite useful.

It will usually be most often at the cost of seeing these more subtle configurations of evaluative "scaffolding" that the most broad dimensions of evaluative meaning get foregrounded in any sustained analysis of policy language. But by identifying the evaluative stances that are foregrounded overall in policy texts, we can begin to see which dimensions propagate "beneath" the most prominent to "support" them. In any case, each evaluative dimension is a way "in" to the axiological stance being most obviously propagated in a given text. Viewing evaluative propagation within and between evaluative dimensions in terms of "logic" has the advantage of separating in analysis what is, in discourse, inseparable: the interdependence between evaluations at all dimensions and levels of axiological propagation.

But there is a problematic question in all of this, precisely because of the complex and subtle interplay between evaluative dimensions: how can any analyst claim to know which evaluative semantics are propagating most strongly in a given instance? How do we know what is supposed to be inferred in the often enthymematic invocation of evaluative syllogisms? How do we explain and identify the contextual materials that organize and propagate evaluations across stretches of text? Unless we claim some inherently superior hermeneutic abilities, while simultaneously assuming that both lay readers and professional analysts can make "sense" of a text's axiological stance, we must say not merely that such evaluative resources exist, but also where they "come from." Moreover, we need to say, or at least acknowledge, how they are propagated and inculcated as meaningful and recognizable axiological patterns. These issues are at the political economic intersection of language, new media, and social perceptions of value. Cultural history, patterns of mediation, patterns of evaluation, and structures of power all combine to provide the historical (or often *ahistorical*) resources that people draw upon to make axiological "sense" of their world.

Mediating evaluative propagation and propaganda

If readers are to make appropriate "sense" of evaluative propagation, they must share a considerable degree of knowledge about specific but often implicit axiologies—propagational "logics" and predicational lexes—within a community. In many ways, notions of "heteroglossia," "discourse formations," "intertextuality," "inculcation," and "evaluative patterns" address the historical nature of specific axiologies.[44] But the central problems addressed by, for instance, the notion of "heteroglossia," are those concerning "the persistent habits of speaking and acting, characteristic of some group, through which it constructs its worldview: its beliefs, opinions, and values" (Lemke, 1995, p. 24). In other words, with an understanding of the heteroglossic nature of language in hand, we can set out to identify the production and reproduction of particular ways in which "people represent the world, including themselves and their productive activities" (Fairclough, 2000). However, and this is all the more important in a globally mass mediated environment dominated by as few as six corporations, heteroglossia, intertextuality, and so on presuppose the existence of shared values systems without explaining *their means of propagation* which is—and has been for at least five thousand years—media technologies and their associated institutions, which are also media forms in their own right. I include here ancient oral and aural technologies as well as the enduring influences of institutionally mediated "knowledge monopolies" that have waxed and waned in their dominance throughout history (Innis, 1950, 1951).

It is unquestionable that the social situatedness of persons is foundational to how they make meanings. However it can no longer be assumed, if it ever could, that people are socialized into local meaning systems, such as families within distinct social and cultural groups, and that "outside" mediation effects "come afterwards," with people merely making of media "content" what they will according to some cultural background that is unaffected by mediation processes. Today's mediations are pervasive, immediate, and global. A global stock of meanings is "part of the family" from the earliest years, and this thoroughly mediated stock is as much a part of the human environment as its water supply (Silverstone and Haddon, 1996). If we are to claim knowledge of a community's axiological resources in political economic analysis, we need to take into consideration precisely how specific ways of evaluating the world are systematically inculcated. The mediated discourses of everyday life are processes "of classification: the making of distinctions and judgements," and processes of mediation are central to these:

> in so far as the media are … central to this process of making distinctions and judgments; in so far as they do, precisely, mediate the dialectic between the classification that shapes experience and the experience which colours classification, then we must enquire into the consequences of such mediation. We *must* study the media. (Silverstone, 1999, p. 12)

This is an important and explicit exhortation, especially during a time when mass mediation processes and political power have merged in an almost seamless manner. Mediation does much to give the impression of credibility and coherence to the system in which we live. In fact the current global system could not exist without its mediation systems (Silverstone, 1999, p. 144). Today, myth, money, politics, and power are conflated in globally mediated systems of meaning. To ignore the institutional and relational aspects of media—the processes of production and distribution in a massified means of inculcation—is at least as serious an omission as ignoring the meanings of mediated "messages."

The neoliberal axiology that underpins most (if not all) of contemporary technology policy is the result of massive propaganda that cannot be ignored in any political economic analysis. That is because it is through mass mediations that people's understandings of "value" or "worth" are shaped, whether in terms of aesthetic, financial, social, or cultural worth:

> Everywhere we hear it said, all day long—and this is what gives the dominant discourse its strength—that there is nothing to put forward in opposition to the neoliberal view, that it has succeeded in presenting itself as self-evident, that there is no alternative. If it is taken for granted in this way, this is a result of a whole labour of symbolic inculcation in which journalists and ordinary citizens participate passively and, above all, a certain number of intellectuals participate actively. Against this permanent, insidious imposition, which produces, through impregnation, a real belief, it seems to me that researchers have a role to play. First they can analyze the production and distribution of this discourse. (Bourdieu, 1998, p. 29)

While I do not agree that it is just a few "intellectuals" that participate actively in the production and distribution of neoliberal discourse, nor that "ordinary citizens" are passive receptacles for axiological inculcation, mass-mediated culture, a significant part of which is populist politics, provides essential normative work in propagating its own *legitimacy*. It has become a centralized, "entertainmentized" system of self-valorizing values.

Because of the convergence of global, instantaneous mediation systems and organized political power, policy has becomes both a means of propagating the desirability of new technologies—insinuating the tools by fiat in schools, universities, offices, laboratories, and communities—and an apparent "victim" of the same technologies, succumbing to industry hype and increasing expenditure on ICT at an exponential rate for very little in the way of visible returns:

> Growth in this market is viewed to be driven by the heightened need for automated security compliance, disaster recovery, and Windows 2000/XP migrations, as well as an increased focus on IT efficiency and cost reductions. The federal government spent $37.1 billion on information systems and services in 2002, and will increase spending at a compound annual growth rate of 11 percent from $37.1 billion in fiscal year 2002 to $63.3 billion in FY 2007. (JB Cubed, 2003)

As well as being an agent for propagating the value of technologies, and for promoting their use in every department of society, it is in policy that the stamp of legitimacy is applied to specific ways of knowing and evaluating the world. The means of achieving these ends are products of history.

Seeing historical role structures in policy

Defining official axiologies is an historically persistent function of sacred institutions and their associated means and institutions of mediation (Mumford, 1944/1973, pp. 100-102). The axiologies that have emerged and subsided during the centuries in which the devices of contemporary policy have been developed do not entirely disappear. Instead they are overlaid upon each other, like geological strata. The voices of past modes of social control speak to us through the ages, pulling the past and the future into the present. Seen as historically and globally mediated artifacts that still "contain" the most ancient historical practices, heteroglossic relations in technology policy usually express the following "role structures" (Halliday, 1978, p. 143), or "voices" (Lemke, 1995, pp. 22-25):

1. **client⇔patron** [*action*: sell/choose/select; *relationship*: the patron speaks on behalf of the client's needs];

2. **beneficiary⇔benefactor** [*action*: give gifts/mercy/permission; *relationship*: the benefactor speaks on behalf of the beneficiary's well-being];

3. **employee⇔manager** [*action*: order/organize/control/plan; *relationship*: the manager directs the actions and attitudes of the employee];

4. **expert⇔idea** [*action*: innovate/transform/inform/define/quantify/identify; *relationship*: the expert speaks on behalf of the idea. Examples include legal expert⇔law; engineer⇔technology; bureaucrat⇔policy, etc.];

5. **soldier⇔officer** [*action*: order/command/coordinate: *relationship*: the officer commands the soldier who is only a means to an end and has no voice in the matter];

6. **priest⇔god** [*action*: dispense salvation, justice, fate, predictions, divine law, and received wisdom; *relationship*: the priest speaks on behalf of an omnipresent, extrajudicial god].

These voices rarely appear alone in the language of policy and politicians today. Rather, they have been developed, refashioned, and drawn upon throughout history by those in power and those seeking to usurp power. In operationalizing these voices, policy authors and spokespersons produce, reproduce, and transform the centuries-old practice of symbolic control. The "voices" have been historically overlaid and refined as effective techniques of social control, one upon the other. Here is an example of the historical heteroglot I am describing:

> In other words, some of these are the ways that—(applause)—what I'm telling you is, things are changing in the Nation's Capital when it comes to invigorating the faith-based initiative, and the Knights [of Columbus] have helped a lot. I appreciate your efforts to level the playing field when it comes to grant-making. And because of your efforts, America is changing for the better.
>
> I needed someone to lead this program, so guess who I turned to? The Knights. (Applause.) I found Towey. Jim Towey is the Director of the White House Office of Faith-Based and Community Initiatives. He's with me. You know what his job is? His job is to help the faith community—by the way, all faiths, all faiths—Christian, Jew, or Muslim—all faiths understand what is possible now. His job is also to make sure the federal government is a hospitable place for faith programs to work with. Let's be frank about it. Many faith-based programs don't want to interface with government. You know why? They're afraid of losing the ability to practice their faith. How can you be a faith-based program if you're not allowed to practice your faith?
>
> Towey's job—(applause)—so Towey has got a big job, it's to change a culture, a suspicious culture, and we're making progress. A suspicious culture in Washington, a suspicious culture in the grassroots. Here's Towey's story. He goes to meet Mother Teresa for the first time. He shows up at one of her homes for the dying in India, and the sister who greeted him assumed he was there to work. (Laughter.) That's what I assume every day that Towey shows up. (Laughter.) So she gave Jim some cloth, and said, go clean the sores of a dying man. He says it changed his life, that experience. He went on to work full-time for the Missionaries of Charity. Incredibly enough, Jim Towey, Director of the Office of Faith-Based Initiatives in the White House, was Mother Teresa's lawyer. I ask you, what kind of society is it where Mother Teresa needs a lawyer? (Laughter and applause.) It's a society that needs tort reform. (Laughter and applause.). (Bush, 2004c)

Here, George W. Bush compresses two millennia of resources into three paragraphs to propagate the *Divinity*, *Desirability*, and the ultimate *Necessity* of re-establishing something approximating the *ancien regime* fusion of Church and State in Western Europe. Knights, saints, lawyers, missionaries, and reformation-sits; government, church, and state; miracles, management strategies, funding agencies, and national interests are all conflated to present an entertaining discourse on the virtues of combining Church and State to remedy an almost complete lack of equitable redistribution.

Supranational policy gets even more complex. Having so many contradictory and antagonistic cultural forces to contend with, and without the comfort of identifiable axiological traditions to draw upon, it is characteristically shot through with logical and axiological contradictions, and not only in terms of its role-structures. Such contradictions are the product of historical interaction—the historical production and reproduction of symbolic power forms—which are institutionally and otherwise technologically mediated on a worldwide basis (cf. Bourdieu, 1991). They are contradictory because each historical "layer" is necessarily set in distinction to its previous and subsequent "layers": each "enlightenment" in history is set in distinction to a "dark age"; each "renaissance" is set in distinction to political and cultural death. I am not asserting a "punctuated," "revolutionary," singular, or linear view of historical progress, although sometimes history can change in those ways. Rather, I am acknowledging that each new form of political control can only be defined as such in distinction to what has gone before.

Turning time into space by means of policy

The pressure upon the most ambitious supranational policy is apparent in its tense system, the most overt linguistic resources for dealing with time. The future-oriented social function of policy forces its authors into a series of future-oriented proposals and propositions that cannot, because of technocratic convention, seem too outlandish from a "presentational" perspective (Lemke, 1995, p. 41). Again, this orientation reflects the spatial bias of new media systems in political economy, and of their treatment in the official domains of intellectual labor from at least the mid-nineteenth century onwards. As James Carey puts it:

> Economics, political science, urban planning, sociology, and the physical sciences charted the problems and challenges of society in space. Even time was converted to space as the social sciences, enamoured of prediction, characterized the future as a frontier to be conquered. Even historians caught the bug using time merely as a container to tell the narrative of progress: politics, power, empire, and rule. (1989, pp. 155–156)

Policy produced by such means cannot, perhaps, help but present a picture of a frozen world comprised of inanimate "things" that need to be worked on by government and industry. In contemporary policy, the classical categories of political economy—land, labor, and capital—have been extended to embrace the intellectual and emotional lives of people, now and into the future, to control the way people will act and interact "in" that future to achieve economic benefits. Of all the classical categories, labor is the most unruly because it is comprised of the thoughts, actions, and words of people. To realize the "promises" of new technologies, labor in all its manifestations must be oriented to the virtues of the coming technological utopia. That is to say, people must be made to act, think, know, and evaluate in politically and economically correct ways if the benefits of new media are to be realized according to current official perceptions of value.

The introduction of management techniques into mainstream policy production processes has further exacerbated the money-minded tendencies of policy, bringing "the strategic plan" into the realm of policy. The strategic plan is a direct translation of time into space; it turns notions of what is into notions of what should be. Because of the intellectual trends Carey describes, the future has become a "place" to be defined, delineated, occupied, and controlled in policy. Yet in purely human terms, the future is not a new place; it is what people will do in future, how they will do it, with whom, and according to which principles. Carey's description of "the future as a frontier to be conquered" is quite overt in policies concerned with new media. It is a feature of policy discourse that can be seen through the lens of axiological analysis, as can the implications of doing so. The methods for axiological analysis I have briefly presented were developed analyzing what appears to be a fairly tired and rigid genre with very ancient roots. The rigidity of contemporary policy gains further from the need to deal with ever larger, faster, and more complex social and technological changes. Because policy is oriented towards what people will do, and because of the spatially biased character of new media, policy authors are required to deal with and shape human potentialities on an ever-larger scale. They are forced into grappling with complex, massive, and dynamic human potential interactions that span the globe and extend indefinitely into the future. The typical scientific textual strategy for taming and simplifying complexity is to use highly compressed nouns and present complex processes as static things. In itself, that grammatical strategy is unremarkable and in many cases quite necessary for doing science. But the need to define, shape, and conquer future social spaces compels policy authors to use scientific discourse to freeze, hide, or elide time as far as possible. In the following chapter, I focus on key devices in contemporary policy discourse that authors use to turn time into space in order to "conquer" uncertainty.

CHAPTER SEVEN

Utopian frontiers of the digital age

> Armed with the techniques of modern science, especially the new measuring de-
> vices of precise clocks and telescopes, a secular priesthood seized hold of the idea
> of a perfect future, a zone of experience beyond ordinary history and geography, a
> new region of time blessed with a perfect landscape and a perfection of man and
> society. Nevertheless, there exists a continuity from the ancient astrologers of the
> temple, tribe, and city to modern scientists, for both are elevated castes who pro-
> fess special knowledge of the future—indeed establish a claim over the next stages
> of human history.
>
> Modern oracles, like their ancient counterparts, constitute a privileged class who
> monopolize new forms of knowledge and alternatively panic and enrapture large
> audiences as they portray new versions of the future. Moreover, modern scientific
> elites often occupy the same double role of oracles to the people and servants of
> the ruling class as did the astrologers of ancient civilization […] modern scientists
> use their capacity to predict the behaviour of narrow, closed systems to claim the
> right to predict and order all human futures. (Carey, 1989, pp. 173-174)

James Carey's characterization of "modern scientists" as merely contemporary versions of the ancient augurs and oracles may seem, *prima facie*,
little more than anachronism put to the service of political economic critique. Yet the oracular functions of contemporary science can be quite clearly
observed in policy through axiological analysis. The oracular function of policy is key in understanding the complex relationships between language, new
media, and social perceptions of value. In the guise of predictive science,
utopian and dystopian predictions are written into policies that affect whole
nations, and in some cases, the whole of humanity. The strong historical links
between the emergence of new media, new social spaces, new utopias, and
new social classes is well-evidenced. However, the bias of any age includes a
tendency to construe its official ways of knowing as eternally correct and
valid, even when they turn out to be otherwise. In such cases, the "past and
present are rewritten to evidence a momentous changing of times in which
particular policies and technologies will yield a way out of current dilemmas,
and a new age of peace, democracy, and ecological harmony will reign"

(Carey, 1989, p. 174). The latest official utopia is no different from any other in history, its advocates' claims no less a matter of faith or chance than those of the ancient oracles. Only the means of presentation and legitimation differ slightly.

The title of Thomas More's *Utopia* is a play on words that can mean both "good place" and "no place." When considering the official utopia of our current age, at least as it appears in policy, More's wordplay takes on a new significance. That is because our contemporary utopia is a future paradise comprised almost entirely of time. Makers of law and policy have developed many ways to create imperatives for action: by directing resources towards or away from certain people; by prioritizing civic objectives; by making or unmaking laws; by brute force; and by mass propaganda. In many ways, though, these are the "blunt objects" of power. A far more ancient, subtle, and perennial method of shaping the actions and attitudes of people is to inculcate prophetic visions for new, unexplored, or unknowable spaces that exist at a time—distant from the here and now; that is, to create paradisiacal values for some imagined future place (Bernier, 1992, p. 199).

Mythically constructed utopias of the official kind, whether imagined or real places, have been a feature of political discourse since the beginnings of history (Noble, 2004; Voltaire, 1764/1972, pp. 141–145). They have been perennial places to aspire to, places where life will be better; where, by "simply passing on through the inevitable steps proposed by whatever particular ideology is in question, we are promised that we will re-enter Eden at a higher, more sophisticated level. Paradise is the first and last destination" (Saul, 1997, p. 41). The official utopias of any age are its most powerful illusions. Their attainment is typically achieved through sacrifice, and the future state of perfection that is the promise of every utopia can only be achieved at the expense of life in the present.

Utopian visions in history that remain influential today include Plato's "next world" (de Santillana and von Dechend, 1962/1999, p. 230); the future "kingdom of priests and ... holy nation" detailed in the Old Testament (Exdodus 19:6 in Küng, 1968/1995, p. 370); the "holy nation" promised by the New Testament (Küng, 1968/1995, pp. 380-383); the promised "holy land" pursued by the crusade-mongers of twelfth-century Western Europe (Cawsey, 1999); the "silk road" of the late middle ages (McNeill, 1987); the mythical El Dorado upon which the South Sea Bubble was built (Morgan, 1929); the gold-fields of nineteenth-century Australia and California (Marx, 1976, pp. 932-940); and "the heavenly cities" of the eighteenth and nineteenth centuries (Carey, 1989, p. 180). Whether they are manifest as the many despotisms that plagued the twentieth century, the religious wars over land in the Middle East since 1947, the all-out competition for economic supremacy promoted by *laissez faire* economics since the nineteenth-century, or the currently unfolding religious wars between the great Mosaic sects in the post-9/11 twenty-first century, our most powerful utopian ideals have had enduring and profound effects upon the whole of humanity. We had best understand them, how they are made, and how they are propagated.

One of the most well-publicized utopias of our contemporary milieu is cyberspace—the global space of interactions facilitated by new media. It is this utopia that is said to contain the riches of a global knowledge economy, the ease of Bill Gates's "friction-free" trade routes, the benefits of direct democracy, and the cornucopia of "moral, social, and material" betterment typical of all utopias (Carey, 1989, p. 180). There are other utopias *du jour*, of course—as yet without specific names—and I include some of these in the following analysis and discussion. In knowledge policy discourse, "frontier" language is used to construct the myth of the golden future. Specifically, a phrasal verb ("opens up") and its various forms (opened up, opening up, open up) is deployed in policy to present a spatialized future. In most cases, this phrasal verb functions as "process metaphor" (McKenna and Graham, 2000, p. 230).

The strange life of metaphorical verbs in policy

Most processes typically pertain to quite specific aspects of human experience (Halliday, 1994).[45] Halliday identifies different "worlds" of human experience to which processes typically refer: "the abstract world of relations" (being); "the world of consciousness" (sensing); and "the physical world" (doing) (1994, p. 108). The phenomenon I am calling *process metaphor* here allows elements in discourse to act simultaneously throughout antithetical realms of human experience. For instance, in trade and technology policy, "globalization" gets to act in all sorts of mystical, relational, conscious, and physical roles, giving the impression that it exists as a godlike force independent of what people do. When used in process metaphorical ways, processes retain their grammatical function as processes, but they are deployed in a way that allows elements to act throughout the various realms of human experience. Process metaphor is a deceptively powerful tool. In policy it is used to construct utopian and dystopian futures, and to present human phenomena as if they acted independently and exogenously upon the whole of humanity on their own accord. The typical structure of process metaphorical syntax relies on two central features: strenuous exercise of the tense system and the embedding of a future oriented, time-based element in the object position of the sentence. The presence of this *irrealis* (i.e., potential or imaginary) object is a key element in "scientifically" constructed utopias. It allows policy authors to manipulate the tense system in a seemingly matter-of-fact way that often hides the prophetic element in their discourse.

Here is an example that is typical of policy promoting the use of new media:

> The transition to a knowledge economy and society over the next few decades
> opens up the possibility of massive productivity gains. (OECD, 1999, p. 1)

In the above example, *opens up* appears to function as a material process: a singular, concrete action. In the case of a more "common sense" use of the same phrasal verb, such as "George *opens up* the shop at 9: 00," the materiality and singularity of the process in this case is clear. However, the authors of the above example from the OECD deploy *opens up* in a process metaphorical way, relating two highly condensed nominal groups, both of which compress a countless complex of actions and relations into static "things": *the transition to a knowledge economy and society over the next few decades* and *the possibility of massive productivity gains*. The process metaphorical use of *opens up* in this example works throughout all domains of experience, and not necessarily in a "material" sense at all.

We can see the rather surprising scope of the process metaphor by substituting other processes that retain the semantic sense of the OECD's proposition: *The transition to a knowledge economy and society over the next few decades [opens up, promises, offers, brings, creates, reveals, shows, presents, indicates, signifies, suggests] the possibility of massive productivity gains*. All of these lexical substitutes would retain, to some extent, the sense that the OECD example conveys, but would constrain the effects of the great "transition" to one, perhaps two, realms of human experience. Compared to the concrete example I provided above, there are few other substitutes that can retain a similar semantic sense: "George [opens up, opens] his shop at 9.00 o'clock." There are no other options. Within the choices that do retain the original semantic sense of the proposition in the OECD example, we see that they would occupy positions on the *verbal* (promises, suggests); *abstract-material* (offers); *relational* (indicates, shows, *symbolizes*); and *material* (creates, brings) planes of human experience. In other words, the process metaphor presents the highly compressed nominal group Head [*The transition to a knowledge economy and society over the next few decades*] as something that will affect every aspect of human experience—the conscious, the sensate, the physical, the logical—by having an *irrealis* nominal group [*the possibility of massive productivity gains*] as its grammatical object.

The substitutive probe I use above shows what sort of "sense" or "action" the OECD authors are trying to convey with their choice of process. So when we see the substitutes—*promises, offers, brings, creates, reveals*, etc.—we see that something like a future treasure, prize, or gift is being all but guaranteed. A transformative Agent with immense powers is implied as guarantor. But the mystical character of such futuristic speculation—a kind of "*I promise you that these new things portend a magical future ...*"—is hidden in the deceptive materiality of the process *opens up*. A distinctive feature of process metaphor is that synonyms for processes, as they are typically used in concrete language, need not sensibly apply. Put differently, lexical synonyms for process metaphorical meanings can "come from," or properly pertain to, completely different realms of experience than those we would expect to see in more "common" usage.

One effect of process metaphor is to animate the products of imagination, allowing authors of policy to present abstractions as if they had supreme power over people. The term *globalization* is exemplary of the twentieth-century *fin de siecle* policy pantheism. Abstractions animated by power elites have long played a large part in the governance of human societies by providing a model for society-wide axiological agendas. They are phenomena as old as history. The gods of our various religions are excellent examples, as are the ethereal utopias they inhabit and promise (Noble, 1994).

From time, to space, to property

> Political economy proceeds from the fact of private property. It does not explain it. It grasps the material process of private property, the process through which it actually passes, in general the abstract formulae which it then takes as laws. It does not comprehend these laws, i.e., it does not show how they arise from the nature of private property. Political economy fails to explain the reason for the division between labour and capital, between capital and land. For example, when it defines the relation of wages to profit it takes the interests of the capitalists as the basis of its analysis; i.e., it assumes what it is supposed to explain. (Marx, 1844/1975, p. 323)

Besides creating omnipotent powers for policy abstractions, another function of process metaphor that pertains specifically to the lexical item I focus on here (that of *open/s/ed/ing up*) is to propagate evaluations of *Desirability* and *Importance* for irrealis spaces, thereby prefiguring their transformation into property. Throughout Western history, there have been a number of significant periods during which the radical redefinition of geographical and social spaces has become central to the future political economic character of societies: during the latter twelfth century when feudal ties were legally formalized throughout large areas of western Europe (Bloch, 1940/1961, pp. 72-73); during the three hundred years or so it took to complete the enclosures movements at which time the land of whole nations was "privatized," providing the property foundations for early capitalism (Hobsbawm, 1962, p. 46; Marx, 1844/1975); and during the early twentieth century when radio bandwidth was first subject to technical definition, allocation, and ownership, becoming the ground upon which twentieth-century nationalisms were built.[46] These are significant transitional periods in history and, if policy is any guide at all, we are quite probably in such a period now.

Of course there have been many other significant periods during which empires, nations, and groups have fought over ideas, faiths, and geographical prizes—literally, over the meaning of space. But these are very different phenomena. I am concerned here with describing the technical definition of concrete, finite, ownable spaces that previously did not exist as such for people. It is quite probable that land would have appeared as a "fluid," ineffable, and unownable space in ninth-century Europe (cf. Bloch, 1940/1961, pp. 39-42). The same most certainly holds for radio bandwidth in the early twentieth century (Childs, 1924; Church, 1939). The creation of space as property—that is, as a concrete, technically delineated area within which active relationships, rights, and obligations are formally defined—is reducible to four basic prerequisites: (i) the technical means to identify and make use of new forms of space, such as electromagnetic spectrum, airspace, trade routes, land, bodies of water, and so on; (ii) the pre-existence of a set of informal relationships within that given space *prior* to the technical division of the space; (iii) legal means for formalizing the definition of space and regulating the relationships therein, including a sufficiently developed legal language and institutional infrastructure; and (iv) the means to patrol and enforce the boundaries, both within and without, as concrete, substantial, "exogenous" spaces and as abstract, time-bound, "endogenous" activity-spaces.[47]

In policy oriented towards encouraging the uptake of new media, new and emerging spaces are being anticipated as the basis of new property forms. From the perspective of political economy, the spatial aspects of human relatedness are being defined in policy by assigning values to the social activities that are a prerequisite of new property forms. Any social space must exist as informal (even invisible) relationships before being formally defined at law as something else: new spaces cannot be brought into existence by law alone. In what follows, I show the social processes that have been foreshadowed in policy as becoming real, ownable activity spaces, each corresponding to specific and existing domains of activity and, consequently, to their associated axiological potentials.

Realis and Irrealis spaces

In dealing with the future in policy discourse, it becomes necessary to distinguish between two distinct types of space, *realis* and *irrealis*. The significance of process metaphor in policy language is that it operates "officially" in the subjunctive, thus binding "large stretches of institutional time and space. It achieves this, first, by orienting its actions towards potentiality ("irrealis") rather than actuality ("realis")" (Iedema, 1998, p. 484). However, while the actuality⇔potentiality cline that distinguishes between potential and actual states is commonly expressed through tense (distinguishing between past, present, and future) and modality (the degree of likelihood attributed to something happening or existing), the functionality of *process metaphor* turns on actuality and potentiality being conflated and buried in the object to which the process is directed, whether the potentiality is realized literally, such as in the words *possibility* and *opportunity*, or whether it is buried in the compressed nominal groups that are typical of the policy genre. Herein lies the aesthetic ruse of process metaphor: when deployed, policy representations of irrealis spaces are presented as concrete *Substances* that exist in the here and now. In other words, policy language turns future time into space, preparing future activity to be turned into property.

"Opening up" new frontiers for the "new economy"

In technology policy, the phrasal verb "open/s/ed/ing up" collocates (typically appears in conjunction) with *possibility/ies* and *opportunity/ies*. The *possibilities* and *opportunities* opening up in policy are overtly spatial in their constitution. They are often construed as the spatial aspects of irrealis states, as the result of ways of being, seeing, and acting in new spaces and as the social realms in which such doings might occur (cf. Fairclough, 2000). Something on the value differentials between the main irrealis objects being "opened up" is in order here. *Possibilities* may be evaluated as positive or negative potentialities in terms of *Desirability*. *Opportunities*, on the other hand, are already potentialities positively evaluated for *Desirability*: *opportunities* arc always *Desirable* potential realities for *someone*. They therefore contain imperatives for a certain amount of action in order that the opportunities be moved from potentiality to actuality. These broadest of evaluative orientations are implicitly and explicitly expressed in policy. Following, for example, is an explicit recognition that *possibilities* may be *Desirable* or *un-Desirable*:

> As with other technologies that have become intrinsic parts of everyday life like the automobile, different physical, social and economic configurations may prevail in distinctive societies with particular traditions, values and political preferences. The Net is no different, *it opens up possibilities, from the ominous to the utopian*, for facilitating the development of new or the consolidation of old social orders. (oecd6: 2,656)

Opportunities, on the other hand, are always *Desirable* potentialities, even if they are not available or recognizable to everyone:

> However, an element of the population is likely to remain excluded from the opportunities opened up by e-commerce for a range of social and economic reasons.
>
> Whilst a number of publicly-funded initiatives, at local, regional and national level, aim to improve the opportunities for this 'e-excluded' group, the Team be-

lieves that better co-ordination of these initiatives is needed—with resources targeted at the most effective programmes—which must also be effectively marketed. (uk_eva2: 32,909)

Here we see the interrelationship between evaluations of *Desirability* and *Importance* for realizing *opportunities*. The hortatory function of policy is expressed as an evaluation for *Necessity*: *initiatives* are required to *improve opportunities* and they *must be effectively marketed*. There is also an indication here that the raw material of the knowledge economy is ignorance: the *"e-excluded" group* must be made to recognize opportunities, something that will be achieved through marketing.

The preconditions for property in political economy

As I state above, there are four preconditions for new spaces to be developed to the point at which they attain political economic status as property. These are a major focus for new media policy. The first and most significant aspect is the technical definition of new spaces. Somewhat surprisingly, this is the least elaborated aspect of space in the corpus. The second is the pre-existence of informal relations in that space. The third is a legal infrastructure for formalizing the relationships, and the fourth is the means to patrol, police, and defend the space. This last aspect is presupposed and typically passed over. Given that the 1998 redefinition of cyberspace as "battlespace" by the US Department of Defense (Brewin, 1998) committed the world's most expensive and destructive war machine to patrolling and policing the boundaries of an ostensibly global space, little more needs to be said on the matter. I firstly focus on the activity spaces— the currently "informal" relationships—that are being prefigured for formalization in the "new economy" before moving on to identify the concrete geotechnical space that is currently being colonized on a global scale, and upon which the foundations of a new form of political economy are to be built.

Making public activity spaces into property

Cyberspace is most often construed as a space created by new ways of doing things, which is merely to say that it is a technologically constituted space:

The information economy opens up new ways of communicating with each other and doing every day activities—and it offers huge opportunities to all Australians.

[...]

And it no longer matters how far away we are from each other, because it takes no time to get there. This is the information society. (cita1: 635)

So, according to Australia's Department of Communication, Information, Technology and the Arts (DCITA), the future activity space of the information economy, with its *huge opportunities*, is created through the destruction of *time* between people. In fact this statement says that the space between people is where *huge opportunities* lie, as they logically must in any process of mediation. In any case, it is a space of new activities into which specific institutions are moving:

> Telecommunications companies ... are moving into e-commerce and application development and finding new value. They are moving more into Internet Protocols and data transmission. This is opening up a whole lot of new opportunities for them ... in this new environment that can mean developing software. (ausbey1: 40,801)

Here are direct and explicit links between what people do, the new *environment* created those activities, and the perceived value that accompanies the creation of new activity spaces.

New media can also bring different social spaces—previously distant institutions and different activity spaces—into contact with one another:

> These channels would help teachers to find workplace assignments and might also offer "job shadowing" or other programs that would expose business executives to the learning environment and build connections that would open up classrooms to the world of work. It is essential that employers gain a fuller appreciation of the complexities and challenges involved in preparing young people for the labour market. (canada1: 34,261)

It is worth noting that *open up* does not function process metaphorically in this instance. Both the realization and possible semantic substitutes are constrained to the abstract-material plane. In this case, a semantic probe reveals that *open up ... to* means, roughly, *expose ... to*: that is, schools *should* be exposed to the world of work; executives *should* be exposed to the learning environment. In the knowledge economy, education is nothing more than *preparing young people for the labor market*. The key process metaphor here also occurs to a slightly restricted extent in the modalized verbal group *might also offer*. Probing *offer* in this case, we find the meaning is something like *allow, create, open up, bring about, mean, facilitate*, and so on. Once again, future opportunities that would exist given the conditions the policy authors outline are presented as valuable artifacts. No explicit evaluation for *Desirability* or *Importance* is necessary: the irrealis promised land of *opportunities* requires only certain forms of action at the right time. The word *would* provides an evaluation for the *Probability* of outcomes related to *exposure*, but becomes an obligatory *should* in the axiological chaining of *would help* ➤ *would expose* ➤ *is essential*. The chain develops its force in "retrospective" propagation (Lemke, 1998, pp. 52-53). The term *is essential* casts its hortatory force back along the chain to propagate the *Necessity* of exposing *schools* to *work*: *would help* ◄ *would expose* ◄ *is essential*. The propositional *would* is thus shifted by retrospective propagation to an hortatory *should* or, more strongly, a *must*.

"Opening up" new ways of seeing, being, and acting

The inculcation of ways of seeing, being, and acting is an inherent aspect of policy discourse (Fairclough, 2000). It is an overt function of new media policy. Certain irrealis spaces are presented as new spaces that would more concretely be seen: *vistas, horizons, perspectives,* and so on:

> In the future, the main possibilities for manufacturers, whose horizons for the moment remain primarily European, will be linked to the expected opening up of the American market .... (fr3: 16,736)

In this example from France, the process metaphor is embedded in a projected nominal group, a disembodied "expectation." The strategic advantage of nominalizing the process metaphor is to hide some nonsense and submerge an admission of dependency. Future *possibilities* for French *manufacturers*, whose *horizons* are currently limited to Europe, *will be linked to expectations* of an irrealis space *opening up*. That is to say, the *main possibilities* of French manufacturers are linked to another set of *possibilities* which are shifted towards higher degree of *Probability* by being *expected* by unspecified persons. Put concretely, this says: *The future opportunities of French manufacturers depend on whether the American market opens up*—an admission of dependency. To be realized as overt process metaphor, this construal would have to read something like *the expected liberalization [opening up; deregulation] of the American market **will open up** the main possibilities for manufacturers.*

The geographical metaphors of *trails* and *paths* provide the nexus between social activity and its legal regulation. In the following example, legal expertise and legal language are the means by which *new paths* can be paved:

> France has a meaningful voice to be heard in this respect, which should amount to more than just exporting its "model" of data protection; given the country's experience in these matters, France must and can put forward propositions that open up new paths. (fr2: 14,231)

New legal *trails* are being blazed in France, ones of a very specific nature and orientation:

> The current positive law covering communications would not be capable of serving as a basis for the entire analysis relating to criminal liability. The first cases brought before the courts open up certain trails which confirm that inspiration can be drawn from foreign examples. It then becomes appropriate to formulate recommendations which are based both on a clarification of the relevant rules and recognition of the role of a joint regulatory body. (fr2: 64,483)

The legal trails being blazed here are concerned with intellectual property, with the ownership of the products of people's minds: "How does one become an owner of productive stock? How does one become owner of the product created by means of this stock? Through *positive law*" (Marx, 1844/1975, p. 295). The legal definition of existing social relations is perhaps the most significant aspect of any transition in human social relations. It is the means by which formal feudalism and the basis of capital, private property, were established (Bloch, 1940/1961, pp. 72-73; Hobsbawm, 1962, p. 46; Marx, 1844/1975). The mere mention of a "knowledge economy" implies new commodity forms and new property laws—intellectual property laws— which depend on the codification and definition of new types of *property*, and thus new spatial domains. New *positive law* is needed to define and own the newly commodifiable products of labor, products of everyday human interaction—thought and language.

Making marketspace

As might well be expected in the neoliberal policy climate of the current age, the most attractive irrealis space being "opened up" is the activity space of *markets*:

Internet opens up global markets.

The market must lead. The government's first job is to remove obstacles, and champion the way ahead.

Setting out a vision and a clear direction.

Where government intervenes, the results must progress us towards becoming a knowledge-driven economy. We must have a sense of urgency. We've won against the odds before ... we can again.

Throughout our history, New Zealanders have shown a remarkable ability to respond in a positive way to world events. Just as the first shipment of refrigerated meat aboard the SS Dunedin in February 1882 opened up new overseas markets for our primary products, so the Internet opens up new markets for our knowledge exports. These include such products as software, technology, education, film, television, Web design, telecommunications, financial services, call centres and others, all of which can travel down the information superhighways to the world at the speed of light. (nzknow1:17,456)

The New Zealand authors are overtly concerned with new "territory"—a market space filled with opportunities. The policy authors cast their government as a pioneering trailblazer. The government must *remove obstacles, and champion the way ahead*. But within the first two sentences of this text, the propositions become either circular or redundant because there are two distinct meanings of "markets." This is evidenced in the two consecutive clauses: *Internet opens up global markets. The market must lead.* In the first sentence, *global markets*, means a global space defined by the activities of producing, buying, and selling commodities. In the second sentence, in which the *market must lead*, refers to market logic, principles, and values, as defined by neoliberalism.

The authors' panic is barely concealed when they say that New Zealand is running *against the odds* and that the government *must have a sense of ur-*

gency about all of this.[48] The clear distinction between geographical and activity spaces becomes evident when the authors claim that a *shipment of refrigerated meat opened up new overseas markets* in 1882. That being the case, the authors are not concerned with the existence of new geographical markets, since none have been "created" for quite some time. Nor could even the most confused person buy into the claim that a *shipment of refrigerated meat opened up new overseas markets* in any literal sense. Here, the process metaphorical function becomes apparent. It is buried under nonsensical prose.

The trailblazing shipment of *refrigerated meat* presumably did not depart all by itself from New Zealand for foreign lands in order to *open up new markets*; it merely *signified* the existence of new markets, or, more precisely: a) the newly acquired ability that New Zealanders developed to keep their products fresh during long sea voyages via the medium of refrigerated ships; b) the pre-existence of commercial and legal relationships between New Zealand traders and institutions in other countries that made trading shiploads of refrigerated meat practical and legal; c) the qualities that made New Zealand's refrigerated meat a desirable commodity for people in other countries; and d) the ability of New Zealand farmers to produce enough meat to establish practical commercial and legal relationships throughout the world. So the use of *opened up* here collapses all sorts of participants, circumstances, relationships, activities, processes, and other abstractions in the strange clause that says *refrigerated meat opened up new markets*. The main point to note here is that New Zealand's historic meat ship and the internet are being used by the authors to conflate very different conceptions of new marketspaces. The nineteenth century was still a time of geographical frontiers and navigational challenges. New land could be found, claimed, and tamed. Many new ways of navigating and traversing the globe, especially in respect of trade, were yet to be developed. The authors confound the very real frontiers of nineteenth-century trade and travel with the metaphorical, irrealis "frontiers" of new media networks.

The most extreme expressions of neoliberal dogma are possible when expectations of the irrealis are too heavily overlaid upon the present:

> With the advent of information and communication technologies, the vision of perfect competition is becoming a reality. Consumers can now find out the prices offered by all vendors for any product. New markets have opened up, and prices have dropped. When businesses can deliver their products down a phone line anywhere in the world, twenty-four hours a day, the advantage goes to the firm that has the greatest value addition, the best known brand, and the lowest 'weight.' Software provides the best example: huge added value through computer code, light 'weight' so that it can be delivered anywhere at any time.
>
> Competition is fostered by the increasing size of the market opened up by these technologies. Products with a high knowledge component generate higher returns

and a greater growth potential. Competition and innovation go hand in hand. Products and processes can be swiftly imitated and competitive advantage can be swiftly eroded. Knowledge spreads more quickly, but to compete a firm must be able to innovate more quickly than its competitors. (nzknow1:3,920)

Here is at least one reason why the "knowledge economy" is treated with such enthusiasm in policy. Contemporary econometrics is well known for its lack of ability to cope with the unpredictable muck of reality (Saul, 1997). New technologies will solve the problems of reality by making *the vision of perfect competition a reality*. The reality is, unfortunately, exactly the opposite of that posited by neoliberal economics. Media ownership concentration is at an historic high (Kellner, 1999; McChesney, 2000). Monopolies appear to be the paradoxical outcome of increasingly *perfect competition*, a point not lost on Marx. Moreover, the product that *provides the best example* of new economy goods, *software*, is perhaps the most monopolistic of all, as evidenced by the many anti-competition suits launched against Microsoft.

The process metaphorical function of *opened up* is perhaps less obvious here, partly because of its past tense, partly because it is agentless, and partly because of the level of abstraction in the single participant, *new markets*. Markets are activity spaces, mass processes involving many people, interactions, places, and things. There are many different kinds of markets: labor markets, financial markets, software markets, commodity markets, fruit markets, geographically defined markets, and so on. We are left unsure as to which *new markets have opened up*. But if we assume that *perfect competition* and consumers having *perfect knowledge* of *prices* are predicated upon *the advent of information and communication technologies*, then the process metaphor becomes more obvious. Put more directly, the relationship is this: *With the advent of information and communication technologies new markets have opened up* [in the first instance, *appeared; come into being; become accessible, etc.*]. But even with that relationship made clear, the metaphorical scope of the process is still not entirely exposed. To see the scope of the metaphor, we need to further consider time and tense, and how these are manipulated in policy to become space.

The temporal relations between ostensibly linked propositions in the second New Zealand text is confusing because of the mixture of tenses deployed: the *present*-ness of *is becoming a reality* and of *can now find out*, conflict with the *past*-ness of *have opened up* and the *future*-ness of *when businesses can deliver their products down a phone line*. We are left unsure as to which elements are predicated upon which others, and of the qualitative aspects of the markets that have previously *opened up*. Presumably, the markets the authors refer to must have been *opened up* prior to *consumers* having complete access to price knowledge. The confusion of past, present, and future, and the consequent lack of clear causal and temporal relationships, makes the propositional content of the passage elusive: while perfect competition is presented as the result of *information and communication technologies*, *new markets* are already presupposed in the availability of perfect price information and product availability. The ability of *businesses* to *deliver their products down a phone line* appears to be set in the future. However, in the next paragraph, *the increasing size of the market* is again *opened up by these technologies*, resulting in more *competition*. Products *with a high knowledge component*—those that can be delivered over the phone—appear in the present.

When all this is unpacked in terms of causal and temporal relations, the metaphorical scope of *opened up* becomes more clear. The market, its products, its producers, and its prices are *already* present: new media *makes these available*; *exposes* them *to* competition; *relates* them to all the others; *signifies* their existence for people, along with their *Significance*; *creates* markets as social and symbolic spaces of interaction; and *facilitates* awareness of all participants in the market process to all others, thus *creating perfect competition*. The superficial singularity and materiality of *opened up* appears to be something that has *already happened*. But it actually collapses and confuses causal relations, uniting past and future happenings, awarenesses, possibilities, knowings, and doings for all the participants in the marketspace of the knowledge economy, thereby bringing into being an econometric utopia: a space in which the reality of perfect competition, perfect information, and the absence of transaction costs are realized.

Drawing the contours of a digital utopia

All of the future spaces that are elaborated to any extent in the large corpus of new media policies I have analyzed are symbolic activity spaces. Whether referring metaphorically to the vague outlines of irrealis spaces, or to currently "protected" social activities, what is said to be "opening up" in policy are *possibilities* and *opportunities* for the further commodification of existing human activities: *education, biological processes, thought, art, language services, cultural production, imagination,* and so on. The most intimate, delicate, and ephemeral expressions of human social interaction are to be drawn from whole nations and sold off as commodities in the "knowledge economy." But the kinds of activities that policy authors posit as the basis of the "new economy" are not new in any way whatsoever. They are existing activities that are to be formally redefined for "removal" into a "new" space.

And it is this largely "undefined" space into which much of human conscious activity is to move which is of most historical significance. It is a *concrete space*, one that certain groups of people have only very recently developed the technological, institutional, and legal means to colonize on a global scale. The concrete space being prefigured as property is electromagnetic space, or bandwidth, or "electrospace" (Hinchman, 1969 in Smythe, 1981, pp. 300-318). Throughout history, the social meaning of concrete spaces has, to a very large extent, characterized each particular age (Marx, 1973, pp. 276-283). Concrete spaces exist independently of what people do. They include land, air, sea, and electrospace. They are fundamental to any new form of political economy. This is most noticeable during recent times in the development of industrial capitalism and its relation to land:

> *wage labour* in its totality is initially created by the action of capital on landed property, and then, as soon as the latter has been produced as a form, by the proprietor of the land himself. This latter then 'clears' … the land of its excess mouths, tears the children of the earth from the breast on which they were raised, and thus transforms labour on the soil itself, which appears by its nature as the direct wellspring of subsistence, into a mediated source of subsistence, a source purely dependent on social relations. (Marx, 1973, p. 276)

Which is also to say that the globally mediated nature of human interaction is epiphenomenal. It first requires the existence of a new "type" of private property. After staring at the ever expanding edge of electrospace, concentrating on the spatial, social, and technical qualities of the electromagnetic spectrum, Dallas Smythe concludes that electrospace "is to communications today as is land to crops and water to fish. It is a peculiar natural resource, one whose politico-economic and social aspects have largely been ignored by social scientists" (1981, pp. 300-318). In short, it is a geotechnical space that can be, and is being, turned into property.

Electrospace barely rates a mention in new media policy. Only once in the 1.3 million word corpus, in an Australian document, is it discussed in terms of "available electromagnetic space," and even then it gets confused with data transfer capacity:

> Bandwidth refers to the range of frequencies, expressed in Hertz (Hz), that can pass over a given transmission channel. The bandwidth determines the rate at which information can be transmitted through a circuit.

> The phenomenal growth projected in electronic commerce will significantly affect the demand for bandwidth. The growth in online transactions for intangibles such as delivery of entertainment and educational products will also fuel demand. In Australia, demand for bandwidth is expected to grow strongly for the retail trade; property and business services; education; and health and community services sectors over the next five years. (au_kba: 7,622)

Although the authors implicitly distinguish between commodity categories— *entertainment*; *retail trade*; *property and business services*; *education*; *health and community services*—and identify electrospace as a medium of sorts, this is a most perfunctory and confused treatment of what is actually being proposed. It collapses three meanings of bandwidth currently in use: the first refers to electrospace, the second to the rate of data transfer, the third to a commodity form. They are far from identical meanings, even though there are relationships between them. Furthermore, none grasp the essential features of electrospace as a geotechnical space that requires sole occupancy to be of any political economic advantage in digital capitalism, like land in industrial capitalism.

A far greater awareness of bandwidth as being concrete space was prevalent when it was first brought to widespread attention in the early proliferation of broadcast radio (Childs, 1924, p. 520). Throughout history, and I see no reason for the current period to be any different, the media environment has been a decisive influence in the distribution of political power, the essence of which is control of people within a particular space (Carey, 1989; Innis, 1951; Mumford, 1962; Smythe, 1981). And power, in the end, is a central focus for any critical approach to political economy. Policy is concerned almost entirely with the *activities* that are or will have been commodified in the next "new economy." That is to say, the function of new media policy is not to identify or explain the foundations of an emergent political economy. Rather, it is to identify the aspects of labor that will be commodified in this new space. These include everything from art and imagination, to education and engineering, to entertainment and research, to practically any kind of symbolic labor whatsoever. As far as policy is concerned, people must act and think in particular ways if their labor is to be made fit for commodification in what will be the "knowledge economy."

Quibbles over the ownership of electromagnetic spectrum may seem mundane in terms of what is being proposed in the policy corpus: namely the commodification of practically everything that defines us as human (and inhuman in many cases). But it should be noted that the global privatization of bandwidth is an historically unique proposal. Electrospace is objective common property, the global enclosure of which is presupposed in policy and apparently needs no explanation. Grabs for whole spectrum blocs have to date been the concern of nation-states: "radio communication is particularly susceptible to national control because, to a much greater extent than other communication media, the radio requires *some* control if it is to serve any human purpose whatsoever" (Church, 1939). But today there is a fully developed system of international institutions that can provide the legal infrastructure to define and formalize social interaction; to make property, commodity, and contract laws; and to enforce these on a global scale.

Until quite recently,

> nations of the world have never departed from the basic "world property" concept
> of the right to use specific radio frequency assignments, such rights have in prac-
> tice been treated as one of the most important bases of politico-economic power
> on a first-come, first served policy. (Smythe, 1981, p. 307)

Today this power is being privatized. Unlike copper wire, fiber optics, or satellite infrastructure, radio spectrum is the non-depletable, concrete resource upon
which any global economy, if it is to exist at all, must eventually be built
(Rosston and Steinberg, 1997). The concrete qualities of electrospace are almost incomprehensible. Because electromagnetic spectrum exists everywhere
all the time at all frequencies, the current bandwidth legislators construe electrospace as a kind of "space in the fourth dimension" which should be left
"open to private exploitation, vesting title to the waves according to priority
of discovery and occupation," but that is not the case:

> Of course, the wave length is not a fourth dimension, for there is also breadth and
> depth of wave (amplitude and frequency) and doubtless the correct analogy is the
> whole electro-magnetic field; but private property in any natural field or wave is
> only a human convention and one that it would be dangerous to extend to *this
> new-discovered continent*. The theory that otherwise it cannot be developed has al-
> ready been demonstrated to be untrue. Otherwise only can it be kept free from
> monopoly. (Childs, 1924, pp. 522-523, emphasis added)

In 1924, electrospace was indeed a "new-discovered continent." Today,
though, it is a continent that has become as conceptually opaque as land, perhaps more so. That is because bandwidth is generally sold as amounts of
time, and because it cannot be seen or touched. It has thus been relegated to
the status of myth. Electrospace is now not widely conceived of as concrete
property, at least not in policy.

Even those officials charged with selling electrospace to private interests
seem confused about the character of the space. The language advocating
spectrum privatization is shot through with all the clarion calls of colonial-
ism, and with all the "pioneering" images that adorn the frontier-conquering
mindset. Consequently, in however an unconscious and confused manner, the
spatial aspects of language are clear and present:

> I truly believe that encouraging more bandwidth, particularly, to residential con-
> sumers in the country, is the next great frontier in communications policy.

> As I was saying, bandwidth is the great ... the next great frontier in communica-
> tions policy. And I want the hallmark of this Commission's work to be that we
> encourage the competitive provision of high speed networks and services using
> any appropriate technology for all Americans wherever they live, at home, at
> work, in schools, libraries, hospitals, whether they live in cities or in rural areas,
> on reservations. Wherever there's demand, there should be bandwidth. (Kennard,
> 1998 in FCC, 1998)

Here again in the US Federal Communications Commission's argument to
"deregulate" bandwidth we see the same expansive aspects of social life im-

plicated as in the policy concerned with proposing the commodification of human activity. But this time the talk is referring to foundational space, *actual space*—newly enclosable property, not something that there can be suddenly *more* of by fiat.

Typically, such talk is accompanied by the liberatory enthusiasms that have accompanied "revolutions" throughout history. Here is another Federal Communications Commissioner bidding farewell to the national character of electrospace:

> I think this is *an extraordinary crossroad* in our intellectual thinking with regard to communication services, and we should keep that in mind. In a sense, the beginning of *crossing the rubicon*, sort of *leaving the world of legacy systems and their inherent limitations* not only in technology and the kinds of communication services we provide to the public, but as well in the regulatory structure that was built up and served well, and to a great degree, administering national policy with respect to those sorts of systems.

> And so, this really is *one of the many opening salvos of an important transition*, both in terms of the way we provide communication services and the way that we regulate them. (Powell, 1998 in FCC, 1998)

Powell is firing off *salvos* as he prepares to *cross the rubicon* into a new land, enthusiastically mixing metaphors and confusing medium, message, national regulation, and service provision with the meaning of private property in electrospace.

The underpinning assumption of the new (de)regulatory push for bandwidth is that, because of the digitally convergent nature of our new technological environment, *modes of communication between people have become qualitatively indistinguishable*: "I would say that if not already, in the very immediate future, it gets rather basic. Bits is bits. Voice is data. Data is voice. Video is data. They're all the same" (Chrust, 1998 in FCC, 1998). There is much in history to refute the Commissioner's assertions that "bits is bits"; radio waves is radio waves; space is space. Such remarks misrecognize mediation, ignoring the fact that as a process it involves people, their cultures, and their historical and extant knowledge economies (cf. Innis, 1951; Silverstone, 1999; McLuhan, 1964). We might as well say "trucks is trucks," regardless of whether they are moving nuclear weapons, wheat, or anthrax. From such a perspective "all roads lead to Rome" and the rest is so much irrelevant noise. With all eyes fixed towards future conquest of social, cultural, intellectual, and legislative activities, and to the conquest and enclosure of the electromagnetic commonwealth, the armies of the faithful march fervently onwards supported by a technologically inspired faith.

"Content" and property policies in the knowledge economy

In all of this—in the privatization of formerly common property and the global commodification of human activity at the most intimate levels—we see an incipient prefiguring of what policymakers and telecommunications industry experts think should happen in the irrealis utopia of the knowledge economy. The symbolic activities of humans are to be commodified and traded within a privatized, globalized electrospace. The unifying principle underpinning both "types" of policy is that it will ideally encompass and commodify *all* aspects of human activity *everywhere*. There is nothing that should not be bought and sold according to neoliberal tenets. The policy concerned with spectrum ownership is oriented to reaching people *wherever they live, at home, at work, in schools, libraries, hospitals, whether they live in cities or in rural areas*, *on reservations*, and so on. Similarly, for policy concerned with those aspects of humanity that are to be modified for, and commodified within, a newly enclosed electrospace, the legislative *vistas* include changing how people *live, learn, work, create, buy* and *sell*. The privately owned, concrete property element will ideally extend to enclose all of humanity; the commodity element will ideally infuse every aspect of what it means to be human. In policy, time and space are conflated in the irrealis utopia that new media policy is creating on a worldwide basis.

It is not surprising to find that policy constructed in an age dominated by fundamentalist neoliberal economics has the most personal aspects of people as the primary focus of the commodification process. We owe such an oppressive global condition to the failure of political economy to understand its object. Nevertheless, neoliberal economics has become very successful in dominating administrative logic and colonizing the channels of public opinion throughout much of humanity. But political economy continues to misunderstand private property, the element on which its claims to expertise are premised, and the foundations upon which any new political economy must be based. To this day, political economy continues to presuppose the property element. That is all the more pronounced considering that we are in the historically unique situation of seeing the creation of new private property on a global scale in the global enclosure of electrospace. It is the largest continuous expanse of property we can possibly realize under existing technical conditions. Consequently we are in the situation of seeing the creation of the largest division of "*property owners* and propertyless *workers*" in history (Marx, 1844/1975, p. 322). Simple possession has nothing to do with the matter. At the same time as "the digital divide" continues to be loudly touted by groups of legislators as the issue that most needs addressing, another related group of legislators are busily working towards the only possible means by which such a fundamental division can be created and sustained for any length of time. Almost the entire body of "knowledge economy" and "information society" policy ignores the creation of this new private property, focusing instead on rationalizing the commodification of human thought, language, art, imagination, communication, creativity, and emotion. These are the labors of the propertyless knowledge worker that will be commodified in the institutional edifices that will control the medium through which all electronically mediated experience must eventually pass. Should full techno-logical realization of the property element prove to be possible (there are doubts that this can be accomplished), the implications cannot be overstated: it would amount to the corporate colonization of every aspect of *propertyless* humanity. Moreover, as basis of political power since radio, the privatization of electrospace is essentially the privatization of political power on a global scale: the privatization (or rather *corporatization*) *of global political power*. What is now only a barely covert influence in world politics must, if the me-dium of political power becomes wholly owned by corporate interests, become an overt and singular influence, leading to outright structural domi-nance on the part of its future owners. Alienation of thought, language, and the most intimate aspects of biology is the apotheosis of a long-standing pa-thology that is based upon the legal definition and ownership of others' lives, of their life energies, and of the products of these. The gene pools of whole nations are now being sold off to private interests (Williams, 2000). The cur-rent process of total enclosure is, or will be, at its most complete if and when the irrealis spaces being claimed process-metaphorically in current technol-ogy policy are allowed to become the basis of positive law. The language of policy *is* the discourse of contemporary political economy.

CHAPTER EIGHT

Eat my head

Consciousness is the total awareness of life which people have. It includes their understanding of themselves as individuals and of their relations with other individuals in a variety of forms of organization, as well as with their natural environment. Consciousness is a dynamic process. It grows and decays with the interaction of doing (or practice) and cognition over the life cycle of the individual in the family and other social formations. It draws on emotions, ideas, instincts, memory and all the other sensory apparatus. (Smythe, 1981, pp. 270-271)

Consciousness can never be anything else than conscious existence, and the existence of men is their actual life-process. (Marx and Engels, 1846/1975, p. 118)

The global privatization of electrospace marks the current period as historically unique in political economic terms. Electrospace has been the basis of national political power for a century. Understanding this fact helps us understand the profound character of the political economic upheavals in which we currently find ourselves. The creation of a global cyberspace amounts to nothing less than the enclosure or "privatization" of consciousness. A full and formally defined cyberspace, at least as it is currently conceived of, must eventually lead to the alienation of human social existence at its most fundamental and definitive levels: the forms of consciousness that arise from social relatedness and lived experience.

Cyberspace is the space in which human decisions are made. As is well known, the "cyber" in cyberspace has very old roots, "Kyber" meaning "helmsman" in Greek. Seen as a global phenomenon, "cyberspace" refers literally to the helm of the vessel in which we are all travelers. This is a point not lost on the United States Military, which aims at "full spectrum dominance":

The ultimate goal of our military force is to accomplish the objectives directed by the National Command Authorities. For the joint force of the future, this goal will be achieved through full spectrum dominance. [...] The label full spectrum dominance implies that US forces are able to conduct prompt, sustained, and synchronized operations with combinations of forces tailored to specific situations and with access to and freedom to operate in all domains—space, sea, land, air, and information. (Joint Chiefs of Staff, 2000, p. 6)

"Information" is tacked on to the end of these "domains," almost as an after-thought (Miller, 2004). But its working definition could not be more specific or expansive:

> *Information operations* is the employment of the core capabilities of electronic warfare, computer network operations, psychological operations, military decep-tion, and operations security, in concert with specified supporting and related capabilities, to affect or defend information and information systems, and to influ-ence decisionmaking. (Department of the Army, 2003)

Little wonder that that the most powerful military force in history recognizes its future is in the dominance of cyberspace—literally, the space from within which control of all previous forms of space is coordinated. Yet even in the most technologically advanced organization on earth, the most powerful space is construed as an aspect of time, namely conscious human engagement with each other and the rest of the world.

Space is a relatively new and therefore difficult concept. Perhaps it is for that reason that it gets largely ignored in studies of political economy. Even when the subject of space is broached, political economy has tended to em-phasize the time aspect, such as labor, the circulation of money and commodities, rent, the depletion of buildings and machinery, the movement of information, and so on (Enke, 1942). But the *meaning* of space is, for the most part, left untouched as a problem. In other words, space—as exempli-fied by land—is generally assumed to be an unproblematic concept; it is the activities that go on within and between particular spaces that most of politi-cal economy focuses on, again because "labor" is the most unruly and unpredictable element in political economy. But the legal definition and own-ership of land is the very basis of private property. Without it, capitalism could not have emerged as a system. The legal and technical redefinition and privatization of land is the historical basis of private property and capitalism. As an idea and a reality, the privatization of land became taken for granted relatively quickly, even though it took more than 300 years and much vio-lence to achieve.

Still, it is quite understandable that space is typically reduced to aspects of human activity because the existence of a set of more or less informal and flexible social relationships within a given space is essential to its formal definition as an objective entity—as freestanding, privately owned and ow-nable property. Put differently, we create the possibility for property only by doing what we do within certain spaces. Consequently, our ideas about the meaning of space are inseparably tied to our experiences of property, work, family, community, and nationality. They are a function of the entire web of activities and relationships in which we are embedded. And this is the central paradox of political economy, as well as the paradoxical flip-side to scientific constructions of the future as a kind of space. We make many kinds of spaces by doing what we do: social space, organic space, symbolic space and geographical space, to name only a few. For example, a workplace conversation can be viewed as creating many different types of social and symbolic spaces all at once: it creates and maintains interpersonal spaces, or relationships between people; attitudinal spaces, or cultures; organizational spaces, within which social behaviors are regulated; and ideational spaces, in which unique ways of knowing are created, preserved, and transformed, such as in a university, a monastery, a legal firm, or a factory.

But these social and symbolic spaces are of a distinctly different type than the much less ephemeral, much more tangible kinds of space that constitute the "common sense" understanding of property, such as the land and buildings in which a workplace conversation takes place. Social and symbolic spaces are activity spaces and are therefore time-bound. Geotechnical spaces—like land, sea, air, and electrospace—exist independently of what people do. They contain and constrain what people do and they share a common aspect in that they can only be occupied exclusively: two different people, or groups, or factories, or cities, or nations cannot occupy the same space at the same time. It is an impossibility. The same holds for electrospace: a particular frequency cannot be used at the same time by different people or organizations. Like land, electrospace must be occupied exclusively if it is to be used for any purpose whatsoever. Electrospace is the geotechnical aspect of cyberspace; it is the concrete arena within which digitized symbolic and social spaces are produced, reproduced, and exchanged.

Electrospace, cyberspace, and political economy

To understand the historical significance of "privatizing" electrospace it is imperative that its concrete nature be understood. For the past decade, electrospace has been steadily "cleared" of its public occupants and "enclosed." The assumption underpinning this trajectory is that internet traffic will "migrate from personal computers to devices like cell phones and hand-held computers," and that the spectrum must therefore be privatized (US to clean up, 2004). Whether or not internet traffic does "migrate" to cellphones and hand-held devices to any significant degree remains to be seen. But the imperatives from legislators and business that bandwidth must be cleared for such an occurrence are very insistent. The advent of radio was the first time people made use of electrospace for the purposes of mass communication. Since then, electrospace has become more and more crowded with the inclusion of television, microwave, infrared, cellphone, radar, and satellite signals.

The public nature of the area currently being sold off (or given away in some cases) is well-evidenced by the nature of its incumbent occupants. For example, in the United States, the Defense Department, "law enforcement authorities and public safety organizations" were asked to "shift" their entire communication systems to other, less commercially "useful" spaces (US to clean up, 2004). That ought to be enough in itself to raise questions about the social efficacy of the global bandwidth privatization. Electrospace is *literal and concrete* rather than virtual and symbolic space; it is just like land. It must be understood as such to understand the historical significance of the current age.

The consciousness of electrospace as a concrete space was far more prevalent when radio first emerged as a dominant medium. What brought this aspect to the fore was a self-conscious sense of nationalism throughout the most technologically advanced countries, especially following the unprecedented slaughters of the first World War. A concern with mass propaganda, most notably in the United States, brought with it the realization that electrospace was essential to the cultivation of nationalism.

It was therefore quickly realized that electrospace is a geotechnical space because it can only be used effectively as a political base if occupied exclusively. Over the last century, it has become the ultimate public resource, as essential to political power as air and water are to the survival of the human organism. The concrete nature of electrospace has slid, for the most part, into the realms of incomprehensibility for people. One consequence is that electrospace is now officially viewed as a commodity by the US Federal Communications Commission (FCC):

> The spectrum sharing plan will further the Commission's goal of efficient spectrum utilization by increasing the number of providers offering services to consumers over the same spectrum, and will promote the deployment of more innovative services to consumers. (FCC, 2004)

Alternatively, legislators treat electrospace like "raw material," or as a kind of other-worldly space that should, according to the tenets of neoliberalism, be privatized to more efficiently realize economic gains. Because of increased technical capacity, electrospace has become a global space. Unfortunately, it has become invisible, both as space and a source of political power. It is sold as quantities of time and understood as such. But in political economic terms, the time aspect is invariably and inevitably tied to labor, to what people do. In any cyberspace, the activities that must be technically redefined, appropriated, and commodified are the products of human consciousness.

Harvesting the labors of consciousness

Like ownership of space, ownership of human activity and its products is a matter of law. The legal distribution of property rights in the ownership of human activity and interaction is perhaps the most overt aspect of any transition in human social relations. John of Salisbury's *Policratus* is historically instructive in this respect. It comes

> just before the important turning-point in institutional development at the end of the twelfth and the beginning of the thirteenth century, when legal precision began to be stamped on a number of previously indefinite relationships, and when feudal independence tended to become consolidated into definite organs of political control. (Dickinson, 1926, p. 309)

Similarly today, new forms of legal precision are being stamped on human social relations at the most intimate levels. There is also a pervasive sense, as there was during the enclosures movement, that there exists an unbreachable and quite conscious distance between the people who define rules for human behavior, for value creation, and for almost all forms of human activity, and those who are bound by those rules but are excluded from making them.

Just as the definition of geotechnical spaces and social relationships are a function of legal expertise, so it is for other social technologies, such as policies that define the legitimacy of money-forms, production technologies, management techniques, and the ways in which legally sanctioned violence (war and punishment) are organized. As such, expert legal and political definitions can also formalize and fix (to a certain extent and for a certain time) meanings of social space. Legal definitions transform informal relationships into formal and legal ones, rendering flexible and variegated social relationships as relatively inflexible symbolic spaces, such as systems of law or management. It was from strenuous and sustained efforts in these directions that the historical development of wage labor became the dominant method of appropriating human energy—human life—or what political economy has called "labor."

This is also the case in what is being called the "knowledge economy," although pre-capitalist labor relations are once again becoming dominant methods of appropriating people's labor (piecework, casualization, and outsourcing). The aspect of social activity which is technologized and commodified in cyberspace is its *conscious* aspect. Not surprisingly, today's most frenetic legal activities are concerned with the ownership of the products of consciousness, or "intellectual property" (see, e.g., WIPO, 2000). With the not-so-gradual development of a global, privately owned electrospace, a practical, artificial, humanity-wide split is being affected— technologically and at law—between labors of the muscle and labors of the mind. The artifacts of consciousness that people produce in the production, reproduction, and transformation of their social spaces are the commodity-forms of any knowledge economy. While the activities and social relations that correspond to new commodity-forms continue to differ in levels of legal and economic formality, the aspects of humanity which are to be formalized in cyberspace include every facet, function, and product of consciousness.

"Information" produced for people, by people, and about people is supposedly the basis of any knowledge economy. As we have seen, art, science, culture, education, communication, and commerce are said by the authors of policy to be the social domains within which knowledge commodities are created. But to focus solely on the commodity-forms produced within specific activity spaces is to miss most parts of the picture, namely their social, biological, environmental, and geotechnical foundations. With increasing attention given to intellectual property regimes, a new formality is being stamped upon existing social and biological relations of globalized humanity. More particularly, legal formality and money values are being placed on the conscious relationships that we have with the array of symbolic artifacts we call our culture:

> So uncritically do we accept the idea of property in culture that we don't even question when the control of that property removes our ability, as a people, to develop our culture democratically. Blindness becomes our common sense. And the challenge for anyone who would reclaim the right to cultivate our culture is to find a way to make this common sense open its eyes. So far, common sense sleeps [...]. The extremism that now dominates [the intellectual property] debate fits with ideas that seem natural, and that fit is reinforced by the RCAs of our day. They wage a frantic war to fight "piracy," and devastate a culture for creativity. They defend the idea of "creative property," while transforming real creators into modern-day sharecroppers. (Lessig, 2004, pp. 261-262)

Today, in the development of intellectual property rights, relations between such human intimacies as words, sounds, and genes are being formalized in laws that are designed to be imposed worldwide (Lessig, 2004; WIPO, 2000, p. 2).

Flippantly defining the products of conscious activity as "goods of the mind," or biotechnological products as wealth derived from the "essence of life," does little to clarify the picture or its implications for what it means to be human (Barlow, 1998). Such a view misses the point that these are already freely existing relations. But these parts of human existence are being technically redefined in legal and political discourse so as to be ownable and sellable as quickly as they fall within legal reach. As such, the redefinition of these relations, and of electrospace, is nothing less than the largest and most pernicious attempt at outright theft by a group of elites in the history of humanity, if only because of the sheer size of the current human population. Individuals are currently buying the gene pools of whole countries, with the governments of Tonga, Estonia, and Iceland selling property rights in their constituencies' gene pools.

Underpinning the global expropriation of human consciousness is a set of contradictions inherent in any knowledge economy, at least as it is currently conceived of by its corporate and legislative designers. These are: the assumed predominance of the exchange-values (money) over production-values, the values of creativity, and the whole range of human values that fall outside the money system; the collapse of distribution and consumption into the same moment as that of production and exchange; and the subsumption of use-value (usability) under the logic of exchange-value (salability). One result is that the production of money becomes an increasingly irresistible imperative. But money is just the idea of value given a (sometimes) physical form—money is itself a product of imagination and discourse. A brief excursion is necessary to comprehend the historical significance of these actual and conceptual implosions.

Human axiologies in the alien realities of cyberspace

Axiologies are the cultural logics through which the value of any given aspect of our environment is produced, attributed, and expressed by people. Axiologies are expressed as patterns of social "preference" and "decision-takings" (Firth, 1951). Axiological patterns are achievements of history—a massive accumulation of normative work. Therefore axiologies specify the *acceptability* of what is perceived to be desirable within a given social domain. Because they are the product of expressed cultural choices, axiologies peculiar to any given social group are only perceptible in distinction to others. In a globally mediated social system, ideally encompassing the whole of humanity, the very concept of culture-specific axiologies takes on very complex dimensions and is a threat to the system it will allegedly nourish. Paradoxically, and perhaps because faced with such vast complexity and cultural differences, the axiological principles of policy have been narrowed to the most singular and simplistic system—price. Discourses of efficiency, growth, progress, and control derive their logics and technologies almost exclusively from this system:

> The more production comes to rest on exchange value, hence on exchange, the more important do the physical conditions of exchange—the means of communication and transport—become for the costs of circulation. Capital by its nature drives beyond every spatial barrier. Thus the creation of the physical conditions of exchange—of the means of communication and transport—the annihilation of space by time—becomes an extraordinary necessity for it. (Marx, 1973, p. 524)

And this is what has happened: exchange value has become an end in itself, and the "annihilation of space by time" is achieved by the *conceptual* shattering of concrete space (electrospace) and social space (human activity) into mediated *time* (conscious labor) through the manipulation of *spatial consciousness*. In policy, the complex of global axiologies has been reduced to expressions of space over time (how fast money circulates globally).

Paradoxically, the larger this number—the closer it gets to a mathematically undefined term, where circulation time equals zero—the greater the perceived efficiency of the system. In similar terms, conscious social activity (the production of social and symbolic space) is measured in terms of "the speed of thought" because, "expressed passively, the magnitude of labour appears as an amount of space; but expressed in motion, it is measurable only in time" (Marx, 1973, p. 321). When understood as time, social space is annihilated by imperatives for faster exchanges. There has never been so much human activity dedicated to the production of consciousness-commodities. Activity is time and time is money. Time is also the most ancient and basic measure of human life: "In Stoic physics there is no simple location, no analytical space," nor did there exist a "common sense" distinction between time and space during the archaic period—"time was the only reality, and space still had to be discovered—or invented—by Parmenides after 500 B.C." (de Santillana and von Dechend, 1962/1999). Space, in its contemporary conception, is a very new concept.

The destruction of space by time takes place by means of increased speed in social exchanges. In axiological terms, this is expressed as a relationship between the fastest possible speed at which perceptions of value can be exchanged across the greatest possible space. Axiological principles have therefore become the primary commodity-forms of knowledge economy production processes. The *production* of mediated perceptions of value across vast geographical and electrospaces is simultaneously an ongoing and immediate complex of consumption (destruction), circulation (distribution) and exchange (realization of price). A paradox of this temporally devastated system is that by decreasing time distances between people, it simultaneously annihilates existing *perceptions* of social space. So in any fully developed knowledge economy, the alienation of conscious human activity from its source, along with the perceived value of that activity, is complete.

Sui generis?

It is a commonplace bias of every age to think of itself as historically unique. At some level, this is necessarily true for every moment in history. But there are very few ages during which the relationships between great masses of people and their concrete spatial environments are redefined on such a far-reaching and fundamental level as is happening today. The privatization of global electrospace distinguishes the current era from any other as historically unique. Such periods combined the "legal" formalization of previously informal networks of social relations with the "legal" redefinition of geotechnical space. While electrospace is generally treated by legislators as little more than a complex time-bound conduit—a medium—for symbolic activities and institutional organization, it is not only that. It is property in the most precise economic definition of the word. Its most incomprehensible aspect is that it can only be traversed at a speed close to that of light. The speed of electrospace is its most confounding aspect. It conflates space and time because of the speed at which it must operate. But electrospace nevertheless retains its concrete spatial characteristics and there is more to grasping political economy than the technical definition and reallocation of property. We must grasp the domains of human activity that legislators are redefining, harnessing, and exposing to commodification in the emergent space: the commodity-forms of the economy and their relationship to their "producers" and "consumers"; the axiological basis upon which exchange, circulation and distribution are premised and enacted; and the global web of institutions that are responsible for defining all of these. Most importantly, we must consider which aspects of human social activity are to be commodified within this space, and whether such aspects *ought* to be legally commodified. And since electrospace is global—in fact our *only* global space—we must understand the relationships of those institutions who would claim ownership over what must become the property base for fiefdoms over the most abstract, intimate, abstract, and concrete aspects of humanity. These are the foundational tasks for any political economic analysis of a global knowledge economy.

CHAPTER NINE

Not the end

The social function of policy is to define the legal limits and principles by which economic resources are produced, evaluated, and distributed in a knowledge economy. Knowledge economy policies, tied as they are to new media, are multi-faceted exercises in applied epistemology: they not only attempt to define "what counts" as knowledge, but also how legitimate knowledge is to be produced: in which social domains "it" is to be produced; how it is to be valued; and, most importantly, what it means to be a knowledgeable person. The distribution of political power and economic values flow directly from such determinations.

The kinds of policy that I have focused on identify and delineate the kinds of activities that can and may be commodified in any future knowledge economy. But that is where the limitations of policy lie in its heuristic value for learning about the "newness" of current social transformations as they relate to new media. Policy focuses almost exclusively on the products of consciousness. In a repetition of its history, political economy, as it is expressed in policy, fails to grasp the historical significance of enclosing electrospace. This is, as I have argued in previous chapters, the most significant aspect of the "new economy" and what will define its character for some time to come.

The ambitious aims of this book are only partially met. I set out to identify relationships between value determination and policy language; to elaborate and demonstrate a method for analyzing evaluations made in policy language; to critically examine the capacity of Marx's political economic method for understanding what might be meant by a knowledge economy under current circumstances; to identify and elaborate historical relationships between new media, language, and social perceptions of value; and to identify relationships and trends that characterize the current period as historically unique. Much work remains to be done to complete these tasks in any comprehensive sense. But I have shown, at the very least, how critical studies of political economy of communication might benefit from critical sociolinguistic analysis, particularly where the development of a new theory of value is concerned. I believe this is of the utmost importance given the extent to which people's lives are currently colonized by money values.

The relationship between policy and value determination is analogous to that of canon law and the first crusades: speakers with the socially sanctioned, delegated, or divine expertise (or mixtures of all of these) can have profound effects on social value systems given favorable circumstances. Hitler and Stalin are recent exemplars, as are Walt Disney and Ted Turner. The first crusades were impossible without a widely propagated value system being set against, and defined in relation to, other demonized ones, as has been the case for totalitarianisms of all kind throughout the twentieth century. Any method for analyzing evaluations in language cannot separate itself from the social and historical contexts in which perceptions of value are produced, manipulated, and expressed. More confusingly, patterns of evaluation themselves get evaluated. And since observation is evaluation to some degree, any description of evaluations in language is an evaluation of evaluations, and therefore confronts the circularity of linguistically focused scholarship of any sort.

Grounding sociolinguistic studies within the conceptual apparatus of political economy mitigates against that circularity to some degree. But it must be acknowledged that political economy is simultaneously an evaluative, normative, and linguistic pursuit. In other words, a *critical* political economy is also a *reflexive* political economy which must attempt, as far as possible, to recognize its own social and historical positioning. So a critique of one's conceptual apparatus is essential. My efforts to understand and explain an emergent political economy have led me to use the fewest categories in the most expansive ways. Time, space, and value are the foundational aspects of the political economic perspective I have put forward here. But those are all just different perspectives on human activity. All human activity produces *something*: the possibilities for, and meanings of, space; the use, ownership, and meaning of time; the attribution, propagation, distribution, and meaning of "value." How these elements are distributed, configured, and understood at any given moment in history defines the political economic character of a system. All these elements of political economy are mediated—institutionally, culturally, socially, and technologically. Having the power to define the meaning of media and mediations is intrinsic to the character of any given historical period, hence my emphasis on the domain of political discourses about the meaning of new media.

Historical relationships between new media, language, and social perceptions of value are neither simple nor direct. With the emergence of new media, dominant patterns of evaluation peculiar to one social domain can be inculcated across vastly different social and geographical spaces, and for different durations throughout these. Cultural disjunctions, though, prohibit the positing of any singular or direct effects in the process of inculcation. Social situatedness and normative historical praxis are the refractive lenses through which propagated and inculcated value systems are transformed and dissipated. Most importantly, societal value systems and the patterns of evaluation through which they are expressed appear to be very resilient, which is to say that they do not simply disappear to be replaced with the next. Rather, new value systems get overlaid upon extant ones, just as new forms of mediation overlay older ones, and new ways of meaning exist within and "on top of" older language practices (Halliday, 1993; Innis, 1951). Rather than conveying a simple sedimentary process, I hope to have conveyed a sense of historical "weaving" and "warping" where axiological praxis is concerned. The resultant cultural fabric will, under certain circumstances, and from certain perspectives, appear to be very new; in other views it may seem positively ancient.

The bias of dominant media constrain and influence, to a surprising degree, the forms and types of meanings we can exchange, and the kinds of evaluations that are emphasized in specific media environments. Different media technologies are biased towards *the meaning* of different aspects of space and time (Carey, 1989; Innis, 1951; McLuhan, 1964; Postman, 1985). As I hope to have shown here, evaluations that are oriented towards spatial aspects of our experience are vastly different to those oriented towards the time element. Institutions, which are also media, also have their biases towards space and time. That difference can be seen in the value orientations between, for example, a town council, the World Trade Organization, and the Roman Catholic Church. The same sorts of differences in patterns of evaluation can be seen between those of a particular family and the education system within which the children of that family are immersed.

Having realized the confounding nature of a globally mediated political economic system, and the inadequacies of the conceptual framework of classical political economy to deal with the most basic phenomena confronting any conception of a "knowledge economy," I found myself driven back upon two of the most ineffable concepts in the human intellectual constellation: time and space. The resultant conceptual formulations therefore remain indistinct, serving only as indicators of possible directions in which political economy might move so as to comprehend the nature of the emergent system. A more developed reformulation of political economy would develop and refine different qualitative aspects of concrete space, social space, and social time, and their significance for grasping the changes in human relations being wrought. While John Armitage and I have emphasized the need to understand the cultural impacts of increased communication speed in political economy, a similar effort is required for conceptualizing different kinds of social space. The break from the conceptual apparatus of classical and neoclassical political economy that such an undertaking requires is radical and massive. It is doubtful whether the language necessary for such an undertaking will exist for some time.

My argument also suffers from the problems of generality. But the subject of a global economy—any aspect of a global economy—will tend towards "grand narrative" theory at the expense of a focus on individual agency and difference. However, and this is important in the context of what I have attempted to do here, historical contextualization of our global political economic system is both necessary and important, not merely because such a system does exist, but because it has become a central focus and rationale for policy decisions at all levels of government. Consequently, the perceived logic and values *of the system itself* has become the basis for political decisions that directly influence the distribution of resources and power throughout humanity. It requires understanding, however vaguely and generally, to begin with. Moreover, definitive specificity as regards the system is neither feasible nor practical because of its transitionary and unstable state at present. But such a transition might provide empirical material for the development of suitably flexible, "empty" categories that can readily adapt to the kinds of changes we are seeing.

A further reason for the generality is the institutional nature of the problems I have confronted. My research is not concerned with specific individuals; it is about patterns of evaluation at a social level. I have focused specifically on the institutions that make laws drawn from scientifically derived propositions. These laws are all directed towards, and have significant effects upon, the whole of humanity. Further, to emphasize the role of any particular individuals in the current trajectory would have a doubly negative and illusory effect: it would attribute far too much power to any individual involved in the complex processes at play in the transformation of global political economy. Conversely, it would diminish and compromise the significant role that institutionalized value systems play during any such period in history. Individuals who make policy have a much shorter life span than do the institutions of policy production.

The neoliberal emphasis on "consensus" as regards the underpinning axiology of policy (unmitigated faith in "free" trade, efficiency, productivity, competition, and so on) is well evidenced by the authors of policy. Exploratory interviews at the OECD and EC produced two notable quotes on the matter: "Our job is to create a hegemony" (July 19, 1999, interview, OECD: Paris); "We're just technocrats. We're here to produce a consensus and create a system. That's all" (July 21, 1999, interview, EC: Brussels). The level of analysis and argument is general because it is tied to the institutional and global scale of the study. That of course does not mitigate against the well-aired problems of generality. That said, I assume the theoretical and analytical perspectives presented here can inform microsociological analyses to some helpful extent.

Notes to future research

The following assertions are testable. Each is an area that bears directly on the problems I have addressed throughout the present work and each provides a rich vein of research for the future.

1. New media are by definition new ways of relating. New forms of relatedness are necessarily overlaid upon older forms, giving rise to conflicts and crises of understanding. This is most obvious when a new medium is oriented towards control over the spatial element. Those using a new medium to propagate ideas and direct human action across vast geographical spaces will invariably encounter cultural resistance.

2. Cultural resistance to new mediations is axiological: it is values-based. Human resistance is a function of a felt need for autonomy, justice, social equilibrium, or all of these. Cultural disruptions from the effects of new media are manifestations of perceived threats to cultural autonomy in the determination of values; of a sense of justice in the formal and informal relationships between people; and of a clear historical tendency in social systems towards a social equilibrium between the separate but interdependent social values that pertain to the definition and meaning of space and time in their many aspects.

3. A medium oriented towards regulating meaning over vast spaces will firstly seem as if it is oriented towards time. The current system is exemplary in this respect because it appears to emphasize the speed of exchanges. However, it is oriented towards the regulation and meaning of vast spaces. Larger social spaces are created at the expense of time between people and groups of people. One consequence is that time appears to be an object of destruction for new media rather than the means by which larger, less stable social spaces are created.

4. In any case, the relationship between time and space will always be confusing because the separation of the two is artificial. The same conceptual artifice is further reinforced because of the strange character of electronic exchange. Since the advent of electronic mediations, the maximum speed at which meanings get moved has been fairly stable. This might lead people to suspect that time has been steadily diminishing in importance. That is not the case, but it points to the very meaning of the word "media," implicating movement at every level: institutions, people, cultures, and the qualitative aspects of any form of communication are intrinsic "parts" of any medium. It also suggests the necessity of an historical orientation for research into relations between political economy and new media because a concern with "newness" is a concern with change.

5. "Old" media are not destroyed by new. New media are parasitic upon the old to a large degree, especially in their early stages. For example, broadcast television is primarily a time-oriented medium. It is an electronic ritual (Postman, 1985). The introduction of video recorders changed that to some degree. But the sense of communion and communality in a time-shared mass spectacle remains very much an essential part of television media. For example, a re-run of Princess Diana's funeral is unlikely to generate a very large audience, whereas its "live" performance was watched by more people than any other televised spectacle in history. Seen from one perspective, institutions are also media. Some are more oriented towards the meaning of space, such as national governments; others are more oriented to the meaning of time, like the Catholic church. All new media impact upon social perceptions of time *and* space to some degree. A functional perspective on mediation (asking, "What are the social functions of this medium?") is therefore implied, since purely structural descriptions of media (asking, "What are the technical aspects of this medium?") tell us little about social impacts.

6. Genres, or content types, are developed within institutions and therefore within the realms of vested interests and axiological traditions. The sermon was developed within the Roman church and claims *Divinity* as its primary value. The "white paper" of contemporary policy has developed in large national bureaucracies and evokes the values of *Expertise* and *Inevitability* (the latter in terms of future policy directions). Genres elicit and solicit expectations, including an expectation of axiological integrity in respect of the institutions within which important public genres develop. The close connection between institutions and genres therefore needs far more investigation, *particularly from the perspective of production*. Moreover, relational categories of media, genres, technologies, and institutions need development. What is a medium from one perspective can be an institution from another; what is a genre from one perspective can be a medium from another. Technology is an equally slippery category that can and must be related to all the others: media, genres, and institutions are technologies in and of themselves, as well as configurations of technologies when seen from another perspective. A full account of genre will necessarily include all these aspects.

7. Because "old" media are never entirely absorbed into the new, they do not disappear. But their social functionality is affected. The invention of paper did not replace vellum, nor did the television replace radio or theatre, nor has the internet replaced paper. Vellum remained the sacred medium, the definitive copy of the sacred texts, for many centuries after paper became available. This remains the case with certain documents. It would be easy to draw an identity between paper and vellum as sequential forms of printed media. However, it would be a "structurally" true but "functionally" false identity.

The cheaper cost of production for paper "democratized" knowledge to some degree in the first instance. The prohibitive cost of vellum ensured a continued monopoly of sacred knowledge. The cheap availability of paper allowed the extant monopoly to extend its legal system across a much wider area. Widespread formal feudalism and its "natural order" were impossible without paper and the agents of canon law in the church. The enlightenment and reformation were impossible without movable type, suitable ink, and paper. Print media, taken as a typological whole, have no inherent effects.

8. "The internet" is not a singular, undifferentiated medium, even though its earliest incarnations appeared as an extension of the printed word. The various aspects of the internet can only be described as social phenomena in functional terms. In this sense it is a stronghold of competing genres held in tension within discrete digital "realms." This gives the impression of "convergence," but that is not the case for the most part. For example, the high levels of security required for personal banking and other more substantial financial transactions ensure that these will remain functionally distinct realms from, say, public chat rooms or listserv groups. Email is an intensely personal yet ambiguous medium; "broadcast" listservs are relatively impersonal. There is a functional force in new mediations that is beginning to exert pressures on genres *within* genres, serving to force distinctions between them in new ways. Rather than convergence of any kind, fragmentation, hybridity, and new genres will be the most visible outcomes of new media.

9. No serious discussion of our new media can ignore their military roots and influence. The military influence is missing from most of what is said about new media (there are of course a few exceptions). It has shaped our new media from the very beginning. The role of the military and the "management" of mass human destruction is a central focus for any further developments in media research. War and its associated atrocities are unlike random violent episodes, such as domestic violence. War is an utterly "rational" undertaking. Today, it is a thoroughly mediated process of "rationally" organized murder, which is, of course, inherently irrational by any measure. These most blatant contradictions will be apparent in new mediations at every level of the military.

10. Critical theory ideally provides insight into the "logic of irrationality" in social organization, such as that connected with "disorganized" violence, and with the organized, "rational" violence that is called war. But armed with experience of irrationality, the dominant forces of humanity operate with full impunity to capitalize upon it. This becomes manifest in the valorization of ignorance, which is plain to see almost everywhere today. Hence ignorance has a social value and can thus also count as an intrinsic part—the negative moment—of any "knowledge economy." Paradoxically, ignorance may even

count as the "raw material" of knowledge. A history of ignorance is in order.

11. Critical social analysis is technique and technology. It necessarily technologizes the object from which it allegedly remains inseparable: social change. The ostensive function of critique is to understand and transform the social world. In accomplishing the first step, critique automatically accomplishes the second. But this does not necessarily (if ever) result in change for the better. Immediately upon doing so, and by being "progressive" and "engaged" with its object, critical theory tends towards its own appropriation by laying bare the inner workings of a social system and provides a means of creating new and more oppressive means of social exploitation.

12. Genre hybridity and "genre chaining" (Fairclough, 2000) are primarily inter-institutional phenomena. At first these will appear as a matter of convergence, like a kind of corporate merger of symbolic modes. But that is to hide the fact that genre hybridity is firstl an expression of institutional conflict over forms of symbolic regulation, which is what genres are (Fairclough, 2000). Today, governments are appropriating the genres of management and marketing. Corporations write policy. That is an expression of conflict over political power, over the right to tell people how to act and interact. The phenomena of genre hybridity and genre chaining are most overt in the processes that promote claims of legitimacy in the public sphere. Being inter-institutional they are primarily inter-axiological.

13. The relation between discourses, media, technologies, and genres can be expressed in terms of duration, as more or less stable patterns of production and reproduction of meaning types over certain amounts of time. Discourses, by which I mean recognizable ways of construing the world according to the interests and values of a particular social group, appear to be much more durable than any genre, medium, or technology. Once again, institutional enclosure of meaning types is foregrounded. Discourses, media, technologies, and genres can be seen as categories that stand in recognizably hierarchical relationships to each other. For instance, an institution cannot be reduced to discourse, nor can genres, media, or technologies. The taxonomic starting point will depend upon the phenomenon being investigated. A full, relational account of these categories is necessary for a political economy of media in a predominantly digital media environment.

14. Karl Marx, Harold Innis, Lewis Mumford, and Dallas Smythe also found themselves driven back upon space and time when considering changes in political economy. This suggests that the classical categories of political economy had already outlasted their usefulness by the mid-nineteenth century. The effects of the telegraph and paper money need to be taken into account to explain and understand Marx, his thought, his influence, and the

social milieu in which he worked. These new media cannot be considered in historical isolation. An understanding of impacts is perhaps best achieved at the initial stages by way of a synchronic "snapshot" focusing on the use and discussion of telegraphic "news" in such places as Vienna, London, Prague, New York, and Berlin. It should be noted that the telegraph and paper money emerged as combined forces at the end of the European imperialist era. There is evidence to suggest a connection between the rise of these media forms and the official end of Empires. There is much to suggest that a "global information overload"—and consequently new conceptions of global human interrelatedness—associated with the telegraph gave rise to the thought of Marx, Mach, Freud, Hertz, Einstein, and Wittgenstein, all of whom were deeply concerned with the limits of expression (Janik and Toulmin, 1973). The implication is that the fundamental relatedness of people, and between them and their environments, was called into question at that time. That is a perennial function of new mediation processes.

15. Just as the church provided the universal spirit for the feudal age, the abstract value systems of corporatist management, mass-marketing professionals, and the principles of the price system provide the elements of a universal, or at least "transnational," belief system for the current age. National forms of association are rooted in geography. The price system has no such boundaries and therefore apparently transcendends nationalism. Managerialism expresses the religious impulse, which has always been "transnational" in its functional orientation. Struggles between religions, governments, and corporations for political and economic dominance over humanity will take place through new and old media. The struggles will also be *dissolved* in such mediations. The forces of corporatism, managerialism, nationalism, and religious fundamentalism, may be (I would suggest that they are very likely to be) destroyed in the process, thus giving rise to new institutions. The successful *engineering* of such institutions, though, is most probably an impossible task. It is more likely that they will be emergent expressions of new systems of human relatedness.

16. Social science is always prone to charges of false determinisms. Media, linguistic, and economic determinism, for instance, are charges that might be laid against the approaches I have taken here. But that is to confuse the means and mode of social enquiry with its stated purpose. Media theory presupposes that new media has social effects. Political economy assumes that the production and distribution of values has social effects. Linguistic enquiry assumes that the way people make meaning has social effects. Causality is inherent to critical scholarship, and the search for causal relatedness mitigates against the barrenness of pure description. Each causal modality of enquiry is nothing more than a kaleidoscopic lens that fractures the social world according to its *functional* aspects: social change seen from the perspective of mediation processes; social

change seen from the perspective of production; social change as linguistically motivated. None of these views is inherently correct or incorrect; all give very different perspectives on social change.

The relationships between language, new media, and social perceptions of value are complex and ultimately indecipherable in any permanent sense. Yet I believe that there are important and deep connections between these elements that are essential for understanding our emergent forms of relatedness in a political economic sense. Marx's critical approach, which is deeply rooted in classical scholarship, remains relevant for understanding the dynamic and ever changing nature of social being. Yet I believe that most of the categories that have been staples for Marxist scholarship throughout the twentieth century—base and superstructure, real and ideal, and even "the capitalist class"—have become irrelevant for understanding current circumstances. The staple categories of Marxist scholarship are, on the best assessment, merely outcomes of the methods he used to analyze his circumstances—results of Marx's study of political economic relations that are almost 200 years old.

Today it is not the muscle-power of people that provides the most highly valued labor forms. Far more intimate aspects of human activity have become technologized and exposed to the logic of commodification. Correspondingly abstract forms of value have developed. Value production, in turn, has become more obviously "situated" in the valorized dialects of "sacred" and powerful institutions, such as legislatures, universities, and transnational corporations. In official political economy, value has moved from an objective category that pertains to such substances as precious metals and land, to become located today predominantly in "expert" ways of meaning and, more importantly, in their institutional contexts of production. These dialects and their products are now propagated and circulated on a global scale at light speed. Legal, political, commercial, and technological developments are key in the appropriation of new, more intangible forms of labor and value.

I began this work with a skeptical view of the actual "newness" of new media and a "knowledge economy." But it appears that the contemporary period might well be a turning point in human history. If so, it most closely resembles the formalization of the feudal system rather than what is now called the Enlightenment. The main elements that prompt me to draw such a comparison are: i) the presence of an international, axiologically consensual, elite group of institutions with the delegated (and undelegated) right to make laws about certain aspects for the whole of humanity, including and especially "intellectual" property law; ii) the "privatization" (or "redistribution") of a global, exogenous, objective space (electrospace); and iii) the redefinition, by a highly concentrated supranational network of legislatures, of international law, of what it means to be human in relation to other humans. These features mark the current period as historically unique, and it is the elements that revolve around global media networks which most obviously give the age its unique character. The current "globalized" system of governance is impossible without its mediation processes and their associated technologies. Any future reformulation of political economy would, I suggest, need to start with mediation processes rather than end with them as a superfluous addendum. The same holds for the analysis of evaluations in language. But any such analysis is doubly confounded by the fact that identifying evaluations in language transforms the often implicit evaluative patterns of a community into analyzable fact-like "objects." Which is to say, the analysis of values in language can never be an ethical or moral project in itself; it can only identify that which is typically construed as (in the last analysis) *Desirable* within a given community. But that is merely a caveat, not a reason to forego the analysis of evaluations. To the contrary, that which is perceived to be most *Desirable* and *Important* in any given context will unquestionably motivate human action. If only to draw attention to the possibility that functional and analyzable relationships exist between language, new media, and social perceptions of value, the contributions of the present work will, I hope, be of some use to future scholars interested in the study of political economy.

Notes

1. For different historical approaches that highlight these phenomena, see Fairclough (2002), Kroskrity (2000), Lemke (1995), and Martin (2000).

2. For a more detailed analysis of the emergence of disciplinarity in this context, see the chapter by Graham (2003) in Weiss and Wodak (2003).

3. For in-depth discussions of this phenomenon, see Firth (1951), Graham (2002), Langworthy Taylor (1895), Lasswell (1941) and Lemke (1998).

4. For Marx's developmental work on his theory of value, see Marx (1973, chap. 1, p. 259) and also Marx (1873/1975, 1844/1975a, 1844/1975b, 1970, 1976, 1978, 1981) and Marx and Engels (1846/1972). Adorno's synthesis of Marx and mass media is best outlined in Adorno (1951/1974, 1964/1973, 1991), Horkheimer and Adorno (1944/1998), and Jarvis (1998).

5. For various discussions of these links see, for example, Adorno (1973, 1994), Bloom (1943), Cook (1982), Fairclough and Graham (2002), Hook (1928a,b), and Warminski (1995).

6. The force of Marx's educational context and content in respect of linguistic scholarship is well recognized in some areas, but entirely disregarded in others (cf. Adorno, 1973, p. 56, 1994, pp. 18-21, pp. 116-118; Bloom, 1943; Colletti, 1975, p. 46; Cook, 1982, p. 530; Grote, 1872; Hook, 1928a, p. 114; Tucker, 1972, pp. xvii-xviii).

7. These discussions have been ongoing for centuries in almost every field of endeavor concerned with the "dual" nature of humans (e.g., Aristotle, 1962/1981, pp. 94-95; Garnham, 1990, pp. 45-53; Harvey, 1973, pp. 13, 22-32; Innis, 1942, 1944, 1950, 1951; Marx, 1973, pp. 100-108; Smith, 1776/1997, pp. 126-132).

8. To my mind, such a point should go without saying. Yet the approaches to doing so remain contentious (cf. Fenves, 1986; Hegel, 1807/1966, pp. 128-129; Makdisi, 1974; Randall, 1940).

9. All theories of value contain subjective and objective aspects, but some, like those of the early mercantilists, and those of the later Austrian school, take up extreme positions along the subjective–objective cline. For clarity's sake, and noting the artificiality of the split, I understand subjective value to be value that is produced or conceived of as agentive, or active, whether in terms of cognitive, emotional, or outwardly physical human activity. Subjective value is value produced by human activity—labor—whether conceptually or in another act of production like, for instance, hunting. Objective value here means passive and essential value. Objective value is value that is conceived of as an essential part of a thing, circumstance, or process. This sort of value exists *a priori* and is conceived of as being independent of human activity.

10. Karl Menger, Freidrich von Weiser, and Eugen von Bohm-Bahtwerk; see Bonar (1888)

for a good overview of their initial impact. There were English, German, and French counterparts to this movement, but they have been eclipsed for the most part, thanks to successes by Hayek (1981) and Schumpeter (1909).

11. Janik and Toulmin (1973) provide a fascinating account of the close cultural and social setting in which these theorists were operating, and which facilitated the emergence of this discourse.

12. For contemporary critiques of these positions, see Saul (1997) and Thurow (1996).

13. See, for example, Galton (1873, 1887, 1901, 1904).

14. The eugenic mindset was so prevalent that H. G. Wells thought he ran the risk of being considered "a crank" to suggest that criminals should perhaps be allowed to breed, and that Galton might not be seeing the whole picture (in Galton, 1904, p. 10).

15. The eugenic worldview flourished during a time when the first electronic mass medium, the radio, became available. Public opinion and social values suddenly became the most valuable of all "commodities" (Hobsbawm, 1994, pp. 142-145 and cf. Innis, 1951, p. 188; Gallup, 1928; Creel, 1941; Bernays, 1928; Lasswell, 1927, 1941).

16. For other interesting discussions on this theme, see also Lemke (1998), Martin (2000), Janik and Toulmin (1973, pp. 194-195) regarding Wittgenstein.

17. See, for example, Malinowski (1921) for a critique of that assumption.

18. This is now changing dramatically. See, for instance, the work of Boyer (2003) and Hart (2000).

19. See Adams (1998), Adams, Alford, and Shanahan (1997), Mullane (1997), and McFeatters (1998).

20. The term "notional" here is meant quite literally. That is, it only exists in the form of a hypothetical possibility.

21. First-order living systems are unicellular. Second-order systems are multicellular organisms. Third-order systems are social systems of multicellular organisms (cf. Maturana and Varela, 1980, 1987).

22. See the Vatican website for details of its communications strategies (www.vatican.vt).

23. The *Presentational* aspect of meaning sees the way a particular community typically construes things in natural or social domains by their "explicit descriptions as participants, processes, relations and circumstances standing in particular semantic relations to one another" (Lemke, 1995, p. 41). The Presentational dimension of meaning is (for perhaps obvious reasons) the dimension that is most readily identifiable as an overt marker of social systemic identity. The manner in which we present ourselves and our ideas to the world—from the language we use, to the clothes we wear, to the way we eat—is both a product of our social histories and a producer of ongoing social systemic identities (Bourdieu, 1998; Lemke, 1995). Social systems are biological and ecological entities. They are, as Lemke (1995) puts it, "ecosocial systems," embedded in relationships with environments of many kinds. People move through many different social systems in their lives, and social systems come in many different sizes and types. Some are more formal and regulated than others, and people act differently in different social environments. A professional bureaucrat will typically act, speak, and dress differently in her working environment than she will at a family party. The Presentational dimension of meaning is not merely an analytical category; it is often a quite conscious and always apparent aspect of our daily existence. The *Orientational* aspects of a community's language refers to how its members orient themselves attitudinally to others and the Presentational content of its

own meanings (Lemke, 1995, p. 41)—literally, how people in a given system evaluate aspects of their world, including what is said. In any given context, certain "ways of representing," or discourses, will be considered more valuable than others (Fairclough, 2002). This is expressed in what Fairclough calls "orders of discourse," dynamic and contested hierarchies of representational practices (1992, pp. 68-69). The Orientational aspects of the sentences contrasted above highlight the different evaluative dimensions of each text. It is the dimension of meaning I am most concerned with throughout this book. The Orientational (or Attitudinal) dimension of meanings within a given social system is expressed in patterns of evaluation—preferences for food, music, ideas, relationships, ways of living together, and so on, however expressed. Orientational meanings simultaneously create, sustain, and change patterns of evaluation within social systems. They are both the basis of social values and their expression. The *Organizational* aspects of meaning reveal how a community construes "relations between elements of the discourse itself" (Lemke, 1995, p. 41). Perhaps more than any of our modes of meaning, the sense we make of language is most often taken for granted. The many ways in which we "fill in the gaps" to provide cohesion for meanings are often quite unconscious. Organizational aspects create cohesion across long stretches of text. They can reinforce elements of a discourse community's thematic formations about a given aspect of the world.

24. For various and useful perspectives on this point, see, for example, McLuhan (1964), Mumford (1934/1963), Noble (1989), and Pacey (2001).

25. "The ability of mental concentration, as well as the absolutely essential feeling of obligation to one's job, are here most often combined with a strict economy which calculates the possibility of high earnings, and a cool self-control and frugality which enormously increase performance" (Weber, 1930/1992, p. 63).

26. For examples of this view, see Barlow (1998), Friedman (1999), and Walker (1999).

27. "World 1" is what the Organization for Economic Cooperation and Development (OECD) calls the wealthiest sectors of the world's wealthiest countries (Coates, 1998, p. 34).

28. This point has been made many times. See, for example, Bourdieu (1991), Castells (1996, chap. 1), Hobsbawm (1998), Innis (1950, 1951), and Marx (1846/1972, p. 139).

29. For detailed discussions, see Bourdieu (1991), Fairclough (1992, p. 216), Innis (1951), Lemke (1995, pp. 60-61), and Martin (1998, p. 429).

30. "The field of power (which should not be confused with the political field) is not a field like the others. It is the space of relations of force between the different kinds of capital or, more precisely, between the agents who possess a sufficient amount of one of the different types of capital to be in a position to dominate the corresponding field" (Bourdieu, 1998, p. 34).

31. Perhaps this is why it seems so strange to people when they hear their own voice on tape for the first time. Such a widespread, unsettling phenomenon cannot be passed off as surprise at hearing a "new" voice for the first time. It is the shock of the most intimate alienation.

32. See also Hyma (1938) for a discussion about the influence of the banks on the Dutch Calvinists, and consequently on large sections of the upper middle classes.

33. While many, like Thurow (1996), see tulipmania as an example of irrational speculation, an alternative view can be found in Garber (1989). He presumes the "impossibility of distinguishing empirically between hypotheses that asset price dynamics are driven by a rational speculative bubble and that researchers have not adequately measured the future

market fundamentals anticipated by market participants" (p. 557). My claim that Holland never recovered from the tulip crash is based on its subsequent failure to maintain the "world-power" status it enjoyed prior to the crash. By other standards, Holland enjoys a flourishing economy.

34. Childs goes on to say that it is "a faulty analysis which discovers some new kind of property in the possibilities revealed by science. Property in real estate is not only exclusive, but inclusive—it embraces all possibilities. A scientific interloper has no more right to start an injurious or offensive commotion among electric or radio vibrations within my space then [*sic*] he has to drive a horse and cart through it or set off a ton of dynamite" (1924, p. 521).

35. I take Hettinger to mean this in a figurative rather than a literal sense. Already, Hitler and Goebbels had begun to use the radio to mobilize and coordinate the physical and conscious activities of Germany's millions. This was well known in the United States and elsewhere at the time.

36. I am excepting those rare individuals for whom mathematics and its associated fields give visceral pleasure.

37. Marx later relabels the phenomenon of "self-realization" to be "self-valorization" because with each cycle, capital appears to increase its value independently (Marx, 1976).

38. Innis's syntax is difficult here, namely " … certainly receives […] a strong psychological impulse to become a fixed habit of thought."

39. That is not an exaggeration. Any study of money and its meaning immediately confronts enormous difficulties. Such debates have been steadily elided in mainstream economics since about 1916, apart from Innis's critique, and more recently that of Saul (1997).

40. For an excellent history of these recurrent phenomena, see Saul (1992).

41. The argument about whether my interpretation of Smith or Darwin is incorrect or perverse is a sidebar to this chapter. Darwin's theory of evolution through natural selection is a macro theory of how species have come into being over many centuries, not a theory of every day change. Adam Smith's mention of the "invisible hand," read in context, has clearly been blown out of proportion in respect of the rest of his theories. Also, most neoliberal readings of Smith entirely ignore his equally important *Theory of Moral Sentiments*. It seems clear to me, whether for better or worse, human beings are, as Aristotle pointed out, social animals. Our survival as a species has relied upon cooperation, not competition.

42. This is a well-documented phenomenon. See, for example, Halliday and Martin (1993), Lemke (1995, pp. 59-65), and McKenna and Graham (2000).

43. The identifying and attributive functions are a complex cline (R. Iedema, personal correspondence, May 2000). The Thing, once enough of its attributes have been elaborated, may take on an identity, either taxonomically or essentially, while a proposition that claims identity may also be sociofunctionally *attributive* and *evaluative* (cf. Aristotle, 1998, pp. 26-27; Fairclough and Graham, forthcoming; Grote, 1872, p. 90; McKenna and Graham, 2000).

44. For various perspectives on this aspect of meaning, see Fairclough (1992, pp. 12-135, 2000), Firth (1953), and Lemke (1995, pp. 22-36, 1998, pp. 34-35).

45. These include: *material* processes, or "processes of doing" such as hit, kick, push (pp. 109-112); *mental* processes, or "processes of sensing" such as think, dream, see, and hear (pp. 112-119); *relational* processes, or "processes of being" and becoming (such as has [x attributes], was/is [a kind of …x], and is like […x]) (1994, pp. 119-138); *behavioral*

processes, or processes that refer to "typically human" behavior such as cough, laugh, shiver, shit (139-142); *verbal* processes, or "processes of saying" such as said, promised, exhort, mean (140-142); and *existential* processes, or those that claim existence for something (142-143).

46. For useful histories on the role of communication and communications in the development of nationalism, see Carey (1989, pp. 225-229), Innis (1951, pp. 81-82), and Smythe (1981, p. 300).

47. Those prerequisites are detailed in many places, though are rarely made explicit. On the need for informal relationships, see Dickinson (1926, p. 308). On the need for legal means, see Bloch (1940/1961, chap. 7). On the need to patrol and enforce boundaries, see Innis (1951, p. 53) and Brewin (1998).

48. The whole New Zealand document is shot through with the same sense of panic, inadequacy, and confusion from the first paragraphs onward. Here is an example:

> "In today's information age knowledge has become the gold standard. If New Zealand is to prosper in the third millennium it is vital that we understand the implications of this change. (para. 1)

> But time is short. Prices for our commodity exports are in decline and we face tight competition for markets. It is unlikely that the traditional foundations of our economy alone—farming, forestry and fishing—can deliver the level of growth needed for our future well being. If we don't change the way we compete in the global economy our way of life and standard of living are at risk. (para. 2)"

Bibliography

Adams, W. (1998, July 30). US chills, Asia fever rocks local. *The Australian*, p. 1.

Adams, W., Alford, P., & Shanahan, D. (1997, October, 23-24). Route hacks $400bn off world shares. *The Weekend Australian*, p. 1.

Adorno, T. W. (1951/1974). *Minima Moralia: Reflections from damaged life* (E. F. N. Jephcott, Trans.). London: New Left Press.

_____. (1964/1973). *The Jargon of Authenticity* (K. Tarnowski & F. Will, Trans.). London: Routledge.

_____. (1991). *The Culture Industry: Selected essays on mass culture.* London: Routledge.

_____. (1994). *Hegel: Three studies* (S. Weber Nicholson, Trans.). Boston, MA: The MIT Press.

Appleby, J. (1976). Ideology and theory: The tension between political and economic liberalism in seventeenth-century England. *The American Historical Review, 81,* (3): 499-515.

Aristotle, A. (1962/1981). *The Politics.* (T. A. Sinclair, Trans.). London: Penguin.

_____. (1998). *The Metaphysics* (H. C. Lawson-Tancred, Trans.). London: Penguin Classics.

Armitage, J. (Ed.). (2000). *Paul Virilio: From modernism to hypermodernism and beyond.* London: Sage.

Armitage, J. & Graham, P. (2001). Dromoeconomics: Towards a political economy of speed. *parallax, 7,* (1): 111-123.

Bagdikian, B. H. (1997). *The Media Monopoly* (5th ed.). Boston, MA: Beacon Press.

Bagwell, S. (1999a, January 30-31). Davos: gabfest on global gloom. *The Australian Financial Review,* p. 9.

_____. (1999b, February 3). Act now on Brazil: Soros. *The Australian Financial Review,* p. 12.

Bales, K. (1999). *Disposable People: New slavery in the global economy.* London: University of California Press.

Barlow, J. P. (1998). *Cybernomics: Toward a theory of the information economy.* New York: Merrill Lynch Forum.

Barr, T. (2000). *Newmedia.com.au: The changing face of Australia's media and communications.* Sydney, Australia: Allen & Unwin.

Basho, K. (1998). *Privacy and the construction of on-line identity.* Available on-line: http://www.communication.ucsd.edu/Kbasho/privacy.html. Accessed December 6, 1998.

Bauman, Z. (1998). On glocalization: Or globalization for some, localization for others. *Book Eleven, 54*: 37-49.

Bernays, E. L. (1928). Manipulating public opinion: The why and the how. *American Journal of Sociology, 33,* (6): 958-971.

_____. (1945). Attitude polls: Servants or masters? *Public Opinion Quarterly, 9,* (3): 264-268b.

Bernier, P. (1992). *Ministry in the Church: A historical and pastoral approach.* Mystic, CT: Twenty-Third Publications.

Beuick, M. D. (1927). The limited social effects of radio broadcasting. *American Journal of Sociology, 32,* (4): 615-622.

Bloch, M. (1940/1961). *Feudal Society: The growth of ties of independence* (L. A. Manyon, Trans., Vol. 1). London: Routledge.

Bloom, S. F. (1943). Man of his century: A reconsideration of the historical significance of Karl Marx. *The Journal of Political Economy, 51,* (6): 494-505.

Blum, A. (1934). *On the Origin of Paper* (H. M. Lyndenberg, Trans.). New York: R. R. Bowker.

Bonar, J. (1888). The Austrian economists and their view of value. *The Quarterly Journal of Economics, 3,* (1): 1-31.

Bourdieu, P. (1984). *Distinction: A social critique of the judgement of taste* (R. Nice, Trans.). Cambridge, MA: Harvard University Press.

_____. (1991). *Language and Symbolic Power* (G. Raymond & M. Adamson, Trans.). London: Polity.

_____. (1993). *The Field of Cultural Production* (R. Johnson, Ed.). Cambridge: Polity.

_____. (1998a). *Practical Reason: On the theory of practice.* London: Polity.

_____. (1998b). *Acts of Resistance: Against the new myths of our time.* London: Polity.

Boyer, D. C. (2001). Foucault in the Bush: The social life of post-structuralist theory in East Berlin's Prenzlauer Berg. *Ethnos, 66,* (2): 207-236.

_____. (2003). Censorship as a Vocation: The Institutions, Practices, and Cultural Logic of Media Control in the German Democratic Republic. *Comparative Studies in Society and History 45*(3):511-545..

BP Amoco p.l.c. (2000). Performance: Health, safety and environmental performance. Available   on-line: http://www.bp.com/alive/index.asp?page=/alive/performance/health_safet y_and_environment_performance. Accessed August 2000.

Brewin, R. (1998, December 2). DOD recognizes info warfare as key battlefield. *Federal Computer Week.* Available on-line: http://www.fcw.com/pubs/fcw/1998/1130/web-infowar-12-2-98.html. Accessed December 11, 1998.

Bullock, A. (1991). *Hitler and Stalin: Parallel lives.* London: Fontana.

Bush, G. W. (2004a). *America's compassion in action: Remarks by the President at the First White House National Conference on faith-based and community initiatives.* Available on-line: http://www.whitehouse.gov/news/releases/2004/06/20040601-10.html. Accessed June 23, 2004.

_____. (2004b). *Executive order: Responsibilities of the Department of Commerce and Veterans Affairs and the Small Business Administration with respect to faith-based and community initiatives.* Available on-line: http://www.whitehouse.gov/news/release s/2004/06/20040601-1.html. Accessed June 23, 2004. Accessed October 30, 2004.

_____. (2004c). *President discusses compassionate conservative agenda in Dallas*: Remarks by the President to the 122nd Knights of Columbus convention, Hyatt Regency, Dallas, TX. Available on-line: http://www.whitehouse.gov/news/releases/2004/08/20 040803-11.html. Accessed October 23, 2004.

Business is booming. (1999). April Credit Risk Supplement. *Risk Publication*. Available on-line: http://www.financewise.com/public/print/crsurveyp.htm. Accessed April, 2004.

Carey, J. W. (1989). *Communication as Culture: Essays on media and society*. New York: Routledge.

Castells, M. (1997). *The Information Age: Economy, society and culture: The power of identity* (Vol. 2). London: Blackwell.

_____. (1998). *The Information Age: Economy, society and culture: End of millennium* (Vol. 3). London: Blackwell.

Cawsey, S. F. (1999). Royal eloquence, royal propaganda, and the use of the sermon in the Medieval crown of Aragon c. 1200-1410. *Journal of Ecclesiastical History, 50,* (3): 442-463.

CBS. (2004). *Marketwatch Scandalsheet*. Available on-line: http://cbs.marketwatch.com/news /features/scandal_sheet.asp. Accessed August 12, 2004.

Center for Responsive Politics. (2004). *2004 Presidential Elections*. Available on-line: http://www.opensecrets.org/presidential/index.asp. Accessed October 23, 2004.

Childs, W. W. (1924). Problems in the radio industry. *The American Economic Review, 14,* (3): 520-523.

Church, G. F. (1939). Short waves and propaganda. *Public Opinion Quarterly, 3,* (2): 209-222.

Clinton, W. J. (1999, March 18). Remarks by the president at radio and television correspondents association dinner at The Washington Hilton. Available on-line: http://www.pub.whitehouse.gov/uri-res/I2R?urn:pdi://oma.eop.gov.us/1999/3/22/3.text.1.

Coates, J. (1998). The next twenty-five years of technology: Opportunities and risks. In Organisation for Economic Cooperation and Development. (1998). *21st century technologies: Promises and perils of a dynamic future*: 33-46. Paris: OECD.

Colker, R. (1998). *American Law in the Age of Hypercapitalism: The Worker, the family, and the state*. New York: New York University Press.

Colletti, L. (1975). Introduction. In K. Marx, *Early Writings* (R. Livingstone & G. Benton, Trans., pp. 7-56). London: Penguin.

Cook, D. J. (1982). Marx's critique of philosophical language. *Philosophy and Phenomenological Research, 42,* (4): 530-554.

Creel, G. (1941). Propaganda and morale. *American Journal of Sociology, 47,* (3): 340-351.

Deans, A. (1998, July 4-5). Rupert Murdoch's intimations of mortality. *Weekend Australian Financial Review*, p. 25.

Department of Foreign Affairs and Trade. (1997). *In the National Interest: Australia's foreign and trade policy white paper*. Barton, Australia: Commonwealth of Australia.

Department of Premier and the Cabinet. (2000). Rationale for change. Available on-line: http://www.premiers.qld.gov.au/about/identity/rationale.htm. Accessed August 18, 2000.

Department of the Army. (2003). *Information operations: Doctrine, tactics, techniques, and procedures*. Available on-line: http://www.adtdl.army.mil/cgi-bin/atdl.dll/fm/3-

13/fm3_

13.pdf. Accessed June 30, 2004.

de Santillana, G. & von Dechend, H. (1962/1999). *Hamlet's Mill: An essay investigating the origins of human knowledge and its transmission through myth.* Jaffrey, NH: David R. Godine.

Dickinson, J. (1926). The mediaeval conception of kingship and some of its limitations, as developed in the Policratus of John of Salisbury. *Speculum, 1,* (3): 308-337.

Dietz, A. (1934). The nature of contemporary propaganda (R. Bytwerk, Trans.). [Das Wesen der heutigen Propaganda. *Unser Wille und Weg, 4*: 299-301.]

Douglas, J. D. (1973). *Introduction to Sociology: Situations and structures.* New York: Mac-Millan.

Durkheim, E. (1933/1960). *The Division of Labour in Society.* Glencoe, IL: Free Press.

Edwardes, W. (1998a). Credit derivatives folly. Available on-line: http://people.delphi.com/riskmanage/credit.htm. Accessed December 5, 1998.

_____. (1998b). *Derivatiphobia: A directors guide to derivatives.* Available on-line: http://people.delphi.com/riskmanage/derive.htm. Accessed December 5, 1998.

Emerson, C. & Holquist, M. (Eds.). (1986). *Speech genres and other late essays* (V. W. McGee, Trans.). Austin, TX: University of Texas Press.

Emery, H. C. (1895). Legislation against futures. *Political Science Quarterly, 10,* (1): 62-86.

Enke, S. (1942). Space and Value. *Quarterly Journal of Economics, 56,* (4): 627.

Fairclough, N. (1989). *Language and Power.* New York: Longman.

_____. (1992). *Discourse and Social Change.* Cambridge: Polity.

_____. (1995). *Media Discourse.* London: Edward Arnold.

_____. (2000). Discourse, social theory, and social research: The discourse of welfare reform. *Journal of Sociolinguistics, 4,* (2): 163-195.

_____. (2003). *Analysing Discourse: Textual Analysis for Social Research.* London: Routledge.

Fairclough, N. & Graham, P. (2002). Marx and discourse analysis: Genesis of a critical method. *Estudios de Sociolingüística 3,* (1): 185-230.

Fairclough, N. & Wodak, R. (1997). Critical discourse analysis. In T. van Dijk (Ed.), *Discourse as Social Interaction: Discourse studies: A multidisciplinary introduction* (Vol. 2, pp. 258-284). London: Sage.

Federal Communications Commission. (1998, July 9). *En Banc Hearing.* Washington, DC: Heritage Reporting Corporation.

_____. (2000). *All About Auctions.* Washington, DC: Federal Communications Commission.

_____. (2004). *Commission adopts spectrum sharing plan to promote the efficient use of spectrum.* Available on-line: http://hraunfoss.fcc.gov/edocs_public/attachmatch/DOC-248343A1.pdf.

Fenves, P. (1986). Marx's doctoral book on two Greek atomists and the post-Kantian interpretations. *Journal of the History of Ideas, 40,* (3): 353-368.

Fenwick, C. G. (1938). The use of radio as an instrument of foreign propaganda. *American Journal of International Law, 32,* (2): 339-343.

Ferguson, J. (1998). Agriculture: A case study in industrial relations reform. *Reform, 4*: 3-6.

Kingston, Australia: National Farmers Federation.

Field, J. A. (1911). The progress of eugenics. *Quarterly Journal of Economics, 26,* (1): 1-67.

Firth, R. (1951). Contemporary British Social Anthropology. *American Anthropologist, 53* (4/1): 474-489.

_____. (1953). The study of values by social anthropologists: The Marrett Lecture, 1953. *Man, 53*: 146-153.

Fogarty, M. (1996). *A History of Value Theory*. Available on-line: http://www.Economics.tcd.ie/ser/1996/mfogarty.htm. Accessed February 1, 2000.

Ford, H. J. (1909). The pretensions of sociology. *American Journal of Sociology, 15,* (1): 96-104.

Freeman, A. L. (2004, October 23). Italy to Raise as Much $9.6 Billion After Pricing Enel Shares. *Bloomberg Worldwide*. Available on-line: http://quote.bloomberg.com/apps/news?pid=10000006&sid=aoyjUpmEP6kU&refer=home. Accessed October 23, 2004.

Freud, S. (1928/1991). The future of an illusion. In A. Dickson (Ed.), J. Strachey (Trans.), *Sigmund Freud: Civilization, society and religion: Group psychology, civilization and its discontents and other works* (Vol. 12, pp. 179-242). London: Penguin.

Friedman, M. & Friedman, R. (1980). *Free to Choose: A personal statement.* Harmondsworth, United Kingdom: Penguin.

Friedman, T. L. (1999, March 28). A manifesto for the fast world. New York Times Magazine, 40-44, 61, 70-71, 84, 96.

Gal, S. (1989). Political economy and language. *Annual Review of Anthropology, 18*: 345-367.

Gallup, G. (1938). Testing public opinion. *Public Opinion Quarterly [Special Supplement: Public opinion in a democracy], 2,* (1): 8-14.

Galton, F. (1873). The relative supplies from town and country families, to the population of future generations. *Journal of the Statistical Society of London, 36,* (1): 19-26.

_____. (1887). Supplementary notes on "prehension" in idiots. *Mind, 12,* (45): 79-82.

_____. (1901). The possible improvement of the human breed under the existing conditions of law and sentiment. *Man, 1*: 161-164.

_____. (1904). Eugenics: Its definition, scope, and aims. *American Journal of Sociology, 10,* (1): 1-25.

Garber, P. M. (1989). Tulipmania. *The Journal of Political Economy, 97,* (3): 535-560.

Garnham, N. (1990). *Capitalism and Communication: Global culture and the economics of information.* London: Sage.

Gates, W. (1996). *Content is King*. Available on-line: http://www.microsoft.com/billgates/columns/1996essay/essay960103.asp. Accessed June 12, 2004.

Gee, J. P. (1992). *The Social Mind: Language, ideology, and social practice.* New York: Bergin & Garvey.

Gee, J. P. & Lankshear, C. (1995). The new work order: Critical language awareness and 'fast capitalism' texts. *Discourse: Studies in the cultural politics of education, 16,* (1): 5-17.

Goebbels, J. (1933). *The radio as the eight great power*. Text of a speech delivered at the opening of the 10th German Radio Exposition (R. Bytwerk, Trans.). Available on-line: http://www.calvin.edu/academic/cas/gpa/goeb56.htm. Accessed September 15, 1999.

Golumbia, D. (1996). Hypercapital. *Postmodern Culture, 7*: 1. Available on-line: http://www.mindspring.com/dgolumbi/docs/hycap/hypercapital.html. Accessed July, 1998.

Gore, A. (2000, January 17). Remarks as prepared for delivery by Vice President Al Gore on Dr. Martin Luther King, Jr. Day, Ebenezer Baptist Church, Atlanta, GA. Available on-line: http://www.pub.whitehouse.gov/uri-res/I2R?urn:pdi://oma.eop.gov.us/2000/1/18/15.text.1.

Graham, L. (1977). Science and values. *The American Historical Review, 82,* (5): 1133-1164.

Graham, P. (1998). Globalist fallacies, fictions, and facts: The MAI and neo-classic ideology. *Australian Rationalist, 46*: 15-21.

_____. (1999). Critical systems theory: A political economy of language, thought, and technology. *Communication Research, 26,* (4): 482-507.

_____. (2000). The ideological context of business: Capital. In J. Harrison (Ed.), *Business Ethics in Australia* (pp.10–24). Sydney: Prentice-Hall.

_____. (2002). Hypercapitalism: New media, language, and social perceptions of value. *Discourse & Society, 13,* (2): 227-249.

_____. (2003). Critical discourse analysis and evaluative meaning: Interdisciplinarity as a critical turn. In G. Weiss & R. Wodak (Eds.), *Critical Discourse Analysis: Theory and interdisciplinarity* (pp. 130-159). London: Palgrave MacMillan.

Graham, P. & Hearn, G. (2000, September). The digital Dark Ages: A retro-speculative history of possible futures. *Internet Research 1.0:The State of the Interdiscipline*. Symposium conducted at the First Conference of the Association of Internet Researchers, University of Kansas.

Graham, P. & McKenna, B. J. (2000). A theoretical and analytical synbook of autopoiesis and sociolinguistics for the study of organisational communication. *Social Semiotics, 10,* (1): 41-59.

Grote, G. (1872a). *Aristotle* (Vol. 1). London: John Murray.

Gunther, J. (1936). *Inside Europe.* London: Hamish Hamilton.

Hacking, I. (1996). Normal people. In. D. R. Olson & N. Torrance (Eds.), *Modes of Thought: Explorations in culture and cognition* (pp. 59-71). New York: Cambridge University Press.

Halliday, M. A. K. (1978). *Language as a Social Semiotic: The social interpretation of language and meaning.* London: Edward Arnold.

_____. (1993). Language in a changing world. In R. B. Baldauf, Jr. (Ed.), *Occasional Paper Number 13* Deakin, Australia: Applied Linguistics Association of Australia.

_____. (1994). *An Introduction to Functional Grammar* (2nd ed.). London: Edward Arnold.

Halliday, M. A. K. & Martin, J.R. 1993a *The Construction of Knowledge and Value in the Grammar of Scientific Discourse: Charles Darwin's The Origin of the Species,* (London: The Falmer Press).

_____. and Martin, J.R. 1993b *Writing Science: Literacy and Discursive Power,* (London: Falmer Press). 13

Harm, M. & Wiehle, H. (1942). The laws of nature and humanity. In R. Bytwerk (Trans.), *Biology for the Middle School for 5th Grade Girls [Lebenskunde für Mittelschulen. Fünfter Teil. Klasse 5 für Mädchen]* (pp. 168-173). Halle: Hermann Schroedel Verlag. Available on-line: http://www.calvin.edu/academic/cas/gpa/textbk01.htm. Accessed

March 24, 2000.

Hart, K. (1999). *The Memory Bank: Money in an unequal world.* London: Profile.

Hartcher, P. (1999, March 13-14). Soros suffers a capitalist crisis of his own. *The Australian Financial Review,* p. 9.

Harvey, D. (1973). *Social Justice and the City.* London: Blackwell.

Haskins, C. H. (1904). The University of Paris in the sermons of the thirteenth century. *The American Historical Review, 10,* (1): 1-27.

Hayek, F. A. (1981). *Individualism and Economic Order.* Chicago: University of Chicago Press.

Hegel, G. W. F. (1807/1966). *The Phenomenology of Mind* (J. B. Baillie, Trans.). London: George Allen & Unwin.

Hellyer, P. (1999). Let's start a war—On mediocrity. Available on-line: http://dove.mtx.net.au/hermann/hellyer.htm. Accessed April 27, 1999.

Herbert, S. (1913). Eugenics in relation to social reform. *The Westminster Review, 180,* (4): 377-386.

Hettinger, H. S. (1934). The Future of Radio as an Advertising Medium. *Journal of Business of the University of Chicago, 7,* (4): 283-295.

Hippler, F. (1937). Film as a Weapon (R. Bytwerk, Trans.). [*Der Film als Waffe. Unser Wille und Weg, 7:* 21-23.] Available on-line: http://www.calvin.edu/academic/cas/gpa/hippler1.htm. Accessed March 24, 2000.

Hobbes, T. (1651). *Leviathan.* Available on-line: http://oregonstate.edu/instruct/phl302/te xts/hobbes/leviathan-a.html. Accessed June 2004.

Hobsbawm, E. (1962). *The Age of Revolution: 1789-1848.* London: Abacus.

_____. (1975). *The Age of Capital: 1848-1875.* London: Abacus.

_____. (1994). *The Age of Extremes: The short twentieth century 1914-1991.* London: Abacus.

Holquist, M. (Ed.). (1981). *The Dialogic Imagination: Four essays by M. M. Bakhtin* (C. Emerson & M. Holquist, Trans.). Austin, TX: University of Texas Press.

Hook, S. (1928a). The philosophy of dialectical materialism I. *The Journal of Philosophy, 25,* (5): 113-124.

_____. (1928b). The philosophy of dialectical materialism II. *The Journal of Philosophy, 25,* (6): 141-155.

Horkheimer, M. & Adorno, T. W. (1947/1998). *The Dialectic of Enlightenment* (J. Cumming, Trans.). New York: Continuum.

Hunston, S. & Sinclair, J. (2000). A local grammar of evaluation. In S. Hunston & G. Thompson (Eds.), *Evaluation in Text* (pp. 76-101). Oxford: Oxford University Press.

Hyma, A. (1938). Calvinism and capitalism in the Netherlands, 1555-1700. *The Journal of Modern History, 10,* (3): 321-343.

Iedema, R. (1999). Institutional responsibility and hidden meanings. *Discourse & Society, 9,* (4): 481-500.

Innis, H. A. (1942). The newspaper in economic development. *Journal of Economic History, 2:* 1-33. [Issue Supplement: The tasks of economic history.]

_____. (1944). On the economic significance of culture. *Journal of Economic History, 4:* 80-

97. [Issue Supplement: The tasks of economic history.]

_____. (1950). *Empire and Communications.* Oxford: Clarendon Press.

_____. (1951). *The Bias of Communication.* Toronto: Toronto University Press.

International Labor Organisation. (1998). *World Report '96/'97.* Geneva, Switzerland: International Labor Organisation.

_____. (1999). *International Labour Organization World Employment Report 1998-99.* Geneva, Switzerland: International Labor Organisation.

Irvine, J. T. and GAL, S., (2000). Language ideology and linguistic differentiation. In F. Kroskrity (ed.) *Regimes of Language: Ideologies, Polities, and Identities* (Santa Fe: School of American Research Press): pp. 35-83.

Irving, L. (1998, December 1). *Forging a connected global village.* Address to the NTCA-World Bank's First International Conference on Rural Telecommunications. Available on-line: http://www.ntia.doc.gov/ntiahome/speeches/ntca120198.htm. Accessed December 12, 1998.

iTulip. (1999). *Background.* Available on-line: http://www.itulip.com/background.html. Accessed April 30, 1999.

Janik, A. & Toulmin, S. (1973). *Wittgenstein's Vienna.* New York: Simon and Schuster.

Jarvis, S. (1998). *Adorno: A critical introduction.* London: Polity.

JB Cubed. (2003). *On technology establishes business development partnership to expand presence within the federal and state governments.* Available on-line: http://www.jbcubed.com/news/news_05072003.htm. Accessed May 7, 2003.

Jessop, R. (2000). The crisis of the national spatio-temporal fix and the ecological dominance of globalizing capitalism. *International Journal of Urban and Regional Studies, 24,* (2): 273-310.

Joint Chiefs of Staff. (2000). *Joint Vision 2020.* Washington, DC: US Government Printing Office. Available online: http://www.dtic.mil/jointvision/jvpub2.htm.

Joint Standing Committee on Treaties. (1999). *Report 18: Multilateral agreement on investment: Final report.* Canberra, Australia: Commonwealth of Australia.

Jones, P. (2004). Discourse and the materialist conception of history: Critical comments on critical discourse analysis. *Historical Materialism, 12,* (1): 97-125.

Keasbey, L. E. (1903). Prestige value. *Quarterly Journal of Economics, 17,* (3): 456-475.

Kellner, D. (1998). Introduction. In D. Kellner (Ed.), *Technology, War and Fascism: Herbert Marcuse* (pp. 1-38). London: Routledge.

_____. (1999). New technologies, the welfare state, and the prospects for democratization. In A. Calabrese & J. Burgleman (Eds.), *Communication, Citizenship, and Social Policy: Rethinking the limits of the welfare state* (pp. 239-256). Oxford: Rowman & Littlefield.

Kennedy, E. (1979). "Ideology" from Destutt de Tracy to Marx. *Journal of the History of Ideas, 40,* (3): 353-368.

Kennedy, P. (1998). Coming to terms with contemporary capitalism: Beyond the idealism of globalisation and capitalist ascendancy arguments. *Sociological Research Online, 3,* (2). Available on-line: http://www.socioresonline.org.uk/socioresonline/3/2/6.html. Accessed October 7, 1998.

Kim, Y. S., Jang, Y. S., & Hwang, H. (2002). Structural expansion and the cost of global isomorphism. *International Sociology, 17,* (4): 481-504.

Kohler, A. (1998, September 26-27). Lessons of history forgotten. *The Australian Financial Review,* p. 60.

Korb, K., Kopp, C., & Allison, L. (1997). Higher education policy in Australia. *Australian Rationalist,* 45: 16-26.

Kothari, V. (2004). Credit derivatives volumes to touch USD 2 Trillion. *Credit Derivative Website.* Available on-line: http://www.credit-deriv.com/crenewsmar02.htm#market_data. Accessed July, 2004.

Kuhn, T. (1962). The nature and necessity of scientific revolutions. In L. Cahoone (Ed.), (1997). *From modernism to postmodernism: an anthology* (pp. 309-325). New York: Routledge.

Küng, H. (1968/1995). *The Church.* London: Burns & Oates.

Langworthy Taylor, W. G. (1895). Some important phases in the evolution of the idea of value. *The Journal of Political Economy, 3,* (4): 414-433

Lasswell, H. D. (1927). The theory of political propaganda. *The American Political Science Review, 21,* (3): 627-631.

_____. (1941). World attention survey. *Public Opinion Quarterly, 5,* (3): 456-462.

Latham, M. (1998). *Civilising global capital: New thinking for Australian Labor.* Sydney: Allen & Unwin.

Lemke, J. L. (1995). *Textual Politics: Discourse and social dynamics.* London: Taylor & Francis.

_____. (1998). Resources for attitudinal meaning: Evaluative orientations in text semantics. *Functions of Language, 5,* (1): 33-56.

_____. (in press). Across the scales of time: Artifacts, activities, and meanings in ecosocial systems. *Mind, Culture, and Activity, 7:* 273-290.

Lennard, W. (2004, 26 January). Bill Gates. *The Guardian.* Available on-line: http://www.guard ian.co.uk/netnotes/article/0,6729,1131775,00.html. Accessed June 11, 2004.

Lepschy, G. (1985). Linguistics. In Z. Baranski & G. Short (Eds.), *Developing Contemporary Marxism* (pp. 199-228). London: The Macmillan Press.

Lessig, L. (2004). *Free Culture: How big media uses techonology and the law to down culture and control creativity.* New York: Penguin Press.

Locke, J. (1696/1989). *Several papers relating to money, interest, trade, &c.* Fairfield, NJ: Augustus M. Kelley.

Lovink, G. (2004). *Uncanny networks: dialogues with the virtual intelligentsia.* Cambridge, MA: MIT Press.

Luhmann N. (1995). *Social Systems.* Stanford, Calif.: Stanford University Press.

Luke, A. (2002). Beyond science and ideology critique: developments in critical discourse analysis'. *Annual Review of Applied Linguistics, 22:* 96 - 110.

MacKay, C. (1841). *Extraordinary Popular Delusions and the Madness of Crowds.* New York: Litrix Reading Room.

Makdisi, G. (1974). The scholastic method in mediaeval education: An inquiry into its origins, law, and theology. *Speculum, 49,* (4): 640-661.

Malinowski, B. (1921). The primitive economics of the Trobriand Islanders. *The Economic Journal, 31,* (121): 1-16.

Mandel, E. (1975). Late capitalism. London: Verso.

Marcuse, H. & Neumann, F. (1942/1998). A history of the doctrine of social change. In D. Kellner (Ed.), *Technology, War and Fascism: Herbert Marcuse* (pp. 93-104). London: Routledge.

Martin, J. R. (1997). Analysing genre: Functional parameters. In F. Christie & J. R. Martin (Eds.), *Genre and Institutions: Social processes in the workplace and the school* (pp. 3-39). London: Cassell.

_____. (1998). Linguistics and the consumer: The practice of theory. *Linguistics and Education, 9*, (4): 411-418.

_____. (1999). Grace: the logogenesis of freedom. *Discourse Studies, 1*, (1): 29-56.

_____. (2000). Beyond exchange: APPRAISAL systems in English. In S. Hunston & G. Thompson (Eds.), *Evaluation in Text* (pp. 142-175). Oxford: Oxford University Press.

_____. and Rose, D. (2003) Working with Discourse: Meaning Beyond the Clause. London: Continuum .

Marx, K. (1843/1975). Critique of Hegel's Doctrine of the State. In K. Marx, *Early Writings* (R. Livingstone & G. Benton, Trans., pp. 57-198). London: Penguin.

_____. (1844/1975a). Economic and philosophical manuscripts. In K. Marx, *Early Writings* (R. Livingstone & G. Benton, Trans., pp. 279-400). London: Penguin.

_____. (1844/1975b). Excerpts from James Mill's *Elements of Political Economy*. In K. Marx, *Early Writings* (R. Livingstone & G. Benton, Trans., pp. 259-278). London: Penguin.

_____. (1875/1972). Critique of the Gotha program. In R. C. Tucker (Ed.), *The Marx-Engels Reader* (pp. 382-405). New York: W. W. Norton.

_____. (1970). *A Contribution to the Critique of Political Economy* (S. W. Ryazlanskaya, Trans.). Moscow: Progress.

_____. (1973). *Grundrisse: Foundations of the critique of political economy (Rough draft)* (M. Nicolaus, Trans.). London: Penguin.

_____. (1976). *Capital: A critique of political economy* (B. Fowkes, Trans., Vol. 1). London: Penguin.

_____. (1978). *Capital: A critique of political economy* (D. Fernbach, Trans., Vol. 2). London: Penguin.

_____. (1981). *Capital: A critique of political economy* (D. Fernbach, Trans., Vol. 3). London: Penguin.

Marx,K & Engels, F. (1846/1972). The German ideology. In R. C. Tucker (Ed.), *The Marx-Engels Reader* (pp. 110-166). New York: W. W. Norton.

Maturana, H. (1995). *The Nature of Time*. Available on-line: http://www.inteco.cl/biology/nature.htm. Accessed November 13, 1998.

_____. & Varela, F. (1980). *Autopoiesis and Cognition: The realisation of the living.* Dordrecht, Holland: Reidel.

Maturana, H. & Varela, F. (1987). *The Tree of Knowledge*. Boston, MA: Shambalah.

Mauss, M. (1925/1990). *The Gift: The form and reason for exchange in archaic societies.* London: Routledge.

McCattell, J. & Galton, F. (1890). Mental tests and measurements. *Mind, 15,* (59): 378-381.

McChesney, R.W. (2000). The Political Economy of Communication and the Future of the

Field. *Media, Culture & Society, 22* (1): 109-116.

McFeatters, A. (1998, February 13). Latest scandal brings Clinton and Hollywood together-again. *Naples News.* Available on-line: http://www.nap lesnews.com/today/editorial/a1 1013j.htm. Accessed June, 1998.

McKenna, B. J. (1997). How engineers write: An empirical study of engineering report writing. *Applied Linguistics, 18,* (2): 189-211.

McKenna, B. J. & Graham, P. (2000). Technocratic discourse: A primer. *Journal of Technical Writing and Communication, 30,* (3): 219-247.

McKeon, R. (1928). Thomas Aquinas' doctrine of knowledge and its historical setting. *Speculum, 3,* (4): 425-444.

McLuhan, M. (1964). *Understanding Media: The extensions of man.* London: Routledge.

McNeil, D., et al. (1997). *The Bubble Project.* Available on-line: http://is.dal.ca/dmcneil/bubb le.html. Accessed July 1998.

McNeill, W. H. (1987). The eccentricity of wheels, or Eurasian transportation in historical perspective. *The American Historical Review, 92,* (5): 1111-1126.

McTaggart, J. E. (1893). Time and the Hegelian dialectic. *Mind [New Series], 2,* (8): 490-504.

Miller, D. (2004). *Information Dominance : The Philosophy of Total Propaganda Control.* Georgetown, ON: Coldtype. Available online at: http://www.coldtype.net/Assets.04/ Essays.04/Miller.pdf

Miller, R., Michalski, W., & Stevens, B. (1998). The promises and perils of 21st century technology: An overview of the issues. In *21st Century Technologies: Promises and perils of a dynamic future* (pp. 7-32). Paris: OECD.

Moore, A. W. (1908). Truth value. *The Journal of Philosophy, Psychology, and Scientific Methods, 5,* (16): 429-436.

Moore, M. (2000, February 9). *Open societies do better: Statement by Mike Moore Director-General, World Trade Organization at the 11th International Military Chiefs of Chaplains Conference.* Geneva: World Trade Organisation.

Morgan, W. T. (1929). The origins of the South Sea Company. *Political Science Quarterly, 44,* (1): 16-38.

Mullane, M. (1997, October 29). Panic sweeps world markets. *Australian Financial Review,* p. 1.

Mumford, L. (1934/1963). *Technics and Civilization.* New York: Harcourt Brace.

_____. (1944/1973). *The Condition of Man.* New York: Harvest/Harcourt Brace Jovanovich.

_____. (1962). *The City in History: Its origins, its transformations, and its prospects.* New York: Harcourt, Brace, & World.

Muntigl, P. (2001). Dilemmas of individualism and social necessity. In P. Muntigl, G. Weiss, & R. Wodak (Eds.), *European Union Discourses on Unemployment: An interdisciplinary approach to employment policy-making and organizational change* (pp. 145-184). London: Benjamins.

National Office for the Information Economy. (1998). *Towards an Australian strategy for the information economy: A preliminary statement of the government's policy approach and a basis for business and community consultation.* Available on-line: http://www.noie.gov.au/reports/index.html. Accessed November 27, 1998.

Neill, T. P. (1949). The physiocrats' concept of economics. *Quarterly Journal of Economics,*

63, (4): 532-553.

Noble, D. F. (1984). *Forces of Production: A social history of industrial automation.* Oxford: Oxford University Press.

_____. (1997). *The Religion of Technology: The Divinity of Man and the Spirit of Invention.* New York: Alfred A. Knopf.

_____. (2004). *Beyond the Promised Land: An essay on the passing of a western myth.* MS.

NSDAP. (1939). First Course for Gau and County Propaganda Leaders of the NSDAP (R. Bytwerk, Trans.). [Lehrgang der Gau und Kreispropagandaleiter der NSDAP. *Unser Wille und Weg, 9*: 124-139.] Available on-line: http://www.calvin.edu/academic/cas/gp a/lehrgang.htm. Accessed March 24, 2000.

OECD. (1998). *Use of information and communication technologies at work.* Paris: OECD Working Party on the Information Economy.

_____. (1999). 21st century economic dynamics: Anatomy of a long boom: Key points of the discussion. In *Expo 2000 OECD Forum For The Future, Conference 2.* Paris: OECD.

Pacey, A. (1999/2001). *Meaning in Technology.* Cambridge, MA : MIT Press

Paul, D. (1984). Eugenics and the Left. *Journal of the History of Ideas, 45*, (4): 567-590.

Penn, F. (1998, January 27). The $exgate millionaire$. *New York Post.* Available on-line: http://206.15.118.165/012798/3149.htm. Accessed January 24, 1998.

Perry, R. B. (1914). The definition of value. *The Journal of Philosophy, Psychology, and Scientific Methods, 11*, (6): 141-162.

_____. (1916). Economic value and moral value. *Quarterly Journal of Economics, 30*, (3): 443-485.

Poole, D. C. (1939). Public opinion and value judgements. *Public Opinion Quarterly, 3*, (3): 371-375.

Poster, M. (2001). *What's the matter with the Internet?* Minneapolis: University of Minnesota Press.

Postman, N. (1985). *Amusing Ourselves to Death.* London: Methuen.

Press, B. (2001, March 16). Bush talks down the economy. Available on-line: http://fyi.cnn.com/2001/ALLPOLITICS/03/16/column.billpress/. Accessed April 12, 2001.

Randall, J. H., Jr. (1940). The development of scientific method in the school of Padua. *Journal of the History of Ideas, 1*, (2): 177-206.

Ranney, A. (1976). "The divine science": Political engineering in American culture. *The American Political Science Review, 70*, (1): 140-148.

Rifkin, J. (2001). *The Age of Access: The new culture of hypercapitalism, where all of life is a paid-for experience.* New York: Penguin Putnam.

Roll, E. (1938/1973). *A History of Economic Thought* (4th ed.). London: Faber & Faber.

Rooney, D. & Graham, P. (2001). A sociological road to applied epistemology: A theoretical and analytical examination of technocratic knowledge policy. *Journal of Social Epistemology, 15*, (3): 155-169.

Rosston, G. L. & Steinberg, J. S. (1997). Using market-based spectrum policy to promote the public interest. Available on-line: http://www.fcc.gov/Bureaus/Engineering_Technolog y/Informal/spectrum.txt. Accessed October 8, 2000.

Ruggiero, R. (1997, September 29). Charting the trade routes of the future. Available on-line:

http://www.wto.org/wto/speeches/sanfran1.htm. Accessed December 18, 1998.

Russell, B. (1919). On propositions. In R. C. Marsh (Ed.), *Logic and Knowledge: Essays 1901-1950* (pp. 285-320). London: Unwin Hyman.

_____. (1911). On the relations of universals and particulars. In R. C. Marsh (Ed.), *Logic and Knowledge: Essays 1901-1950* (pp. 105-126). London: Unwin Hyman.

Samarajiva, R. (1996). Surveillance by design: Public networks and the control of consumption. In Mansell, R. & Silverstone, R. (1996), (Eds.). *Communication by design: The politics of information and communication technologies*: 129-156. New York: Oxford University Press.

Saul, J. R. (1992). *Voltaire's Bastards: The dictatorship of reason in the West.* Maryborough, Australia: Penguin.

_____. (1997). *The Unconscious Civilization.* Maryborough, Australia: Penguin.

Schulze-Wechsungen. (1934). Political Propaganda (R. Bytwerk, Trans.). [Politische Propaganda. *Unser Wille und Weg, 4*: 323-332.] Available on-line: http://www.calvin.ed
u/academic/cas/gpa/. Accessed March 24, 2000.

Schumpeter, J. (1909). On the concept of social value. *Quarterly Journal of Economics, 23,* (2): 213-232.

Shaw, G. B. (1904). Discussion (pp. 21-22). In F. Galton (1904). Eugenics: Its definition, scope, and aims. *American Journal of Sociology, 10,* (1): 1-25.

Sherden, W. (1998). *The Fortune Sellers: The big business of buying and selling predictions.* New York: Wiley.

Silverstone, R. (1999). *Why Study the Media?* London: Sage.

_____. & Haddon, L. (1996). Design and the domestication of information and communication technologies: Technical change and everyday life. In R. Mansell & R. Silverstone (Eds.), *Communication by Design: The politics of information and communication technologies* (pp. 44-76). New York: Oxford University Press.

Slaughter, M. & Swagel, P. (1997). Does globalization lower wages and export jobs? *Economic Issues Paper 11.* New York: International Monetary Fund.

Smith, A. (1776/1997). *The Wealth of Nations* (Books I-III). London: Penguin.

_____. (1776/1999). *The Wealth of Nations* (Books IV-V). London: Penguin.

Smythe, D. (1981). *Dependency Road: Communications, capitalism, consciousness, and Canada.* Norwood, NJ: Ablex.

Solomon, N. (2000, January 13). AOL Time Warner: Calling the faithful to their knees. *Earth Beat.* Available on-line: http://www.fair.org/media-beat/000113.html. Accessed November 12, 2000.

Standage, T. (1999). *The Victorian Internet: The remarkable story of the telegraph and the nineteenth century's online pioneers.* London: Phoenix.

Stark, G. (1930). *Modern Political Propaganda* (R. Bytwerk, Trans.). Munich: Verlag Frz. Eher Nachf. Available on-line: http://www.calvin.edu/academic/cas/gpa/stark.htm. Accessed March 24, 2000.

Stevens, A. C. (1887). 'Futures' in the wheat market. *Quarterly Journal of Economics, 2,* (1): 37-63.

Sukenick, R. (1996). Avant-PoPoMo now. *Electronic Book Review, 2.* Available on-line:

http://www.altx.com/ebr/ebr2/2sukenick.htm. Accessed July, 1998.

Swann Harding, T. (1937). Are we breeding weaklings? *American Journal of Sociology, 42,* (5): 672-681.

Sweezy, A. R. (1934). The interpretations of subjective value theory in the writings of the Austrian economists. *The Review of Economic Studies, 1,* (3): 176-185.

Symmons, J. M. (1938). The value of life. *The Economic Journal (Notes and Memoranda), 48,* (192): 744-748.

Taylor, O. H. (1951). Schumpeter and Marx: Imperialism and social classes in the Schumpeterian system. *Quarterly Journal of Economics, 65,* (4): 525-555.

Tetzlaff, D. (1991). Divide and conquer: popular culture and social control in late capitalism. *Media, Culture and Society, 13*: 9-33.

Thompson, E. P. (1980). *The Making of the English Working Class.* London: Penguin.

Thurow, L. C. (1996). *The Future of Capitalism: How today's economic forces will shape tomorrow's world.* St. Leonards, Australia: Allen & Unwin.

Tucker, R. C. (1972). Introduction. In R. C. Tucker (Ed.), *The Marx-Engels Reader* (pp. xv-xxxiv). New York: W. W. Norton.

Tylor, E. B. (1877). Mr. Spencer's *Principles of Sociology. Mind, 2,* (6): 141-156.

Urban, W. M. (1908). Science and value. *Ethics, 51,* (3): 291-306.

US to clean up wireless mess. (2000, October 16). *Sydney Morning Herald,* p. 40.

van Dijk, T. (1994). Discourse and cognition in society. In D. Crowley & D. Mitchell (Eds.), *Communication Theory Today* (pp. 107-126). Cambridge: Polity.

Varela, F. (1992). Autopoiesis and a biology of intentionality. In B. McMullin & N. Murphy (Eds.), *Autopoiesis and Perception: A workshop with ESPRIT BRA 3352* (pp. 4-14). Dublin: Dublin City University. Available online at ftp://ftp.eeng.dcu.ie/pub/alife/bmc m9401/varela.pdf

Viner, J. (1948). Power versus plenty as objectives of foreign policy in the seventeenth and eighteenth centuries. *World Politics, 1,* (1): 1-29.

Voltaire. (1764/1972). *Philosophical Dictionary* (T. Besterman, Ed. and Trans.). London: Penguin.

Walker, M. (1999). *Address to the Australian Institute of Political Science.* Available on-line: http://www.abc.net.au/rn/talks/8.30/mediarpt/mstories/mr980813.htm. Accessed January 7, 1999.

Ward, L. F. (1895). Static and dynamic sociology. *Political Science Quarterly, 10,* (2): 203-220.

Ware, N. J. (1931). The physiocrats: A study in economic rationalization. *The American Economic Review, 21,* (4): 607-619.

Warminski, A. (1995). Hegel/Marx: Consciousness and life. *Yale French Studies, 88*: 118-141. [*Depositions: Althusser, Balibar, Macherey, and the Labor of Reading.* New Haven, CT: Yale University Press.]

Wasko, J. (2001). *Understanding Disney: The manufacture of fantasy.* London: Polity.

Weber, M. (1930/1992). *The Protestant Ethic and the Spirit of Capitalism.* London: Routledge.

Weinberg, J. (1968). Abstraction in the formation of concepts. In P. P. Werner (Ed.), *Dictionary of the History of Ideas: Studies of selected pivotal ideas* (Vol. 1, pp. 1-9). New York: Charles Scribner and Sons.

Wells, J. (1936). Political propaganda as a moral duty (R. Bytwerk, Trans.). [Politische Propaganda als sittliche Pflicht. *Unser Wille und Weg, 6*: 238-241.] Available on-line: http://www.calvin.edu/academic/cas/gpa/moralpro.htm. Accessed March 24, 2000.

White, A. D. (1896/1960). *A History of the Warfare of Science with Theology in Christendom.* New York: Dover.

White, L., Jr. (1940). Technology and invention in the Middle Ages. *Speculum, 15,* (2): 141-159.

_____. (1965). The legacy of the Middle Ages in the American Wild West. *Speculum, 40,* (2): 191-202.

White, L., Jr. (1974). Technology assessment from the stance of a medieval historian. *The American Historical Review, 79,* (1): 1-13.

Williams, R. (1976). *Communications* (3rd ed.). London: Harmondsworth.

Williams, V. (2000, November 22). Biotech Firm Buys Tonga's Gene Pool. *The Adelaide Advertiser*, p. 2.

Witts, P. (1998, August 4). The Net Effect. *The Australian*, p. 32.

Wodak, R. (2001). From conflict to consensus? The co-construction of a policy paper. In P. Muntigl, G. Weiss, & R. Wodak (Eds.), *European Union Discourses on Unemployment: An interdisciplinary approach to employment policy-making and organizational change* (pp. 73-114). London: Benjamins.

World Intellectual Property Organization. (2000, September). *Joint recommendation concerning provisions on the protection of well-known marks adopted by the assembly of the Paris Union for the Protection of Industrial Property and the General Assembly of the World Intellectual Property Organization at the thirty-fourth series of meetings of the assemblies of the member states of WIPO.* Geneva: WIPO.

Corpus documents cited

Advisory Council on Science and Technology Expert Panel on Skills. (1999). *Stepping up skills and opportunities in the knowledge economy.* Report to The Prime Minister's Advisory Council on Science and Technology. Ottawa: Her Majesty the Queen in Right of Canada. [corpus code: canada1]

Commission on Strategic Development. (2000). *Bringing the vision to life: Hong Kong's long-term development needs and goals.* Hong Kong: Commission on Strategic Development. [corpus code: hongkvis]

Council of State. (1997). *Legal issues raised by the development of the internet.* Paris: Office of the Prime Minister. [corpus code: fr2]

Department of Communication, Information, Technology and the Arts. (1998). *A strategic framework for the information economy: Identifying priorities for action.* Canberra, Australia: Commonwealth of Australia. [corpus code: cita1]

Department of Communication, Information, Technology and the Arts. (2000). *E Commerce beyond 2000.* Canberra, Australia: Commonwealth of Australia. [corpus code: ausbey1]

Directorate General for Competition. (1995). *Green paper on the liberalisation of telecommunications infrastructure and cable television networks.* Brussels: European Commission Directorate General XIII: Telecommunications, information market and exploitation of research. [corpus code: eugpv16c]

High-Level Group on the Information Society. (1994). *Europe and the global information society: Bangemann report recommendations to the European Council.* Brussells: European Commission. [corpus code: eu3]

Information and Communication Legal and Technical Department. (1999). *France in the information society.* Paris: Government Information Department. [corpus code: fr3]

Luu, N., Mathur, S., Williams, P., O 'Connor, M., & Nation, J. (2000). *Knowledge-based activities: Selected indicators.* Canberra, Australia: Commonwealth of Australia. [corpus code: au_kba]

Miller, R. (1997). *The Internet in Twenty Years: Cyberspace, the next frontier?* Paris: OECD. [corpus code: oecd6]

Miller, R. (1998). The promise of 21st century technology. *The OECD Observer, 214.* Paris: OECD. [corpus code: oecd7]

Minister for Information Technology's IT Advisory Group. (1999). *The knowledge economy.* Wellington, New Zealand: Ernst and Young. [corpus code: nzknow]

Ministerial Council for the Information Economy. (1998). *Towards an Australian strategy for the information economy: A preliminary statement of the government's policy approach and a basis for business and community consultation.* Canberra, Australia: National office for the Information Economy. [corpus code: noie1]

Ministry of Industry, Employment and Communications. (1999). *Fact sheet on the Swedish Government's Budget Bill for 2000, presented to the Parliament on 20 September, 1999 to strengthen its position as a leading IT nation.* Stockholm: Ministry of Industry, Employment and Communications. [corpus code: sweden1]

Performance and Innovation Unit. (1999). *E-commerce@its.best.uk.* A performance and innovation report. London: Office of the Prime Minister and Cabinet. [corpus code: uk_eva2]

Prime Minister's Office. (1999). *Greece in the information society: Strategy and actions.* Athens: Prime Minister's Office. [corpus code: Greece1]

Totland, N. (1994). *Central government information policy: Main principles.* Helsinki: Ministry of Government Administration. [corpus code: Norway1]

Index

A

Ability, 128
aboutness, 15, 74
Adelphia, 103
Adorno, 6, 28, 33, 80, 86, 87, 88, 92, 104, 107, 108, 109, 119, 189, 199
Advertising, 61, 80, 105
alienation, 33, 68, 73, 90, 92, 113, 114, 168, 175, 192
anthropomorph, 68
Appropriateness, 128
Aquinas, 66
Aristotle, 15, 31, 32, 39, 53, 54, 189, 193
attitudinal patterns, 56
Australia, 3, 23, 106, 148, 155, 162
Austrian school, 44, 45, 189
Autopiesis, 69, 70. 72, 74, 75, 76
autopoietic, 69, 72, 75, 76, 81
autopoietic organization, 72
axiological, 8, 20, 21, 22, 24, 30, 50, 119, 120, 123, 126, 127, 128, 129, 139, 140, 141, 142, 144, 146, 147, 151, 152, 156, 174, 175, 176, 179, 181, 182, 185
axiologies, 20, 22, 27, 29, 49, 120, 124, 126, 127, 128, 130, 134, 140, 143, 174, 175

B

Bacon, 51
baht, 73
Beauty, 58
Bernays, 55, 56, 57, 59, 61, 190
Bill Gates, 82, 83, 95, 149
Bolingbroke, 42
Bourdieu, 16, 81, 85, 88, 89, 92, 94, 114, 142, 145, 191, 192
brand, 81, 159
Britain, 101, 105
Bush, 116, 117, 118, 144

C

California, 23, 148
camera obscura, 44
Capital, 6, 73, 86, 144, 174
capitalism, 3, 4, 5, 12, 23, 73, 101, 113, 152, 161, 162, 169
Carey, 76, 108, 127, 128, 145, 146, 147, 148, 149, 162, 179, 194
circulation time, 7, 8, 20, 96, 97, 100, 175
clock, 13, 76, 77, 82, 87, 102, 150
Coates, 90, 91, 192
Colker, 3
Colletti, 32, 189
commodification, 3, 9, 15, 26, 69, 71, 73, 74, 82, 85, 87, 97, 161, 163, 164, 165, 166, 176, 187
Comprehensibility, 128, 139
computers, 79, 170
conceptual fetishism, 33
Consistency, 58
consumers, 82, 120, 160, 164, 171, 176
consumption, 4, 18, 19, 70, 80, 83, 84, 85, 97, 113, 119, 174, 175
corporate mergers, 6
Correlata, 35
cotton, 79, 113
creationist, 50
credit derivatives, 71, 73
Creel, 55, 64, 80, 190
cultural laborer, 6
culture industry, 6, 80, 115
currency, 13, 68, 85, 103
cyberspace, 11, 23, 106, 118, 149, 154, 168, 169, 170, 171, 172, 174

D

Darwin, 32, 50, 121, 193
debt, 8, 10, 71, 101, 103, 109, 110, 111, 112
Deprivation, 57

Desirability, 39, 54, 128, 131, 134, 136, 137, 138, 139, 144, 151, 153, 154, 156
Destutt de Tracy, 39
dialectical analysis, 34
Dialectics, 17, 33, 34, 35
digital media, 6, 8, 185
discourse community, 33, 78, 192
Divinity, 58, 144, 182
division of labor, 79
DNA, 82, 85, 110
DOD, 106
dot com crash, 12
doxa, 36, 37
durable commodities, 70, 79
Durkheim, 52

E
economic incentives, 80
El Dorado, 101, 148
Electrospace, 106, 161, 162, 163, 164, 165, 166, 168, 170, 171, 173, 174, 175, 176, 177, 187
empiricism, 51
Endoxa, 33, 34
Engels, 30, 36, 44, 49, 73, 86, 168, 189, 199
England, 39, 42
Enlightenment, 39, 50, 187
Enron, 103
equipment, 42, 79
Equivocation, 35
eugenic sociology, 50, 62
eugenics, 50, 51, 52, 62
Euphoria, 58, 102
evaluative biases, 19, 20
Evolutionary Philosophy, 50
Expediency, 58

F
Fabianists, 51
faith-based, 116, 117, 144
family tree, 75
film industries, 80
financial sector, 71, 82, 103
first principles, 33, 34
First World War, 55
Firth, 16, 52, 53, 54, 174, 189, 193, 199
Ford, 50, 80
France, 39, 42, 156, 157
Freud, 44, 49, 185

G
Gallup, 55, 60, 190
Galton, 50, 51, 52, 95, 190
Germany, 28, 52, 57, 61, 193
Global Crossing, 103
global village, 75
globalization, 6, 68, 75, 112, 115, 125, 149, 151
globalized, 18, 19, 23, 68, 69, 93, 119, 120, 132, 133, 165, 173, 187
gold, 17, 23, 37, 41, 48, 61, 63, 101, 103, 127, 148, 194
Golumbia, 3
Greece, 93, 110, 115, 136, 139
Greeks, 32, 33
Greenleaf, 51
Grundrisse, 18, 33

H
Harrington, 51
Harvey, 28, 29, 30, 125, 189
Hegel, 28, 31, 32, 33, 35, 36, 189
HIH, 103
historical materialism, 31
history, 193
Hitler, 52, 61, 80, 178, 193
Hobbes, 37, 66, 68
Holland, 100, 192
homo sapiens, 62
Horkheimer, 6, 80, 88, 107, 108, 109, 189, 199
Humorousness/Seriousness, 128
Hypercapital, 3
hypercapitalism, 3, 6, 12, 14, 18, 20, 21, 63, 71, 80, 81, 82, 83, 84, 87, 88, 92, 96, 97, 99, 109, 113, 114, 118

I
ICT, 12, 102, 142
Idealism, 32, 33
identity, 13, 30, 39, 44, 46, 73, 74, 75, 78, 84, 88, 126, 183, 191, 193
IMF. See International Monetary Fund. See International Monetary Fund
Indulgence, 57
industrial machinery, 80
industrial revolution, 93
information and communication technologies, 12, 159, 160
information revolution, 93
Innis, 7, 16, 19, 44, 47, 60, 76, 89, 92, 93,

99, 100, 103, 104, 105, 107, 108, 109, 110, 113, 127, 141, 162, 165, 179, 185, 189, 190, 192, 193, 194
institutional, 9, 15, 18, 20, 22, 29, 38, 68, 89, 119, 124, 136, 137, 142, 152, 153, 161, 166, 172, 176, 180, 181, 184, 185, 187
intellectual labor, 81
Intellectual Property, 15
International Monetary Fund, 6, 13
Internet, 102, 155, 157, 158
IP. See Intellectual Property
irrealis, 10, 125, 136, 149, 150, 151, 153, 156, 157, 159, 161, 165, 167

K
Kant, 28, 33
Keynesian, 63
Kmart, 103
Kuhn, 53

L
laissez faire, 3, 149
language, 191
Lasswell, 55, 56, 57, 58, 61, 189, 190, 199
Legality, 58
legislatures, 6, 63, 127, 187
Leisure, 80
Lemke, 9, 15, 33, 36, 53, 55, 56, 58, 68, 70, 74, 76, 96, 124, 125, 126, 128, 129, 133, 134, 136, 141, 143, 145, 156, 189, 190, 191, 192, 193, 199
Leviathan, 66
lexico-grammatical, 78
liberal socialists, 51
liberalism, 39, 42, 62
Liberalism, 39
linen, 79
linguistification, 17, 26, 30, 38, 63, 65
Locke, 39, 41

M
Malinowski, 52, 190
manual labor, 81
Marx, 5, 6, 7, 10, 14, 17, 18, 28, 29, 30, 31, 32, 33, 35, 36, 37, 42, 43, 44, 47, 49, 64, 67, 70, 71, 73, 79, 80, 81, 83, 85, 86, 87, 88, 90, 93, 96, 97, 100, 104, 109, 110, 114, 148, 151, 152, 157, 159, 161, 166, 168, 175, 177, 185, 187, 189, 192, 193, 199

Marxist, 7, 14, 28, 187
Materialism, 32
materialist, 7, 14, 32, 92, 97
Maturana, 69, 72, 73, 77, 84, 190
Mauss, 52
McLuhan, 14, 75, 119, 165, 179, 192
mediation, 14, 16, 18, 19, 20, 22, 26, 28, 54, 64, 65, 69, 70, 74, 75, 88, 98, 116, 127, 140, 141, 142, 143, 155, 165, 179, 182, 186, 187
mercantilist, 17, 41, 42, 100
meta-organismic, 68, 72
modes of *distribution*, 93
Monetary System, 43
Morality, 58

N
national debt, 112
National Socialist, 61, 62
Natural Order, 40
natural selection, 51, 122, 193
neo-Hegelian, 32
neoliberalism, 121, 123, 158, 171
New Zealand, 158, 160, 194
Newton, 39, 101, 104, 122
Normality, 50, 52
Normativity, 50, 54, 139

O
objectification, 33, 87, 88, 90
objective, 189
Omnibus, 58
Organizational, 76, 77, 191
Orientational, 76, 77, 191

P
Padua, 36
Perry, 47, 48, 49, 126
Petty, 51
phenomenological capital, 79, 86, 95
Physiocratic, 42
Physiocrats, 39, 42, 43, 45, 47
plant, 15, 62, 79
Plato, 23, 148
Poincaré, 114
postmodern, 14
predicates, 129
Presentational, 76, 77, 191
printing press, 88, 93, 119
Probability, 58, 139, 156
process metaphor, 149, 150, 151, 153, 155,

156, 160
production, 190
Propaganda, 6, 12, 17, 54, 55, 56, 57, 61, 62, 64, 80, 85, 95, 140, 142, 148, 171
Propriety, 58
protest, 33, 68
public opinion, 17, 54, 55, 56, 60, 80, 113, 166
Pythagoras, 114

R
race hygiene, 52
radio, 23, 55, 59, 62, 80, 93, 99, 102, 105, 106, 119, 152, 162, 163, 165, 166, 170, 171, 183, 190, 192, 193
Reading, 81
Realis, 153
reification, 33
Relata, 35
Relation, 34, 189
Reuter, 102
Ricardo, 47
Rifkin, 3
Roman Catholic Church, 75, 179
roubles, 73

S
Salisbury, 66, 172
satellites, 79
scholastics, 32, 33, 36
Schumpeter, 46, 190
September 11, 2001, 63
seven deadly sins, 91
Shaw, 51
Significance, 128, 132, 160
silver, 17, 37, 48
Smith, 36, 37, 42, 43, 44, 47, 67, 121, 189, 193
social anthropology, 52, 53, 54
social Darwinism, 40, 62
Social Darwinism, 40, 50
social hieroglyphic, 43
social metabolism, 70, 71
social value, 46, 47, 178
socialism, 51
sociocognitive, 70, 106
sociolinguistics, 15, 35, 52
South Pacific, 101
Spain, 101
specialist dialects, 5

Stalin, 52, 178
statists, 51
steel, 79, 94
subjective, 40, 41, 42, 43, 45, 46, 47, 48, 49, 50, 52, 55, 58, 59, 62, 189
Sukenick, 3
symbolic value, 52, 70
symbolic wealth, 95
synchronic, 60, 75, 185
Syntactic propagation, 136
systemic capital, 79, 80, 82, 83, 86, 87, 88, 92, 96, 97
Systemic capital, 79, 80, 86, 96
Systemic cognition, 72

T
Technicalization, 39
Technology, 9, 10, 11, 75, 137, 155, 183
tech wreck. See dot com crash
telegraph, 93, 100, 102, 111, 185
Television, 106
Temple, 51
The Culture Industry, 6
The Origin of The Species, 50
The Wealth of Nations, 43
Third Reich, 52
totalitarianism, 63
tulipmania, 100, 192

U
USSR, 52
Usuality, 128, 139
Utility, 128
utility curves, 44
utility theorists, 45

V
valuational patterns, 55
value, 189, 193, 199
Varela, 69, 72, 77, 84, 190
von Weiser, 48, 190

W
Warrantability, 128, 131, 133, 136, 138, 139
Wealth, 37, 42, 67
World Bank, 13, 89
World Trade Organization, 6, 13, 179
World War II, 63, 80
Worldcom, 103
writing, 13, 14, 29, 81, 90, 93

General Editor: Steve Jones

Digital Formations is an essential source for critical, high-quality books on digital technologies and modern life. Volumes in the series break new ground by emphasizing multiple methodological and theoretical approaches to deeply probe the formation and reformation of lived experience as it is refracted through digital interaction. **Digital Formations** pushes forward our understanding of the intersections—and corresponding implications—between the digital technologies and everyday life. The series emphasizes critical studies in the context of emergent and existing digital technologies.

Other recent titles include:

Leslie Shade
  *Gender and Community in the Social
  Construction of the Internet*

John T. Waisanen
  Thinking Geometrically

Mia Consalvo & Susanna Paasonen
  Women and Everyday Uses of the Internet

Dennis Waskul
  Self-Games and Body-Play

David Myers
  The Nature of Computer Games

Robert Hassan
  The Chronoscopic Society

M. Johns, S. Chen, & G. Hall
  Online Social Research

C. Kaha Waite
  *Mediation and the Communication
  Matrix*

Jenny Sunden
  Material Virtualities

Helen Nissenbaum & Monroe Price
  Academy and the Internet

To order other books in this series please contact our Customer Service Department:

(800) 770-LANG (within the US)
(212) 647-7706 (outside the US)
(212) 647-7707 FAX

To find out more about the series or browse a full list of titles, please visit our website:

WWW.PETERLANGUSA.COM